Policy into
action

Also of interest from the Urban Institute Press:

Social Experimentation and Public Policymaking, edited by
David Greenberg, Donna Linksz, and Marvin Mandell

Welfare Reform: The Next Act, edited by Alan Weil and Kenneth Finegold

Reality and Research: Social Science and U.S. Urban Policy since 1960,
edited by George Galster

edited by
Mary Clare Lennon
and
Thomas Corbett

Policy into
action

Implementation Research and Welfare Reform

THE URBAN INSTITUTE PRESS
Washington, D.C.

THE URBAN INSTITUTE PRESS
2100 M Street, N.W.
Washington, D.C. 20037

Library of Congress Cataloging in Publication Data

Policy into action : implementation research and welfare reform / edited
by Mary Clare Lennon and Thomas Corbett.
    p. cm.
Includes bibliographical references and index.
    ISBN 0-87766-714-4 (pbk. : alk. paper)
    1. Public welfare administration—United States. 2. Public welfare—United States.
3. Welfare recipients—Employment—United States. 4. United States. Personal
Responsibility and Work Opportunity Reconciliation Act of 1996. I. Lennon,
Mary Clare. II. Corbett, Thomas, 1944-
    HV95.P654 2003
    361.6'0973—dc21

                                                                    2003001391

Printed in the United States of America

THE URBAN INSTITUTE is a nonprofit policy research and educational organization established in Washington, D.C., in 1968. Its staff investigates the social, economic, and governance problems confronting the nation and evaluates the public and private means to alleviate them. The Institute disseminates its research findings through publications, its web site, the media, seminars, and forums.

Through work that ranges from broad conceptual studies to administrative and technical assistance, Institute researchers contribute to the stock of knowledge available to guide decisionmaking in the public interest.

Conclusions or opinions expressed in Institute publications are those of the authors and do not necessarily reflect the views of officers or trustees of the Institute, advisory groups, or any organizations that provide financial support to the Institute.

Contents

Preface xi
Barbara B. Blum

1 Implementation Studies:
From Policy to Action 1
Thomas Corbett and Mary Clare Lennon

**PART ONE: Understanding the
Implementation Challenge** 15

2 Perspectives of the Ultimate Consumers:
Policymakers and Program Managers 21
Joel Rabb and Don Winstead

3 Conceptual Underpinnings of
Implementation Analysis 39
Pamela A. Holcomb and Demetra Smith Nightingale

4 Three Generations of Implementation
Research: Looking for the Keys to
Implementation "Success" 57
Thomas Kaplan and Thomas Corbett

**PART TWO: Using Analysis to Understand
            Implementation** **73**

5 Field Network Studies 81
    Irene Lurie

6 Performance Analysis 107
    Lawrence M. Mead

7 Street-Level Research:
    Policy at the Front Lines 145
    Evelyn Z. Brodkin

8 Client-Based Ethnographic Research
    As a Tool for Implementation Analysis 165
    Kathryn Edin

9 What Lies behind the Impacts?
    Implementation Research in the
    Context of Net Impact Studies 193
    Kay E. Sherwood and Fred Doolittle

**PART THREE: Using Data to Understand
                Implementation** **233**

10 Approaches to Data Collection for
      Implementation Analysis 239
      Leanne Charlesworth and Catherine Born

11 Use of Administrative Data for
      Implementation Research 281
      Robert M. Goerge

PART FOUR: Pursuing Excellence **299**

12 Where We Go from Here 303
      Rebecca A. Maynard and Thomas Corbett

About the Editors 321

About the Contributors 323

Index 327

Preface

Publication of this volume has been cosponsored by the University of Wisconsin's Institute for Research on Poverty (IRP) and Columbia University's Research Forum on Children, Families, and the New Federalism at the National Center for Children in Poverty (NCCP). IRP and the Research Forum have been motivated by a strong interest in promoting sound research and in improving research methodology. Both organizations also encourage collaboration among and between researchers, policymakers, and practitioners, and are committed to fostering the exchange of information across disciplines.

These shared concerns led IRP and NCCP to host a forum on February 16, 1996, for almost 100 researchers and policymakers. Funded by the Foundation for Child Development, the meeting was designed to examine the implications for research created by wholesale changes in the Aid to Families with Dependent Children (AFDC) program as a result of waivers already granted in almost every state by the Bush and Clinton administrations. Subsequently, in November 1996, IRP hosted a meeting in Madison, Wisconsin, at which selected researchers presented potential options for describing and measuring the changes that were occurring. A publication entitled *Evaluating Comprehensive State Welfare Reform: The Wisconsin Works Program*, edited by Burt Barnow, Thomas Kaplan, and Robert Moffitt (Rockefeller Institute Press 2000), incorporates that meeting's deliberations.

With the passage of the Personal Responsibility and Work Opportunity Reconciliation Act of 1996 (PRWORA), and the devolution of decisionmaking concerning welfare and other social policies that the act engendered, far more attention was focused on the value of implementation evaluations. As a result, IRP and the Research Forum convened a group of researchers and policymakers who were knowledgeable about process and implementation evaluations. Meeting in October 1997, the group discussed problem areas related to definition, measures, and methodologies, and agreed that a need existed to (1) articulate a general framework for planning and carrying out implementation evaluations; (2) develop a common terminology and language about these methods; and (3) advance general standards and strategies for answering key process questions.

Following the October 1997 meeting, a core group of participants communicated by teleconference calls to develop a strategy for achieving the objectives that had been identified. This core group, now comprising the volume's authors, met twice more, in September 1998 in New York City and in May 1999 in Arlington, Virginia. With support from the office of the Assistant Secretary for Planning and Evaluation of the U.S. Department of Health and Human Services and from the Joyce Foundation, papers were drafted, expertly edited by Betty Evanson of IRP, and vetted by the group during 1998 and 1999. Finally, in October 1999, the papers were presented for review and discussion at a forum in Washington, D.C. Each paper was amended based on suggestions from discussants and meeting participants. The revised papers have become the chapters for this book, which is greatly enhanced by the editing skills of Felicity Skidmore. The meetings were organized by staff of the Research Forum and IRP and benefited from Dawn Duran's organizational skills.

This volume includes 12 chapters by 17 authors. The volume's purpose is to describe a range of methods that can be used to understand the processes that produce changes in policies and programs. Discussion is limited to ways the methods described can be applied to studying the effects of PRWORA. We are well aware that extensive work has been done or is needed in many fields outside of income security, but this work has been driven by the immediacy of the demands for information about the implementation of PRWORA. We do, however, believe that many of the principles set forth in these chapters are relevant to other fields and hope that they will be applied.

Finally, many lessons can be drawn from the development of this volume. First, each chapter has been enhanced by the collegial and collaborative interchange of information and advice among the authors and other participants in the various meetings that led to this volume. Second, collaborative efforts take time and commitment; these authors were exceptional in their efforts to produce materials that will enhance process and implementation evaluations. Third, prescience is important: This book would simply not exist had Thomas Corbett at IRP not identified early on how much we needed to advance an understanding of the value of well-designed process and implementation evaluations. His prescience deserves recognition, as do the many contributions of Mary Clare Lennon, whose perseverance brought this complicated initiative to completion.

Barbara B. Blum

1

Implementation Studies
From Policy to Action

Thomas Corbett and Mary Clare Lennon

This book focuses on evaluative strategies that, in effect, explore the translation of plausible concepts into functioning policies and programs. The techniques further evaluate how well the policies and programs work in all their administrative and management dimensions and, in some instances, examine how the policies and programs are experienced both by intended beneficiaries and by those who carry them out. This group of techniques is known by a variety of names: implementation studies, process evaluations, discrepancy analyses, and even qualitative studies. The various labels connote subtle differences in the underlying research question. For example, implementation studies are thought to focus on newer policies and programs, whereas process evaluations look at their more established counterparts. But the lack of common terminology can be confusing. Because much of the content of this book focuses on the implementation of recent changes in welfare policies and programs, we label the entire array of techniques *implementation analysis* throughout the book.

Purposes of the Book

The book has three salient motivations. These are to encourage a dialogue about developing a conceptual framework for understanding the role of implementation analysis, including its scientific and intellectual contributions; to bring together recent advances in implementation analysis that have yet to be widely recognized as having important common characteristics and goals; and to recognize the importance of timing. Passage of the Personal Responsibility and Work Opportunity Reconciliation Act (PRWORA) in 1996 accelerated fundamental policy and program changes in the social welfare arena in ways that are transforming the institutions and organizations underpinning our systems of social assistance. Arguably, this revolution substantially increases the importance of implementation analysis in the program evaluation world.

The Translation of Proposal into Program

Public programs translate policy intent into action in ways designed to achieve specified goals and reach intended target populations. Among other research questions of interest, program evaluations provide the means for learning whether programs have been implemented as intended by the policy, how they actually work, how well they are achieving the goals envisioned for them, and how well they might work in other environments. Program evaluations have two distinct conceptual dimensions: implementation analysis and impact analysis.

Implementation analysis seeks to understand the program in its own right. It does so by exploring a number of fundamental questions about how systems function—what the real (as opposed to nominal) goals of the policy are, whether those goals are internally consistent and shared among multiple stakeholders, what administrative and management procedures are engaged in the pursuit of the goals, whether they reflect the intent of the program designers, how well the program is achieving its goals, how policy is changed by frontline staff decisions, and whether clients are reacting to the program in ways intended by its designers.

Impact analysis encompasses the research question most commonly associated with program evaluations—whether the program or policy has the desired effect on critical outcomes. In the welfare reform context, the traditional outcomes have been economic—hours worked, earnings, welfare receipt—but they have also included social outcomes such as marital stability and fertility decisions (U.S. Department of Health and Human Services 1983). Because impact analysis is designed to attribute causation, this approach is in essence comparative. It requires a measure of the counterfactual—what would have happened to the outcomes of interest if the program had not existed or if different services, policies, or programs were in place. The gold standard of impact analysis is a design that randomly assigns members of a target population either to the program being evaluated or to control (counterfactual) status. The outcomes of the program being evaluated can then be compared with the outcomes under the alternative program configuration, and the net impact derived. These experimental designs, if done well, typically can deal with selectivity issues (e.g., only motivated individuals "choose" to participate in a welfare-to-work program) that bedevil causal attributions in most non-experimental analyses.

But impact analyses, even when using rigorous experimental methods, are not absent cautionary concerns. Unless the impact of a program is large, dramatic, and immediate, net impact evaluations need data collected at regular intervals over a considerable period from a large number of participants to reliably assess program-induced changes in behavior. Moreover, it is often difficult to control cross-group contamination—the spillover of an intervention to the control group. In addition, there are some interventions that intend to alter the policy signals experienced by target populations. Random assignment, in most cases, dilutes the new signals by making exposure to the new program more like a lottery—people might get to play by the new rules or they might not. Both contamination effects and diluted signaling effects result in a conservative bias in measuring impacts.

One of the most persistent cautions attached to conventional experiments has to do with the difficulties associated with untangling the causal chain. For example, if we do not obtain significant experimental effects, that is, non-chance differences between the experimental and control group, we cannot really be sure that the intervention is a failure. Perhaps the new policy or program was never really implemented as intended, or was implemented in ways that the sponsors would hardly recognize. On the other hand, positive findings can also leave us with unanswered questions. Which component of an intervention might be disproportionately affecting outcomes? Is the nominal policy or program change really causing the effect, or is the cause some associated change in the way things are done outside the "experimental" intervention? Is there a way to tease out evidence that different dosages (strength of the intervention) or delivery mechanisms or contextual attributes would enhance performance? These questions, and many others, require that we peer into the "black box" of program and policy implementation—the way things really work.

When done well, implementation analyses can supplement and complement impact evaluations. They can yield more immediate evidence— suggestive evidence on program-induced change and rather detailed hypotheses on how different components of the program might contribute to overall effects. But as we shall see in the subsequent chapters in this work, implementation analysis encompasses a variety of research questions and techniques that make unique contributions to our knowledge base. And although the range of questions pursued and techniques used is varied, good implementation work should be rigorous and should conform to the accepted standards of science.

In short, both implementation and net impact evaluation techniques are essential weapons in the evaluation arsenal necessary for a comprehensive understanding of a policy or program, each with its own role to play.[1] The methods and standards for impact analysis are well established, however, whereas major recent advances in implementation methods still need to be compiled into a systematic body of knowledge. This book begins to fill that gap, using as its primary examples implementation approaches as applied to evaluations of the 1996 welfare reform initiative. The next two sections of chapter 1 provide context for subsequent chapters. We shall first review the changes that helped produce the new reform environment and then summarize the welfare evaluation history of the 1980s and 1990s.

The AFDC Waiver Programs: A Brief History of Evaluation Expectations

The growing importance of implementation studies in welfare research reflects the revolution experienced over the past decade or so in the way we deliver social assistance.

The welfare reform ideas of strengthening incentives for recipients to work, paying more attention to preparing them for work, and instituting work requirements for cash recipients and/or penalties for noncompliance had been germinating at the federal level and in state capitols well before PRWORA's passage in 1996. States were eager to put these ideas into practice. Federal officials wanted to learn about their impacts without exploding the federal welfare budget. Out of these mutual interests was born an era of waivers where variations of certain federal laws and regulations governing Aid to Families with Dependent Children (AFDC) were systematically explored. Under that system, the U.S. Department of Health and Human Services granted waivers to states to implement changes to their welfare systems under demonstration conditions, with the requirement that the waiver programs be rigorously evaluated.

The waiver program allowed two important things to happen. First, it devolved some decisionmaking to the states while retaining some control of federal matching funds because waivers required that states not spend more on their new systems than they would have under their previous AFDC program. The matching fund issue is important here. The AFDC program had always provided an open-ended subsidy to states that mitigated the financial consequence to the state's budget of its own decisions regarding its AFDC program. It needs to be remembered that state variation did not start with PRWORA, or even with the waiver program. State welfare programs had always had a hand in setting their own eligibility rules and benefit levels above federal minimums, and the federal subsidy had always been open-ended (i.e., with no federal limits on the total amount of matching funds a state could receive for its AFDC program). That is unlike the block grant system now in place, which provides a fixed amount of federal funding to states. The block grant amount is based on a state's AFDC caseload in the mid-1990s, in effect shifting fiscal responsibility to the states if caseloads and costs were to dramatically increase.

The second thing the waiver program accomplished was to relax the principle that all members of the target population in a state should be treated the same. This change permitted states to implement their reforms for particular groups of welfare recipients and in particular parts of the state. Therefore, the federally mandated evaluations could compare the outcomes for recipients of the waiver program with a good measure of the counterfactual—outcomes for recipients with the same characteristics on average as waiver participants who were still under the state's regular AFDC program. Similarity between the two groups was ensured through a client selection process that assigned AFDC caseload members or applicants randomly either to the waiver program or to the traditional AFDC status in that state. This is the classic standard for impact analysis, as noted earlier in the chapter. Random assignment ensures that the two groups do not differ systematically in characteristics that could affect program outcomes (Orr 1999; Rossi and Freeman 1993).

The waiver evaluations contributed valuable information on the average net impacts of the specific waiver programs. Because the basic components of the AFDC program were similar across states, suggestive conclusions could also be drawn about the differential impacts of different state waiver programs. The conclusions about differential impacts, in turn, allowed conclusions about which types of waiver programs were the most effective in producing the desired impacts on work effort, earnings, and welfare receipt.[2] The waiver evaluations also taught us more than we knew before about the impacts of particular components of some of the programs—such as various job search assistance techniques, positive and negative financial incentives tied to certain behaviors (the latter called sanctions in the welfare context), mandatory versus voluntary program participation, and generous versus less generous earnings exemptions (called disregards in the welfare context), among other things.

But the impact findings were years in the making and did not always identify the particular processes through which waiver interventions actually influenced the outcomes of interest, that is, which elements were the most (and least) powerful parts of the program being evaluated. Knowing that a combination of program factors together led to an average program impact, but not having the information necessary to identify which factor(s) caused the impact (or, indeed, whether the intervention as implemented was close to what was intended, either in design or in intensity) illustrates the black box issue introduced earlier.

The waiver experiments used the combined efforts of implementation and impact analysts to address the black box problem. But the implementation parts of the analysis were typically not funded generously enough to provide rich process information. They were also, for the most part, done in isolation from one another and without any general analytic consensus about how they should be done. Further, the results of the implementation components of the evaluations were given considerably less public attention than the impact results and were virtually ignored as having potentially important contributions to make, in their own right, to the public policy debate.

In the current evaluation environment, impact evaluations are virtually never mounted without an implementation evaluation component. But the implementation work is too often done by analysts who have been trained primarily in impact evaluation techniques and have learned whatever they know about implementation analysis on the job. Some of the most intensive implementation studies, in contrast, have been done with no impact component, by evaluators who not only have little experience with impact studies but also often have little interest in them. The evaluation community now has the task of identifying the complementarities of the two approaches and highlighting opportunities for them to come together.

The New Policy World

PRWORA formally ushered in the new welfare policy world presaged by states during the waiver era of reform. It made important changes to the Supplemental Security Income (SSI) program for children, Food Stamps, the child support enforcement and child care systems, and child nutrition programs. Other changes were directed at policy domains that intersected existing programs and policies, for example, restricting assistance to immigrants and reducing nonmarital births. Most policy and public attention, however, has focused on the Temporary Assistance for Needy Families (TANF) program, which has replaced AFDC, the primary cash income support system for poor families with children that was established as part of the Social Security Act in 1935.

TANF is a block grant program that gives states substantially increased responsibility, within more limited federal rules, both for development of their own welfare programs and for the budgetary consequences of their policy and program choices. The most significant federal provisions include five-year lifetime limits on cash assistance receipt, work requirements for welfare recipients after two years of continuous cash support, and financial penalties for states that fail to meet steadily more stringent federal requirements for the proportion of the cash assistance caseload in an allowable work activity. PRWORA also made substantial cuts in several purely federal support programs—including Food Stamps and Supplemental Security Income—and mandated restrictions on assistance formerly provided to immigrants legally allowed to live and work in the United States (some of the latter cuts were subsequently relaxed).

The sweeping reforms embodied in PRWORA are, however, more than a set of new policies. They are, at least in part, the culmination of a set of profound changes transforming the character of government and the structure of social policy in the United States. These deep currents of change are captured by a new set of three R's: the interrelated themes of redirection, reinvention, and reallocation.

Redirection

The redirection theme involves the transformation of public assistance for poor families with children from a system of cash support on the basis of economic need to one aimed at fostering individual and community change. The goals attached to the new concept of support for poor families have multiplied over time. At the local level, they may include communities coming together to improve parenting, family formation, family functioning, and decisionmaking with respect to fertility and sexual activity. Some proponents of reform also anticipate that the redirection of welfare policy will help heal dysfunctional communities, restore public confidence in social assistance programs, and eventually result in better transitions into adult roles by poor and disadvantaged children.

Reinvention

The reinvention theme embraces the transformation of public management from a focus on inputs and protocols for action (tightly allocated resources for specified purposes and explicitly spelled out procedures for which tasks should be done and how) to outputs (how organizations choose to allocate the resources they have to work with and how well the choices they make accomplish the goals they set). Proponents of the new focus argue that greater freedom for managers to structure the processes by which they shape and deliver services will enhance program efficiency and responsiveness. The reinvention theme also emphasizes accountability for results and working within market forces. Some proponents go so far as to challenge the presumption of a public sector monopoly on the provision of assistance.

Reallocation

The reallocation theme encompasses the shifting of program and policy authority from higher levels of government to levels closer to the problems being addressed, not only from the federal level to the states but also from states to localities. The new flexibility afforded to lower levels of authority, proponents suggest, substantially increases both cost-effectiveness and the responsiveness of programs to need—by putting the decisionmaking closer to the particular circumstances of the need. At the extreme, this theme is reflected in a new sense of professionalism on the front lines of welfare agencies where workers now exercise considerable discretion rather than merely carry out the rules formulated in Washington or the state capitol.

This combination of changes is producing a fundamental shift from a bureaucratic, centralized mode characteristic of an income transfer program to a professional mode suited to programs directed at complex behavioral change. Outcomes of interest in the new policy environment include not only the more traditional economic outcomes—poverty, earnings, work effort, welfare receipt—but a variety of other dimensions of behavior. These, as implied by the redirection theme discussed above, include new client attitudes to work versus welfare, new attitudes on the part of program personnel in helping clients reach long-term independence (rather than issues related to benefit payment calculation), and new attitudes of the nation's poorer parents toward themselves, their children, and the quality of their family lives. Also of importance are child well-being, fertility, and family formation.

The fundamental reforms to the nation's support system for low-income families embodied in PRWORA have provoked intense debate. Advocates predict changes for the better, not only in people's behavior with respect to employment, earnings, and welfare receipt, but also in their psychological and social well-being and, as a result, family and community functioning. Other observers predict changes for the worse, particularly in poverty among families with children and the strains associated with it. A strong public consensus has emerged from the debate that we, as a society, must begin at once to understand the implications of these changes. That task is made more complex by expected major differences among state approaches, given increased state flexibility in determining policy and program design. Because of the pressing need for feedback on such broad trends in society's approach to public assistance, the authors of the subsequent chapters anchor their discussions of implementation evaluation issues and techniques in the new welfare reform context.

Implications for Evaluation

Under the old welfare regime, policy functioned in a more set-piece fashion. Uniform federal rules and processes were modified by states only at the margin, and usually only under selected circumstances. Change was slow and linear. Consequently, the research questions were relatively limited in nature and typically could be answered by conventional experiments. For example, would a new job search policy lead to increased employment and lower welfare utilization?

Now, program and policy purposes, including the institutional mechanisms for achieving these ends, are exploding across the social welfare landscape. In essence, reform has become more of an evolutionary process and less a periodic, distinct event. Over the past several years, state and local officials have been quite successful in moving low-income adults into the labor market. But many recognize this as only the first step in the reform agenda unleashed by PRWORA. New entrants must be kept in the labor market through a variety of work supports; functioning two-parent families need to be nurtured and promoted; and the communities in which low-income families reside must be strengthened.

Early on, more farsighted policymakers considered the ultimate purpose of reform to be the prevention of dependence in the first instance, by promoting independence through prudent investments in children, families, and communities. Today's reform landscape has moved closer to this early vision. For example, in seven upper Midwest states, proportional spending on what has been termed family stability issues increased threefold between fiscal year 1996 and fiscal year 2000. Many of those dollars are directed toward investments in children and youth or efforts to stabilize families. Moreover, the future of reform is even more likely to emphasize family functioning if the goals embodied in the administration's TANF reauthorization proposal eventually become law. The proposal, titled *Working Toward Independence,* stresses child well-being and healthy marriages as important ends to be pursued by the states.

We can see that TANF agencies increasingly concentrate on complex, behavior-focused interventions, which tend to be dynamic and longitudinal—seeking fundamental change over time in those served. Interventions tend to be multidimensional—addressing several issues simultaneously as they seek to encourage positive behaviors and discourage those that are counterproductive. If welfare workers in the emerging era are to be effective, they must eschew bureaucratic rules and adopt professional norms.

As this happens, the organizations within which workers function will become structurally flatter and less hierarchical. Agency boundaries themselves will become porous as interagency agreements and one-stop models emerge. Malleable and plastic institutional forms that can respond quickly to new challenges, that are more entrepreneurial in their approaches, will supplant traditionally static and risk-aversive welfare systems. Distinct program and funding streams, the "silo" approach to social policy, will be merged into networks of social assistance. Within agencies, horizontal patterns of communication—dialogue among peers—will become more prominent, and discretion at the operational level will replace traditional command-and-control organizational strategies.[3]

What does all this mean for those responsible for evaluating reform? Basically, a new set of questions now moves to the front burner. We must know much more about the institutional responses to reform, about the new service delivery systems that emerge, and about how policies are filtered through workers empowered with new discretion. At the extreme, policy and rules may be less important than people and organizational cultures in the new world of social assistance—how agencies and workers and clients interact and communicate. In consequence, we must learn much more about the character of interactions at the front lines, how workers and service consumers relate to one another.

These questions are not easily addressed by impact analyses. Rather, we must invest heavily in evaluation strategies that get inside the skin of the new welfare world. This, in turn, requires that we have the methods and strategies to do implementation studies well, with the kind of rigor expected of science. But implementation studies seldom have received the attention devoted to conventional experiments. Often, they are considered little more than an add-on, a nicety to be done as resources permit. But in the new world of welfare, they can easily be seen as an essential analytic tool for understanding what is going on.

Unfortunately, standards for what constitutes good work are not universally accepted. Too often, implementation work is viewed as subjective and interpretive, the purveyors of implementation methods as practicing craft rather than science. We believe it is time to enhance the reputation of implementation work and to improve the quality of that practice. We intend this work as a starting point toward rectifying those ends.

The Content of the Book

The potential of implementation research is clear—as is the pressing need for the evaluation community (1) to define both the strengths and the weaknesses of various approaches to implementation analysis and

(2) to promote quality standards. The contributors to this volume have written their chapters with these goals in mind.

- Part One (chapters 2–4) presents the perspectives of policymakers and program managers, provides an overview of the concepts and analytical approaches that guide implementation research generally, and gives a sense of the historical development of implementation analysis.
- Part Two (chapters 5–9) discusses how particular implementation analysis approaches can be used to help understand a variety of dimensions of program implementation.
- Part Three (chapters 10–11) deals with types of data, methods of collecting them, and their utility for implementation research.
- Part Four (chapter 12) concludes the book with a discussion of what the foregoing chapters tell us about how to pursue quality implementation analysis and with a suggested set of priorities for future research efforts.

Together, the conceptual and empirical contributions of the chapters highlight the critical importance of implementation analysis in understanding how social policy is translated into practice, and the fundamental value of this evaluative approach to understanding the range of program and policy changes embodied in recent changes in welfare policies. We believe that the authors demonstrate the utility and centrality of implementation analyses within the spectrum of evaluation research methods.

NOTES

1. Some analysts contest this perspective. They argue that the nature of the PRWORA changes has increased the need for implementation analysis but reduced the need for net impact evaluation, because the primary focus has changed from client impacts after the program to compliance during it. For example, see Mead's discussion in chapter 6.

2. Some waiver experiments introduced more than one program variant into the experimental design.

3. Recently, states have been experiencing increasing economic constraints. We are not sure how this will affect state variation in welfare regimes. However, we expect that these changes should increase attention to administrative and management practices

that are effective, underscoring the importance of implementation research of the types laid out in this volume.

REFERENCES

Orr, Larry L. 1999. *Social Experiments: Evaluating Public Programs with Experimental Methods.* Thousand Oaks, Calif.: Sage Publications.

Rossi, Peter H., and Howard E. Freeman. 1993. *Evaluation: A Systemic Approach.* Newbury Park, Calif.: Sage Publications.

U.S. Department of Health and Human Services. 1983. *Overview of the Seattle-Denver Income Maintenance Experiment Final Report.* Washington, D.C.: Office of Income Security Policy, Assistant Secretary for Planning and Evaluation. May: 1–17.

PART ONE
Understanding the Implementation Challenge

The first part of this book provides the reader with context for thinking about implementation studies. In particular, the three chapters afford insights into how such analyses are used, how the evaluation community thinks about such work, and how thinking about implementation analyses has evolved over time.

Perspectives of the Ultimate Consumers: Policymakers and Program Managers (chapter 2). Joel Rabb and Don Winstead discuss the tensions facing the public policy/management community as they make policy and program choices. Examples from the Ohio and Florida AFDC waiver programs illustrate the types of evaluation information that proved particularly useful to those states in making policy and improving programs.

Practitioners, note the authors, have one fundamental criterion for judging the worth of evaluation information: Does it tell them something that is useful in making policy and program decisions that affect people's lives? But the interest of practitioners in this fundamental question is mediated by the environment in which they must make their decisions—where the primary considerations tend to be highly political trade-offs between competing values, needs, and desires. Evaluation evidence can help sort out the range of possibilities but seldom dictates the direction taken.

Within that major constraint, persons working at the strategic policy-making level are interested in both impact and implementation findings—

with impact findings from completed evaluations often more welcome and of greater use than impact findings from their own evolving initiatives. The reason is partly that impact findings come in well after the crucial policy and program decisions have been made, but partly that such findings can second-guess decisions that have been made, upon which reputations and careers have already been staked. Persons working at the operational program management level, in contrast, are inherently more interested in implementation findings. These findings are not only more timely, they are fundamentally more useful to program managers, because they can show where the program is working well and provide guidance in making mid-course corrections.

The distinction between strategic and operational thinking may be clear at the conceptual level, but the authors warn that it no longer corresponds straightforwardly to federal versus state and local actors. Devolution has thrust the state and even the local level into debating and deciding on questions of ends as well as means.

Conceptual Underpinnings of Implementation Analysis (chapter 3). As Pamela Holcomb and Demetra Nightingale discuss, most implementation analysis approaches depend largely on inductive logic. That is, reasoning from individuals to a relevant universe often plays a major role—in contrast to deductive forms of analysis, which reason from a conceptual framework to the particular observations being analyzed. A conceptual framework can help the design of an implementation project, but the ultimate analysis involves organizing and categorizing information and using the resulting findings to further refine the initial framework. Implementation studies are commonly used to reach the following analytic objectives: develop program typologies, generalize conditions and experiences in particular sites to a broader universe, and distill potentially promising approaches (best practices) for particular types of jurisdictions or particular types of individuals.

Implementation analysis draws from the theories underlying many academic disciplines—especially those related to organizational behavior, social networks, economic behavior, and group dynamics—as well as accumulated knowledge from similar implementation studies already completed. Such theories help refine research questions, clarify units and levels of analysis, isolate relationships among factors that affect implementation, and allow intellectual feedback to refine all of these. Findings, especially in the case of multiple studies using similar conceptual frameworks, can also be used to generate what is termed grounded theory—

grounded because the refinements emerge from analysis of real-life program experiences rather than from logical deduction.

A number of dimensions are common to well-designed implementation studies, despite the widely varying disciplinary and methodological perspectives that characterize the field. First, they seek to understand— rather than provide simple descriptions of—the issues and relationships of interest to policymakers. Second, they involve using knowledge accumulated from prior studies to refine old and contribute to new theory. Third, they use both qualitative and quantitative analyses to gain understanding of the wider environment in which the program is operating. Fourth, they recognize the primacy of implementation (rather than impact) by using a program, institution, system, or organization as the unit of analysis. Finally, they use multiple methods of data collection to help maintain the general standards of quality common to all methods of research and analysis.

Three Generations of Implementation Research: Looking for the Keys to Implementation "Success" (chapter 4). Thomas Kaplan and Thomas Corbett review the history of analysts' efforts to assess implementation success or failure from an overall perspective: Did the program succeed or not? If not, why not? And what principles increase the chances of success? The general verdict of the Kaplan and Corbett review is that such questions may be too general to be ultimately fruitful in understanding implementation issues.

Before the 1970s, though implementation studies were not unknown, the focus of public policy was on policy design as laid out in legislation or regulation. The implicit assumption was that the details of implementing the policy designs into well-functioning programs would take care of themselves. Failure of the War on Poverty programs of the late 1960s and early 1970s to show much battle success led to a reappraisal and the verdict of many that the failure was rooted in inadequate implementation. This led to what has been called the "first generation" of implementation studies, which used single case studies to look for factors that could explain such failure.

By the early 1980s, a second generation of researchers had begun to criticize these early implementation studies, as relying too heavily on single case studies and on an overly hierarchical concept of implementation as a process of diffusion from top policymakers to operational staff. The former criticism led to efforts to draw generalizable conclusions from implementation studies across multiple program types. The latter led to study of the patterns of influence within organizations at every level of the administrative process. These approaches were greeted by yet a third generation of analysts as useful but lacking in scientific rigor. The new call was for development of clear, testable hypotheses followed by multiple-site, multi-program research to verify or falsify them, in the hope of discovering law-like implementation patterns—a hope that has not been fulfilled.

Implementation analysts have now come to expect less in universal rules for enhancing implementation. Rather, they are heeding a more general lesson—to study process issues at every level of implementation, each in its own right, and to value systematic description rather than demand overall predictive capacity. Subsequent chapters illustrate the range of current approaches and the contribution of each to overall program understanding.

2

Perspectives of the Ultimate Consumers

Policymakers and Program Managers

Joel Rabb and Don Winstead

When asked to build an evaluation component into proposed program legislation, the bill's sponsor balked: "If you don't know the program is going to work, why are you asking me to sponsor it?" This question captures the essence of the dilemma inherent in the public management perspective on evaluation. In the evaluation world, analysts start as agnostics. In the policymaking world, legislators must advocate a position and defend it against all opposition. Program managers live in both worlds, but uneasily. They want to know whether a program is a good one and how to make it better. But they must always focus on operational reality. They have to make programs work.

This chapter lays out the perspectives of the people who have to make policy and run programs, the dimensions along which public managers and evaluators can best collaborate, two state case studies of implementation evaluation initiatives in which one or the other author was involved, and the authors' answers to several more general questions about the public management-implementation research nexus.

Public Management Perspectives on Evaluation: Strategic versus Operational Levels

Two major perspectives characterize the public management function: strategic and operational. At the strategic level, public management involves the formulation of public policy. Those in the business of policy formulation are generally elected and/or senior appointed officials, and their focus is on goals and objectives. At the operational level, in contrast, public management involves the implementation of programs and processes designed to achieve the goals and objectives set at the strategic level. Implementers are generally senior appointed officials and classified civil servants, and their focus is on running programs.

Unlike the ideal taught in graduate school—of an orderly distillation of public wants, needs, and desires into comprehensive rational policies and scientifically based social programs—the formulation of public policy and the implementation of social programs are only part science. They are also part art, part belief, and part guess. Public policy formulation is the business of mediating among competing public wants and desires. And the atmosphere in which such decisions are made is highly charged by the alchemy of political influence. Evaluation research can have some impact on the discussion insofar as it points out the possibility or implausibility of certain public policy goals. It less often informs the direction of political choice and future policy. It can, on occasion, help us sort out the direction we want to go, but is not the foremost currency in a political discussion of goals.

To the extent that public management has the luxury of using evaluation evidence, both impact and implementation findings are considered relevant, with the relative emphasis on the two types of evidence differing between policymakers and program managers.

Policymakers are frequently interested in impact studies, because they answer basic questions about what can achieve the results in which they are interested. They want strong evidence about programs that have produced the results they want to achieve. And impact evaluation is the best source of information on what makes a difference in people's lives. But they tend to be impatient about how long it takes to get impact results from the programs they have authored. The impermanence of political leadership puts a great deal of pressure on early results. But the time needed to produce impact results can span political administrations and terms of political leadership. The consequence of this reality is that promising programs and policies cannot be sustained without frequent short-term results. These are most often the product of implementation research.

In addition to the advantage of speed, policymakers are also interested in implementation results in their own right. Such evidence helps describe the program they may be interested in adopting and can help them estimate the resources that will be required. Once a particular policy has been formulated, they are also interested in formulating major implementation targets (such as implementation of regulations, information systems programming, and program start dates) and determining whether they have been met. But it is the early availability of implementation results that make them most attractive to policymakers.

Program managers are intrinsically interested in issues of process and implementation. They want to understand the conditions under which a program imported from another state or locality has achieved its published results. And they are much more concerned than policymakers about how the program is operated at the local level. For example, do program staff members understand the program parameters? Do recipients understand the program as intended? Are the processes in place those that were planned? How long will it take to do staff training? How will implementation milestones be tracked and monitored? Program managers are the collectors of data that provide indicators on the short-term success of the program. They are also often responsible for collecting data before the impact analysis is complete, to satisfy policymakers that the program is working.

Conventional wisdom used to be that the policymaking function basically took place at the federal and sometimes the state level, with the program management function taking place principally at the state and local levels. Under such an arrangement, it could be generally assumed that federal and state officials were interested primarily in impact studies and state and local officials in implementation studies. In the current policy environment, however, those distinctions are increasingly blurred. The very concept of devolution means that many of the strategic decisions previously made at the federal and state levels are delegated to local officials, who now debate and decide questions of both ends and means. As such, the process of devolution has increased, and changed the composition of, the customer base for evaluation research among public managers. Before the AFDC waiver process of the late 1980s, for example, few state governments were interested in either implementation or impact research. Before passage of welfare reform in 1996, few local governments were interested in either.

The Public Policy–Evaluation Relationship in the Welfare Context: History and Current Practice

A Brief History of Public Welfare Policy Research

Before the 1980s, public welfare policy research was largely an academic undertaking, done primarily to satisfy the questions of sociologists and economists about the prevalence, incidence, and precursors of poverty. Broad national evaluations such as the income maintenance experiments in the 1970s were financed by federal funding and attracted considerable federal attention. But the market for social research was limited at the state level and practically nonexistent at the local level. Because questions of equity, efficiency, and effectiveness for entitlement programs were typically fought out in the legal arena, with changes made as the result of successful suits, public officials were generally much more attuned to judicial decisions than to research evidence. Occasionally, large departments, agencies, or programs would hire accounting firms to help them deal with issues of efficiency and automation of program processes. But that was about it, until the critical thinking of the 1980s on the role and function of public assistance noted in chapter 1 brought major change.

Suddenly, the issues facing public managers changed from a focus on administrative efficiency and fairness to questions about incentives and the purpose of the public assistance system. Stimulated in part by research showing that welfare receipt was temporary for many people but a way of life for many others (Bane and Ellwood 1986), people began to ask: Does welfare support cause people to remain poor? Do people who receive assistance have a social obligation to work toward self-improvement and self-sufficiency? Is the public assistance system supposed to be a way of life or a temporary stage on the road to a better life? Policymakers began to ask program managers how the system could change in ways that shortened a family's stay on welfare, and the Reagan administration began to experiment with welfare as we knew it through the AFDC waiver program described in chapter 1. Wisconsin, New Jersey, and Ohio were the first three states approved for federal waivers under this newly focused effort, which required states to use rigorous experimental evaluation of their AFDC waiver initiatives to find ways to transform welfare from a system of cash benefit provision to one that fostered behavioral change.

In the process, social researchers and policy developers were thrust into a new relationship, as state governments sought the help of research organizations that were experienced and expert in large-scale experimental-control research designs. The financial principle of cost-neutrality was the shotgun that enforced the marriage between state welfare policy people and evaluators. Although many dedicated public policy managers now strongly support the need for sound research into what we do, many would have largely avoided academic research on the subject of welfare had it not been for the budgeters' determination that the waiver process not become a giant pork barrel for states with creative marketing skills.

Although the initial collaboration between researchers and public policy managers was undoubtedly forced, it has had a number of important benefits. It has worked to narrow the cultural differences between the two groups and removed some of the doubts and fears that might have precluded close voluntary collaboration. And it has provided new tools to help the public policy manager to manage more effectively and provided the information needed to satisfy increasingly inquisitive legislatures and media.

Models of Interaction between Public Managers and Researchers

The two worlds now join in at least three models of interaction: participatory, collaborative, and contractual. Each is described briefly.

PARTICIPATORY MODEL

Under this model, public managers are often asked to fill out questionnaires, provide program data, or participate in a study focused on a particular topic. The agency has no financial stake and limited control of results. It is encouraged to participate to the extent that it feels the results will be useful to the organization. Likely agency cooperation is a function of labor required, importance of the information to the agency, and agency trust in the research organization involved.

COLLABORATIVE MODEL

Under this arrangement, public managers enter into collaborative research projects with universities or with the federal government and a research consultant. These collaborative arrangements are among consenting partners where the results are clearly perceived as important by both partners, the ground rules are set in advance, and the partners agree to collaborate on the basis of those ground rules. These arrangements generally require larger commitments of financial resources, time, and information than do participatory ones. They are generally high profile, with commitment of foundation and public funds to the investigation of important social problems, and with financial arrangements developed to offset the evaluation costs involved. Collaborative projects require high-level commitment of the agency involved and come out of trust in the partners and commitment to the research goals. Developing such partnerships requires time.

Maintaining them requires skills around consensus building and problem solving to continually reconcile the interests of the public agency, the funding agent, and the research organization.

CONTRACTUAL MODEL

Under this model, the public manager, by way of a competitive Request for Proposals (RFP) process, purchases services directly from a university or other organization to assess or evaluate a certain issue or problem. The relationship between the agency and the contractee is negotiated through the contracting process. And the public agency typically has much more direct control than under the previous two models over what information is produced, how it is interpreted, and how it is publicly released. Agencies interested in improving performance through scientifically credible research will provide researchers appropriate freedom and resources to produce a quality product.

Examples of Research That Policymakers and Program Managers Use

The two case studies discussed next illustrate the range of evaluation evidence that can prove useful to program operators. Both are case studies of programs implemented under the AFDC waiver alternative that became available in the 1980s. The first focuses on implementation evidence that helped improve an Ohio waiver program's ability to achieve its objectives. The second discusses two findings from a Florida waiver program that informed the policy design of Florida's statewide welfare reform program.

Ohio's Learning, Earning, and Parenting (LEAP) Program

Ohio was one of three states to submit waiver applications and gain federal approval in 1987, the first year of the federal AFDC waiver program. Ohio's Learning, Earning, and Parenting (LEAP) program represented one of the first efforts to use waivers to promote behavioral change intended to prevent long-term welfare dependence.

Formulating the LEAP policy was based on both political strategy and research evidence. On the political side was growing public concern about the incidence of teen pregnancies, positive public opinion about enforcing mandatory school attendance by children of welfare recipients, and concern that interventions not be harsh or unfair to teens. On the research side was evidence that more than half of those receiving welfare for more than eight years had conceived their first child as an unmarried teenager and that teen parents are at high risk of second pregnancy. Little was known about interventions that reduced teen pregnancy and promoted school attendance.

With these factors in mind, LEAP was designed to feature the following basic provisions. Teen parents on public assistance would be required to attend school. Teen parents would be provided case management, supportive services, and child care to support school attendance. Teen parents would receive a monthly bonus of $62 if they attended school and a monthly penalty of $62 if they had more than two unexcused absences.

The Ohio Department of Human Services (ODHS) hired the Manpower Demonstration Research Corporation (MDRC) to evaluate LEAP (Bloom et al. 1991; Bos and Fellerath 1997). Because the waiver program required an independent evaluator approved by the federal Department of Health and Human Services (HHS), the relationship between ODHS and MDRC was collaborative. The relationship proved helpful in identifying critical implementation issues as well as needed changes in the policy that guided the LEAP program. The following highlights the types of implementation issues we faced and the help in resolving them that we received from the evaluation team.

Identifying Teen Parent Cases and Understanding the Program's Reach

Since the benefit issuance database did not separately identify teen parents who were part of their parents' AFDC benefit unit, the evaluators provided valuable technical assistance in improving the information system and in assisting counties to locate teen parents. Even when we had implemented improvements in our system of locating teen parents, we discovered that the number of such parents under age 18 was much lower than was the common perception. The second-pregnancy rate of teen parents was higher than expected, however. In addition, the evaluators helped us understand that, despite all our good intentions, the LEAP program process was touching only about two-thirds of the teen parents in the caseload. This helped us identify high- and low-performing counties and helped target technical assistance to the low-performing ones (typically those that did not have staffs dedicated to LEAP but allocated LEAP responsibility among AFDC case managers more generally).

DEVELOPING A UNIFORM METHOD OF CALCULATING BONUSES AND SANCTIONS TO TEEN PARENTS

We had not anticipated that attendance requirements and record-keeping would vary widely from school district to school district. We had to solve this problem for both administrative reasons (to provide equitable bonuses and penalties) and research reasons. Evaluation staff helped develop a uniform method of attendance tracking and bonus/penalty calculation.

MEASURING THE EFFECTIVENESS OF INTENSIVE CASE MANAGEMENT

In addition to the problem of locating teen parents among the caseload, the ongoing implementation evaluation identified several other problems that required attention if program functioning was to improve. Two deserve particular mention here. First, interviews with case managers and teen parents revealed that both parents and boyfriends were often impediments to school attendance because they perceived that their control over the young woman in question was threatened. Second, child care use among teen parents was far below our expectations. At the suggestion of the evaluators, who had determined that the school busing pattern in the Cleveland public school randomly assigned children to different high schools, we developed a test to determine the effectiveness of intensive case management to overcome these and other barriers. The Cuyahoga County Department of Human Services helped develop a series of intensive case management interventions in half the high schools. This intervention increased school attendance and graduation rates (GED and regular high school).

CHANGING POLICY BASED ON EARLY FINDINGS

Early findings indicated that low school attendance was due at least in part to two factors: regulations permitted pregnant teens to be exempt from program requirements, and teen parents were choosing to take the sanctions rather than comply with the program requirements. Identifying these factors enabled us to make policy changes to the LEAP program that were based on statistically reliable data (in contrast to how much public policy is formulated). Medical exemptions were substantially curtailed, with the pregnancy exemption requiring documentation of medical necessity. In addition, grade completion bonuses were raised to $62 per year and the high school graduation bonus to $200; and the maximum penalty for extensive noncompliance was raised to include the removal of the teen parent and child from the AFDC grant.

HELPING PROVIDE INFORMATION TO KEY CONSTITUENCIES

The ability of the evaluator to obtain media coverage of the project made a crucial contribution to keeping the allegiance of relevant policymakers throughout the project. Results from the LEAP program appeared in state and national newspapers as well as major periodicals. This helped communicate the results to major policymakers in the state, which, in turn, helped sustain the program through a transition from one political administration to another. Statistical information is critical, but some policymakers tend to distrust it. This group needs anecdotal evidence— the stories that put a human face on the statistical package. The interviews that were part of the implementation analysis helped identify the needed examples of LEAP's success in "helping participants triumph over adversity."

LEARNING A PRACTICAL LESSON: NOT ALL ISSUES GET RESOLVED

However great the collaboration, problem solving, and mutual admiration between researchers and public policy managers, certain areas remain conflictual. A major one in our case was ownership of the evaluation data. ODHS wanted an internal database for departmental research and a public access file, free of identifying data, that other researchers could use. But creating these files would have required the use of identifying information to link evaluation survey data with other relevant data sets. MDRC was unwilling to provide that information, given their pledge of confidentiality to the teen parents and what MDRC perceived as the risk of self-incriminating information being used by ODHS for potential fraud investigations (despite all protestations of ODHS to the contrary). We lost. The public access database was created without information from the personal interview data collected as part of the net impact evaluation.

The Family Transition Program in Florida

In 1993, the Florida legislature passed legislation directing that federal waivers be submitted to authorize a welfare reform demonstration, named the Family Transition Program (FTP), that included changes in eligibility rules to make work pay and enhanced funding for case management, support services and child care, and strict time limits for AFDC families that included able-bodied adults. Full implementation of the demonstration began in May 1994, with MDRC engaged to evaluate it.

The Florida Department of Children and Families (DCF) sought to accomplish both tactical and strategic objectives through MDRC's evaluation evidence combined with supplemental evaluative information gathered by DCF. Key elements of this approach included implementation feedback from MDRC's field observation, participant surveys, and case file review; early impact data from the Department's analysis of AFDC, food stamp, Medicaid, and child care benefits administrative data; longer term impact data from MDRC's analysis of administrative files; and the qualitative experience of families.

In August 1995, MDRC produced the first in a periodic set of reports (Bloom 1995; Bloom et al. 2000). The timing of this early implementation report, which provided the first systematic feedback on the demonstration, was fortuitous. Every educator is familiar with the concept of a student's teachable moment. A similar concept operates in the public policy realm. Sometimes legislative initiatives reach a point where action is going to be taken, regardless of evidence. In these circumstances, any evidence forthcoming, however preliminary or rough, is a thousand times more valuable than the best possible evidence that is not yet available. Florida's debate over welfare reform in the latter part of 1995 was one of those moments.

In the fall of 1995, the Florida Senate formed a Select Committee on Social Services Reform to study issues of welfare reform. In late October of the same year, the governor decided to develop a comprehensive statewide welfare reform plan for submission to the legislature in early 1996. As planning for what ultimately became Florida's Work and Gain Economic Self-Sufficiency (WAGES) program moved into high gear, early findings from the FTP pilot became one of the important inputs into the new program's design. Two decisions, in particular, were influenced by FTP evaluation findings: sanctions policy and the generosity of the earnings disregard.

Sanctions Policy

The FTP waiver program did not change the sanctions rules operating under the regular AFDC and food stamps programs. Under those rules, noncompliant families had their AFDC grant reduced by about $61 a month. But that was reflected as an income loss in the food stamp benefit calculation that increased the food stamp benefit amount by about $20 a month. Thus, the effective sanction for noncompliance was only about $40 a month. Months while sanctioned were, however, counted under FTP rules as contributing toward the time limit.

MDRC data confirmed program staff perceptions that the sanctions policy was not effective in improving program compliance—both because the net effect, given the food stamp benefit increase, was not large, and because some clients were using the system by being noncompliant just until sanctions were about to be imposed and then complying, only to repeat the noncompliance cycle later.

Although the general finding of gaming was not surprising or new, the role of sanctions in a time-limited program was unexplored territory. As we focused on this issue, reports from frontline managers were increasingly insistent that noncompliance was not distributed evenly across the caseload. Those who began program noncompliance early in their program participation were those who were most likely to approach the time limit without good prospects for economic independence. Case managers reported being frustrated that current sanctions policy gave them no leverage to enforce meaningful participation early enough in the program to get certain individuals on the right path and avoid their reaching the time limit with few options for fostering independence. Those findings led directly to the decision to raise the sanction for noncompliance under the WAGES program to encompass the whole family benefit.[1]

EARNINGS DISREGARD

The inherent challenge in setting an earnings disregard is to increase the reward for working without breaking the assistance budget. The regular AFDC program disregarded the first $30 of earnings a month and then an additional one-third of the remaining earnings for four months. The FTP demonstration increased the disregard to the first $200 of monthly earnings and then one-half of the remaining earnings for as long as the individual remained employed.

Our original reason for this increase was to provide a stronger incentive to work, although we were aware of two potential pitfalls. First, the higher earnings disregard would let people stay on assistance longer, which seemed somewhat at odds with the idea of time limits. Would this confuse the time limits message? Second, would we be able to afford the increased cost? We felt relatively safe in trying this policy out in a demonstration context. But it is doubtful that we could have put such a provision into the statewide program without a good sense of the potential cost consequences. Here, again, the FTP evidence saved the day.

First, we heard from MDRC of more general findings that the effects of poverty on children were particularly bad if children grew up in deep poverty of long duration. The less deep the poverty and the shorter the stay in poverty, the less drastic the negative effects. This offered validation of our policy to raise the disregard. Increasing family income to keep the family out of deep poverty would be worthwhile, even if the family did not escape poverty entirely (a relevant concern in a low-grant state such as Florida).

But could we afford it statewide? Here evidence from the waiver demonstration became important. Although MDRC had no impact evidence yet available, the Department had established a benefit tracking system to enable us to produce the federal cost-neutrality reports that were a waiver program requirement. That evidence showed that the higher proportion of people working under FTP than under AFDC more than offset the increased benefit cost due to the more generous earnings disregard. At the same time, early implementation evidence from the evaluation suggested that FTP participants were more likely to understand the negative incentives (time limits and sanctions) than the positive ones. This suggested to us that our demonstration cost results were probably conservative and could even be improved with more effort devoted to helping participants understand the generosity of the earnings disregard. The combination—potentially beneficial effects on children of more family income plus evidence indicating that raising the disregard would not break the bank—led us to include the more generous disregard in our proposal for statewide welfare reform, which was successfully incorporated into the state's WAGES program.

Pointers for Effective Interaction between Public Managers and Evaluators

The policy/program and evaluation worlds have certain similarities. Both begin with assumptions that are to be tested, and both wish, other things being equal, to improve policy design and program implementation. But it is important to recognize that other things are not equal and that the fundamental goals of the two groups are inherently different. The following points highlight relevant differences:

- In the public policy/program arena, as has been said, "Success has a thousand fathers; failure is an orphan." In the research world, both success and failure have value.
- The public manager categorizes facts as either beneficial or detrimental to the cause at hand. The researcher tries to establish the facts objectively.
- The public manager is required to provide information, make decisions, and react on short notice. The researcher is required to wait until the evidence is fully developed before drawing firm conclusions.
- The public manager develops a practical sense of what will and will not work based on the bump and grind of daily experience. The researcher is reluctant to generalize from the immediately relevant experience.
- In any interaction, the public manager worries about how the facts are going to be interpreted and presented and whether the evaluator understands the organization's adversaries and allies. The researcher is worried about whether the necessary access to information and key processes will be provided, about whether scientific standards will be honored and supported, and about how critical he or she can be before that stance affects the ability to get good information.

In light of these important differences, we as public managers have a few pieces of advice (1) to help evaluators position themselves to get the information they need for their work and (2) to foster the maximum use of their findings in the public arena. We couch our advice in the form of answers to questions we are frequently asked.

The Types of Implementation Analysis That Are Most Helpful to Public Managers

We single out three types of implementation research that are particularly useful to public managers: syntheses of previous research, case studies, and ongoing implementation research.

Syntheses of previous implementation efforts are invaluable to policy managers in both the formulation of strategies and the adjustment of programs already in operation. These products should describe the range and variation of previous program efforts that are related to the policies or programs in question. They should also include a distillation of relevant effects on similar policy goals achieved by other programs.

Good case studies can assist policy managers with the details needed to design operational interventions. To be effective, these studies must have succinct executive summaries that include clear discussions of implementation issues, design elements, and results. Case studies that describe the implementation process and key program elements are useful to public managers. They can be informed by previous research as well as ongoing research on current implementation efforts.

Ongoing implementation studies of current efforts can inform program managers about the efficiency and effectiveness of program approaches. Further, they can point out unintended consequences of the program, which may be positive or negative. Ongoing studies can also help public managers become aware of the extent to which a program is actually reaching its intended clientele, identify design flaws and implementation difficulties, and point to ways to strengthen the program.

The Relative Values of Impact Evaluation versus Stand-Alone Implementation Studies

Both have value. The case studies we discuss in this chapter focus on implementation studies done as part of impact evaluations. But we also use implementation findings obtained in other research contexts. Our sanctioning discussion, for example, references a recent survey of sanctioned individuals that was done without any connection to an impact evaluation. And Florida State University has performed surveys of former WAGES participants to gather information about child care use, sanctions, and reasons people leave welfare. These were done with no impact evaluation connection and all have provided information of use to us.

External versus Internal (Agency) Evaluations

State and county agencies now have access to more administrative data than we could ever hope to analyze. We use internal data for decision-making, but we do not like to do formal evaluations in-house. Experience has taught us that the media and legislators too frequently see agency evaluations as not being objective—particularly if the findings are positive. It makes no sense to commit to the time and expense involved in an evaluation unless the results will be accepted as valid. Outside evaluations are preferable for this reason, and we place a premium on the proven integrity and credibility of the evaluator. Administrators understand the difference between marketing and evaluation. Having evaluations done by outside organizations with a proven track record enables everyone to recognize this distinction.

Rating In-State versus Out-of-State Evaluation Resources

In many states, Florida being one of them, state purchasing rules allow agencies to work with state universities without having to go through all the competitive procurement procedures that would otherwise apply. This gives us an incentive to work with in-state universities as long as they can perform the type of evaluation we need. If they cannot, or we are not confident they can do the best job, we will almost always use a competitive procurement process involving an RFP and a formal evaluation of the bids received. In this case, there is no particular advantage to being an in-state bidder. Proposal procedures are always "done by the book" and the only way a bidder can influence the outcome is to submit the best proposal.

Does the Cost of Research Affect Decisions?

The cost of research can be high, but is generally a lot less than the cost of operating without the information. We tend to assess the cost of a potential research study in one of two ways. If there is a specific budgetary ceiling for a project, we structure the RFP to ensure that the bidders stay within that ceiling. Otherwise, although cost is a factor in assigning points in the rating of a proposal, it is not the major one. As long as we remain within whatever budget constraint exists, issues such as proven competence, expertise, and credibility are weighted more heavily than cost. When we are purchasing file folders or pencils, decisions tend to be based on relative cost. For evaluations, we tend to decide on the basis of ability to produce a quality product.

Barriers Researchers Must Overcome to Obtain Access to Agency Information, Staff, and Data

Two important factors influence our willingness to participate in outside evaluators' research: whether the findings will be worth the investment of time and whether the project requires access to client data.

During the implementation of welfare reform, state agencies received surveys or questionnaires from literally dozens of researchers (hundreds of students with term papers to write are included). Sorting through all the requests is difficult and time-consuming. Getting us to focus on moving a request to the top of the stack requires making a compelling early case for the reason the results will be useful, either to the program or in understanding issues of general interest in the field. If the research presumes the outcome, it is likely to be found meritless. If the researcher is doing structured interviews with administrators in 10 states to document implementation issues, we are likely to find a way to participate.

For client data, if they are available or can be made available in an aggregated form without too much time or expense, there will be little problem. But if a researcher needs access to disaggregated data that are confidential, the individual is likely to have trouble gaining cooperation because of legal and ethical constraints (which often take a good bit of legal research to sort out). Researchers who want access to confidential data must be prepared to show clearly how the project satisfies the requirements of state and federal law and how it will ensure that the information will be safeguarded. Those conditions are possible to meet, but the cause will be advanced if the requestor has done the necessary homework. If the agency cannot provide client-identified information, there may still be ways to provide access to disaggregated data with identifiers removed. If researchers come armed with answers to the obvious confidentiality questions, they will have better odds of getting the information they need.

The Most Useful Way to Present Evaluation Findings

To make research accessible and useful to public managers, the writer must make major messages short and clear. The executive summary should be honed to get to the basics very quickly; more than two or three pages probably will not be read. One of the strengths of the research on children and poverty that was so important to the designers of the Florida FTP waiver program was its clear message: "Deep and persistent poverty is bad for kids." Even someone with an attention span measured in nanoseconds could understand that. Also, graphics should be used wherever possible. A clear graph is worth all the spreadsheets in the world.

Finally, there should be no confusion between research and advocacy. Advocates for a position should be straightforward. Tufts University recently published a critique of state implementation of welfare reform that used obsolete measures (like AFDC grant levels) to grade state performance (Center on Hunger and Poverty 1998). The report was released during a National Governors Association meeting, apparently for political effect. We do not know of a program administrator in the country who took the findings seriously. If the study's authors were looking for one-news-cycle publicity, they got it. If they wanted states to use their report as the basis for action, the effort was wasted.

NOTES

At the time this chapter was written, Winstead was welfare reform administrator with the Florida Department of Children and Families. The views expressed do not necessarily reflect those of either the Florida Department of Children and Families or the U.S. Department of Health and Human Services.

1. A recent survey of sanctioned individuals in the WAGES program indicates that this stronger penalty is having the intended results (Crew and Eyerman 1999).

REFERENCES

Bane, Mary Jo, and David T. Ellwood. 1986. "Slipping Into and Out of Poverty: The Dynamics of Spells." *The Journal of Human Resources* 21(1):1–23.

Bloom, Dan. 1995. *The Family Transition Program: An Early Implementation Report on Florida's Time-Limited Welfare Initiative.* New York: Manpower Demonstration Research Corporation.

Bloom, Dan, Hilary Kopp, David Long, and Denise Polit. 1991. *LEAP: Implementing a Welfare Initiative to Improve School Attendance among Teenage Parents.* New York: Manpower Demonstration Research Corporation.

Bloom, Dan, James Kemple, Pamela Morris, Susan Scrivener, Nandita Verma, and Richard Hendra. 2000. *The Family Transition Program: Final Report on Florida's Initial Time-Limited Welfare Program.* New York: Manpower Demonstration Research Corporation.

Bos, Johannes, and Veronica Fellerath. 1997. *LEAP: Final Report on Ohio's Welfare Initiative to Improve School Attendance among Teenage Parents.* New York: Manpower Demonstration Research Corporation.

Center on Hunger and Poverty. 1998. "Are States Improving the Lives of Poor Families? A Scale Measure of State Welfare Policies." Medford, Mass.: Tufts University.

Crew, Robert E., Jr., and Joe Eyerman. 1999. *After WAGES: Results of the Florida Study.* Tallahassee: Florida State University.

3

Conceptual Underpinnings of Implementation Analysis

Pamela A. Holcomb and Demetra Smith Nightingale

Since the 1996 enactment of PRWORA, studies on the implementation of welfare reform (as well as implementation studies in other policy/program areas) have proliferated.[1] Some of the studies are incorporated into formal evaluations, some focus on specific features of welfare reform programs, and many simply document what is going on in this dynamic policy arena. Implementation analysts welcome the new attention. But the recent proliferation of such studies accentuates the need for a dialogue among academics, evaluation analysts, and policymakers about methodological rigor and policy usefulness.

This is no straightforward challenge. Debate continues on the scope and dimensions of policy analysis and about the role of analysts, and even the role of social science overall, in public policy development and administration.[2] Furthermore, as noted in chapter 1, the practice of implementation analysis has evolved mainly through studies that are accumulating separately in different policy areas, with only limited sharing and communication across policy areas or between analysts in traditional academic environments and those in the wider policy research community.

Analysis of policy and program implementation, whether specifically referred to as implementation analysis or otherwise labeled, is not grounded in theory from any single academic discipline. Instead it draws theories, methodologies, and concepts from a number of different disciplines. Although no common conceptual models or frameworks are generally accepted guides to the design of implementation studies (in contrast, for example, with studies seeking to identify causation), experienced implementation researchers often have models and frameworks they have developed and modified over the course of several studies.[3]

This chapter summarizes some of the main conceptual underpinnings of implementation analysis and provides an overview of the types of studies and the range of welfare policy issues that implementation research addresses. The discussion here does not offer a comprehensive review of the theoretical developments. Rather, it provides a general policy and research context and defines some terminology that is key to understanding the methods and analyses elaborated on in subsequent chapters of this volume.

Implementation Analysis Defined

Research that describes and explains how programs, policies, and procedures are translated into operation goes by different names: implementation research, process analysis, management research, organizational analysis, case study research, or simply qualitative research (the last being somewhat misleading, because implementation analysis can combine qualitative and quantitative aspects).[4] The terminology and conventions used often reflect the particular analyst's substantive area and academic discipline.

Recognizing that these terms lack a common definition and are sometimes used interchangeably, the terminology established in chapter 1 is followed here. That is, the term *implementation analysis* is used as an umbrella term referring to a range of studies that address the ways public policies are developed and implemented—from the early stages when legislation is formulated and regulations developed, to the actual delivery of services at the grass roots level, and all administrative, political, and operational stages in between. Thus, implementation analysis is a category of research within the broader domain of policy analysis.

Although the importance of implementation analysis is increasingly recognized, confusion remains about this category of research on several dimensions, including philosophical underpinnings, disciplinary foundations, and methodological approaches.

The philosophical dimension is captured in the intensifying debate about the dominant role of positivism in much public policy research.

The traditional research criteria of validity, reliability, and objectivity originate from positivism, described by Devers as "a philosophy that proclaims the suitability of the scientific method to all forms of knowledge (natural and social) and gives an account of what that method ideally entails . . . accompanied by a broad commitment to the idea that the social sciences should emulate the natural sciences" (Devers 1999, 1157). Disciplines that are primarily quantitative in approach, such as economics, adhere fairly strictly to positivist criteria in design and analysis. In contrast, disciplines that focus more on analyzing phenomena of social constructs, such as individual feelings, subjective experiences, and various personal perspectives, are more likely to emphasize qualitative research.

A growing cadre of post-positivists are questioning the validity of positivist standards for research on inherently social issues, often endorsing the establishment of special criteria for the standards that should guide studies that are essentially qualitative—rather than presuming that the traditional standards that emerge from positivist scientific perspectives will suffice (Devers 1999). Concerns raised by proponents of a post-positivist paradigm for policy research and qualitative analysis, particularly since the late 1980s, offer an important forum for understanding some of the confusions surrounding key dimensions of implementation analysis, even though they do not resolve them.

In any case, implementation analysis of policies and programs does not fit neatly into either a positivist or a post-positivist paradigm, in large part because the types of questions analysts are called upon to address have both quantitative and qualitative aspects. At a basic level, for instance, implementation research seeks to *explain* and *describe* how closely actual implementation meshes with original intended policies, why discrepancies or modifications occur, and what (if any) effect implementation has on subsequent policy decisions. This is generally done by examining the key aspects of a program or policy intervention to learn what it intends to accomplish, how it changes as it is implemented through various parts of the system, and how it works in reality.

Implementation analysis ideally recognizes the organizational dynamics involved in program implementation, which include routine, ongoing adaptation, and modifications. Discrepancies between original design and subsequent operations may occur because of some failure of implementation, but they more often reflect normal organizational responses to operational experiences. Qualitative, contextual, and interpretive analyses are all essential for fully understanding a program because many different perspectives (e.g., those managing programs, those delivering services, those receiving services) are involved. Often these types of studies also take into account external factors, such as the economic, demographic, or political climate, which may shape the way a program is implemented, influence program outcomes, or both. Analysis of these external factors involves inherently quantitative methods.

Similarly, implementation research often focuses on the details of program processes: understanding the internal dynamics and structure of a program, the organizational context in which the program operates, how clients enter and move through the program, and how the program is structured and managed. Describing and analyzing the process generally involves dividing program services or client activities into discrete components, documenting how the components fit together in client flow, and obtaining a variety of perspectives from people inside and outside the program on the strengths and weaknesses of the various components. A combination of qualitative and quantitative analysis, here again, is likely to produce a more accurate and comprehensive description and assessment of the process than either might produce alone.

Welfare reform at the beginning of the 21st century is an ongoing, dynamic process that is creating a variety of institutional, systemic, and administrative changes within and outside welfare agencies. These, in turn, raise a number of questions and issues on which it is important for implementation research to focus. Table 3.1 lists three major types of implementation studies, along with the primary foci of each, and shows how the chapters in Part Three of this volume fit into the typology depicted in the table.

Theoretical Dimensions of Implementation Analysis

No single research design, philosophical paradigm, or theoretical model underlies the branch of study we call implementation analysis. Further, there is no standard set of research questions or library of data collection instruments. (Nor, as discussed in the next section, does any single academic discipline dominate the field.) That said, however, and with due recognition of the concerns of both positivists and post-positivists, it is generally agreed that well-designed implementation studies should rely on an analytic process that, though not rigidly bound by existing theory,

Table 3.1. Selected Types of Welfare Implementation Studies

Major study types	Primary implementation focus	Chapter examples
Institutional analysis	• Formal stages of policy implementation, from conceptualization to institutionalization • Administrative and systems change: structural, political, cultural dimensions • Details of procedures, practices, organizations, and management • Operational practice: service delivery procedures, line operations, client flow • Promising practices and program models	• "Field Network Studies," Lurie (chapter 5) • "Street-Level Research: Policy at the Front Lines," Brodkin (chapter 7)
Program management	• Program outcomes and performance • Program evolution, policy refinement/formulation, performance improvement	• "Performance Analysis," Mead (chapter 6)
Observational	• Client/customer perspective on policies and programs • Staff perspective on policies and programs • Ecological context of policies and programs	• "Client-Based Ethnographic Research As a Tool for Implementation Analysis," Edin (chapter 8) • "Street-Level Research: Policy at the Front Lines," Brodkin (chapter 7)

is guided by a theoretical framework that serves not only to structure the conduct of the study but also to present its results and findings. At the same time, implementation researchers must use such frameworks flexibly, to incorporate into their analyses the perspectives of a variety of "actors" in the policy or program process.

Theory is defined by *Webster's Third New International Dictionary* as "the general or abstract principles of a body of fact, a science or an art . . . the coherent set of hypothetical, conceptual, and pragmatic principles forming the general frame of reference for a field of inquiry . . . a plausible or scientifically acceptable general principle or body of principles offered to explain phenomena." In practice, different academic disciplines use and refer to theory in different ways. In such disciplines as economics, for example, there is a body of generalizations, principles, and assumptions that form the core of generally accepted scholarly theory. That theory has been tested, refined, and validated through much scholarly research and can be reliably used to conduct empirical analysis. Disciplines such as anthropology and sociology, in contrast, begin with the view that theories can continuously evolve and expect conceptual models and frameworks to draw on a variety of concepts, or combinations of theories, to help define categories of variables appropriate for a particular study and further refine theory in the context of that study.

Another way to think about such differences is to note that disciplines differ in the relative emphasis they place on deductive versus inductive analysis. Deductive analysis uses general theories and principles to guide analysis of consequences or outcomes, such as individual net impacts. The "consequences" are thus deduced from general principles. Inductive analysis, in contrast, involves reasoning from a part to the whole, from individuals to a relevant universe.

Implementation analysis techniques place relatively strong, though not total, emphasis on inductive approaches. Studies usually (although not always) involve documenting or assessing in considerable detail one or more programs (or agencies or study sites, etc.), and often apply that knowledge to a broader or higher purpose. A conceptual framework can help guide the design of an implementation analysis project. But the ultimate analysis typically involves organizing and categorizing information to address the issues of interest and using the resulting findings and observations to further refine the framework. Implementation studies are commonly used, for example, to reach the following types of analytic objectives:

- to *develop program typologies* or models based on studies in selected sites or programs;
- to *generalize conditions or experiences* in selected sites to a broader universe of sites (e.g., identify whether or how particular legislative or regulatory provisions are being implemented; or identify political, environmental, or organizational factors that are affecting implementation); and

- to *suggest "best practices" or potentially promising approaches,* in particular types of jurisdictions or for particular types of individuals, based on analysis and observation in selected sites.

Using theory-based frameworks and predominantly inductive analysis, therefore, program implementation studies can simultaneously be both *knowledge based* and *theory based* to produce defensible conclusions. Such carefully designed studies stand in contrast to less formal efforts that do not use formal fieldwork protocols and involve visiting a few convenient sites, meeting with local administrators, touring a program, and possibly speaking with clients. Although one might obtain a valuable sense of "what is going on" from a study like this, it is not based on a conceptual framework and lacks methodological rigor—which prevents it from adding credibly to the knowledge base.

An implementation study of even one program in one or a few sites (i.e., case studies), if well structured, can build the knowledge base and contribute to theory. Multiple or iterative studies improve these prospects. For example, repeating studies focusing on the same program, agency, or service delivery strategy provides researchers with improved understanding of program intricacies, which often allows data collection instruments and measures to be standardized and improves the validity of findings. Patton (1997) suggests that combining inductive analysis with a user-focused approach to theory can help implementation researchers work with users (e.g., policymakers, program administrators) to make their "theory of action" explicit, including goals, mission, objectives, and expectations. Sherwood and Doolittle (chapter 9 of this volume) describe similar approaches that allow both testing the theoretical assumptions and observing the reality of program operations.

Similarly, "theory of change" approaches are increasingly used in research on community-building initiatives, which typically have multiple objectives, multiple stakeholders, and programs operating at various levels—that is, neighborhood, community, city, institutions, regions (Connell and Kubisch 1998). Researchers applying this approach devote considerable attention in the initial stages of a project to articulating various perspectives about objectives and about how the change process occurs. In effect, there are often many "theories" of change, each of which is incorporated into the definition of short-term and long-term outcomes that are ultimately tracked over time by researchers. Fully documenting and assessing the process and progress toward outcomes requires under-standing all applicable perspectives about change.

Thus, theory enters into implementation analysis at multiple points:

- Specifying the study design: conceptual framework, hypothesis development, levels of analysis;
- Developing data collection protocol: program/site selection, instrumentation methods;
- Clarifying and then applying the analytic approach: units and levels of analysis, types of analysis; and
- Building theory and refining concepts and frameworks for subsequent studies.

Disciplinary Contributions to Implementation Analysis

Implementation analysis draws from many academic disciplines. Table 3.2's non-exhaustive list illustrates the variety of disciplines underlying implementation studies that are particularly evident in implementation studies of welfare reform issues. As can be seen, such studies benefit from a range of theories from a variety of academic disciplines, especially those of organizational behavior, social networks, economic behavior, and group dynamics. The conceptual framework for particular implementation studies, or sets of studies, is developed from some combination of disciplinary approaches such as those appearing in table 3.2.

Urban Institute implementation studies of welfare-to-work programs, for example, have drawn extensively from organizational theory and systems theory to build a conceptual framework that incorporates both a macro- and a micro-organizational perspective. This conceptualization can be likened to studying a three-dimensional entity such as a sphere.

To understand how a program fits within its broader environment, one would view the sphere as a whole—its shape, its form, its movement or change over time, its proximity to other spheres, and the like. This macro-implementation analysis perspective examines the larger environment in which a program operates and the external factors that can affect program operations and outcomes. For a welfare-to-work program, this might include understanding various institutional and community contexts such as economic and demographic characteristics; the political, bureaucratic, and community environment, including relevant federal

Table 3.2. Theoretical Contributions to Welfare Implementation Analyses

Academic discipline or area	Selected theories, concepts, and methods
Political science	Implementation theory, political behavior, political culture, governance theory
Sociology	Social network theory, bureaucratic behavior, group dynamics/behavior, phenomenology, child and family development
Organizational development	Organizational behavior, management theory, network theory
Public administration	Public management theory, performance analysis, program budgeting/accounting
Economics	Microeconomic behavior and theory, macroeconomic theory, labor economics, welfare economics, economic development theory, industrial relations
Public finance	Cost-benefit analysis, fiscal federalism
Anthropology	Ethnography, cultural dynamics
Evaluation	Evaluability assessment, individual impact analysis, program outcomes analysis
Operations research	Systems analysis, decision theory, simulation analysis, group dynamics
Law	Constitutional law, labor law, civil rights, family law, administrative law, legislative development
Psychology	Cognitive development, communication, relationships
Social work	Social work practice, social work administration
Public policy	Policy process, policy analysis, simulation, public management, program evaluation

and state regulatory and policy decisions; current and past activities of other agencies that may influence program operations and outcomes; the local labor market; and the local employment/education/training and social services system.

A macro-implementation approach to examining welfare reform would thus include studies designed to track or analyze how a new national policy is being implemented nationwide by observing the emerging system in selected states or sites. Field network studies (such as those described by Lurie in chapter 5) adopt a macro perspective, as does the multistate *Assessing the New Federalism* project at the Urban Institute (see Burt, Pindus, and Capizzano 2000). The primary objective is to understand the process of change in the nation, and the method for acquiring that understanding is to track and analyze a sample of jurisdictions. Secondary objectives include documenting and explaining in considerably more detail the change process as it plays out in the selected states.

A micro-implementation approach is necessary to fully understand and analyze specific functions and processes. This implies the need to "slice" the sphere to examine how it operates internally. The micro-organizational implementation perspective involves documenting in detail service delivery procedures, management functions, client flow, staff responsibilities, and other activities or processes within a program that help define its operations. Mead's performance analysis (chapter 6) and Brodkin's street-level analysis (chapter 7) take micro-organizational approaches to different slices of the sphere. Even when focusing on a slice, analysts should not ignore the form and features of the sphere as a whole.

Many implementation studies use a macro perspective and several micro perspectives simultaneously. For example, a cross-site study (Holcomb et al. 1998) of Work First programs as components of state welfare policy reform was concerned primarily with describing and assessing the implementation of strict work requirements and short-term job search. From a micro perspective, this involved documenting all steps of the welfare intake, eligibility, and employment assistance procedures followed by specific caseworkers in a sample of local welfare offices and analyzing client participation data. But full understanding of the implementation of work requirements also required consideration of the macro-organizational context within which each local program operated. This involved examining contextual factors important in each site and across sites, such as the condition of the local economy and labor market, changes in state policies, local organizational support for state policies, and variations in operations across offices in the same state.

Thus, no one standard conceptual framework can be applied to every implementation study. Each study involves developing a framework that draws on relevant intellectual theory, either from established academic disciplines or from accumulated knowledge from past studies of similar programs/policies. Theory can help refine the research questions, clarify units and levels of analysis, isolate relationships among factors that affect implementation, and allow intellectual feedback to refine and build theory. Earlier findings, especially from multiple studies using similar conceptual frameworks, can then be used to generate "grounded" theory—

grounded because the refinements emerge from analysis of real-life experiences of a program.[5]

Common Features and Key Research and Design Issues across Implementation Studies

Recognizing that there is no one standard design for an implementation study, the chapters in this volume suggest a number of features that many welfare studies have in common, despite different disciplinary and substantive perspectives and methodologies. Some studies employ a top-down design to analyze policy development and program structure (see Lurie's discussion in chapter 5); others adopt a "street-level" approach from the bottom up (see Brodkin's discussion in chapter 7) to assess service delivery. Process studies that are incorporated into formal experimental-design evaluations (see the Sherwood and Doolittle discussion in chapter 9) are discussed, and examples of program performance analysis are described (see Mead's discussion in chapter 6). A number of common themes run through them. That commonality provides a useful basis for beginning to clarify what implementation analysis is, and to suggest important dimensions common to well-designed implementation studies:

- A primary stated objective is to further the policy community's "understanding" of issues of interest (rather than just provide simple description), such as how policy is interpreted in practice; how practice affects program performance; and what similarities and differences exist across programs, across staff and work units, across locations, and over time.
- Research and analysis designs are based on theory but are dynamic. That is, they use knowledge accumulated over time from prior studies, and refine and contribute to subsequent theory building. This is the case even in studies that also include theory-driven deductive analysis for testing hypotheses, such as process components of formal evaluations of program impacts on individuals.
- A combination of qualitative and quantitative analyses is used.
- The design and analysis take an institutional perspective—meaning that a program, institution, system, or organization is the unit of analysis.
- Multiple methods of data collection are used.

- Conscious efforts are made to maintain general standards of quality in research and analysis methods (e.g., validity, reliability, objectivity).

Although the exact research questions addressed by implementation analysis will vary according to the overall research objectives of a given study, some general categories of inquiry commonly explored by implementation and process research in the welfare area can be categorized as follows:

- *What are the major goals and assumptions underlying the policy that was adopted?*
  What are the policy's underlying premises and assumptions? What is the policy intended to accomplish?
- *What is the organizational and service delivery structure and context in which the policy is operationalized?*
  How is the organization structured? What are staff roles and responsibilities? What organizational arrangements and linkages are in place to deliver services? What types of interagency and inter-program interactions and collaborations are involved?
- *How are key management functions carried out and what role do they play in the program?*
  How is program planning structured? Who is involved? What types of management information are used and for what purposes (e.g., planning, monitoring, performance analysis, performance improvement, evaluation)?
- *What is the sequence and timing of client activities?*
  How do clients learn about and access services? How do clients move through a program (e.g., intake, eligibility determination, work orientation, activities)? How does client flow differ based on client characteristics? How is a client's progress tracked and monitored?
- *What role do contextual factors play in shaping program operations and client outcomes?* Labor market conditions? Fiscal/budgetary conditions? Political environment? Historic program experience?

The relative emphasis placed on these (and other) questions, and the methods used to provide the desired information, will vary depending on other important design aspects of an implementation study. For instance, implementation studies may have a broad or narrow focus. They may focus on one specific policy (e.g., implementation of time limits or sanctions) or on a range of policies incorporated under one broad program strategy (e.g., moving welfare recipients into employment), or on a multipronged and complex initiative that spans a range of programs and organizations (e.g., comprehensive state welfare reform initiatives). Each provides useful but different levels of information. In-depth studies on a single topic or narrow set of related topics can illuminate how a particular policy works (or could be improved). Broader implementation studies, such as those commonly linked with comprehensive state welfare reform evaluations, provide a better understanding of whether and how the various pieces of the welfare reform initiative fit together.

Another important dimension of implementation research concerns whether the intervention being examined operates in one site/geographic area or multiple sites/geographic areas. Multisite implementation studies enable researchers to identify common patterns and trends by comparing the implementation of an intervention across locations (see Lurie's discussion in chapter 5).

It is also particularly important to be sensitive to the time in which an implementation study takes place; research findings can be different depending on whether the analysis captures a program or intervention at start-up or steady-state. The initial phase of implementation is likely to encounter an array of operational difficulties. Conducting an implementation analysis during that period can yield useful early input and feedback to program administrators. It can also provide early implementation lessons on barriers likely to be encountered and ways barriers might be avoided or overcome for those interested in replicating a similar program model or procedure elsewhere. However, answering the larger question of whether a program has been implemented as intended requires conducting analysis only after the program has reached a steady-state level of operations.

Fundamental Challenges for Implementation Research in the Current Welfare Reform Environment

Interest in and demand for freestanding welfare-related implementation research that is not coupled with any formal evaluation of net impacts on individuals is increasing rapidly. This increase occurs in part because the current round of welfare reform includes greater emphasis on changing the way in which the welfare system operates and is organized—the very types of questions and issues for which implementation research is particularly well suited. In addition, the descriptive dimension of implementation analysis is considered valuable by itself, and policymakers and/or administrators are anxious to learn what is actually happening in the field. There is also much greater interest than before in whether and how written policies are being translated into operational realities and how much variation in practice occurs across states with policies that, on paper, seem similar.

This intensified interest emanating from welfare reform provides great opportunities for analysts in the area to contribute to the theoretical development of implementation theory that has evolved in various academic disciplines over the past three decades. The recent interest in this type of research, however, also presents welfare implementation analysts with three important challenges.

1. *The need to use theory- and knowledge-based approaches, even if sponsors are impatient with such issues.*

As argued throughout this chapter, implementation studies that are both theory based and knowledge based contribute importantly to understanding how public policies are carried out at all levels of government policymaking and program operations. Implementation analysts can simultaneously contribute to building theory and knowledge and to describing and documenting program procedures and administrative practices. Study designs and methodological approaches can be continuously refined—and potentially become more standardized—based on the experiences that emerge from conducting multiple implementation studies over time in particular policy or program areas, such as welfare reform. Given the inherently qualitative nature of much implementation analysis, the understanding requires a conscious commitment by researchers to strive for the most theoretically based designs possible and to use clearly specified data collection and analysis tools, at the same time that they incorporate flexibility into their studies. Flexibility is important, because the particular combination(s) of factors that shape and influence implementation are too varied to depend on a single method of implementation analysis. Structure is important to avoid the risk of producing little more than a mass of interesting but disorganized qualitative information, with little utility or credibility.

Unfortunately, the sponsors of implementation studies are often not interested in making sure that the studies they sponsor are theory or knowledge driven. Particularly in times of major change, such as the current welfare reform environment, policymakers and administrators are concerned with obtaining rapid operational insights to help make policy decisions. This high degree of interest results in strong support and encouragement for implementation studies. But it also raises concerns about the increasing call for and proliferation of quickly completed "best practices" studies.

To minimize the tendency of these studies—and all implementation studies—to become primarily anecdotal, it is important to use multiple sources of data and multiple types of analysis. Implementation research typically relies heavily on interviews with state and local policymakers and program administrators or staff, or both. But information obtained from interviews analyzed in conjunction with other sources of data—such as observations of client and staff interactions, program participation data, or focus groups with clients—can produce a much more accurate and methodologically sound description and assessment of how a policy actually works in practice than can interview data alone. Mead (chapter 6) provides an excellent discussion of the need to combine interview data with other data sources. Charlesworth and Born (chapter 10) and Goerge (chapter 11) discuss the strengths and weaknesses of the range of data sources used in implementation studies.

2. *The need to make clear to users that implementation research is not designed to yield individual net impact findings.*
The evaluation community is increasingly recognizing that implementation analysts can contribute to the theory and knowledge base at the same time that they are describing and documenting program procedures and administration. However, the fundamental purpose of implementation research is not to make causal links between program factors and individual outcomes.

However intensely grounded implementation studies are, they cannot supplant net impact analysis (i.e., the effect of the program on individuals above and beyond what would have happened without the program), and the implementation evaluation community needs to make this clear to sponsors and users of their work. But implementation research can, and should, suggest and speculate about plausible explanations for why individual outcomes turn out the way they do, by clarifying the links between a range of factors and individual outcomes. In the context of a net impact evaluation, for example, implementation analysis can help clarify whether an unexpected negative outcome reflects an ineffective policy or simply that the program was not fully or correctly implemented. Sherwood and Doolittle (chapter 9) discuss this type of implementation research in detail.

3. *The need to withstand pressure to produce implementation findings of doubtful quality because of the demand for speed.*
The public management community's growing interest in implementation research occurs not only because of what it has to offer substantively. It also happens, as stressed by Rabb and Winstead (chapter 2), because of a perception that implementation analysis can produce quick results. Implementation researchers need to satisfy the demand for timely and useful findings while sustaining the standards of quality and integrity required of all credible research. Analysts and sponsors of research must consciously consider and balance quality versus perceived utility, recognizing that studies that fall victim to haste at the expense of rigor are not useful in the long run.

This is as important in quick turnaround studies initiated by public agencies as it is in studies designed to tackle questions of primary interest in academia. The quality of implementation research is strengthened when studies draw upon more than one methodological approach and use more than one source of data—whether they be qualitative, quantitative, or both. And by conducting theory-based studies, even with tight time constraints, implementation analysis can avoid substituting anecdotes for quality research and still address the need for immediate information that can benefit policymakers and program managers alike.

NOTES

1. In the welfare field see, for example, Brock et al. (1997); Brodkin (1997); Holcomb et al. (1998); Mead (1996); and Mitchell, Chadwin, and Nightingale (1980).
2. For a thoughtful discussion of the recent dialogue about policy analysis, positivism, post-positivism, and the role of social science, see Lynn (1999a).
3. Many analysts continue to contribute to the accumulating development of theory-building research practice. See Bardach (1996) and Lynn (1999b).
4. See, for example, Connell and Kubisch (1998) and Cummins (1999).
5. Patton (1997) refers to this as an inductive approach to theory; Yin (1994) calls it "analytic generalization."

REFERENCES

Bardach, Eugene. 1996. *The Eight-Step Path of Policy Analysis: A Handbook for Practice.* Berkeley, Calif.: Berkeley Academic Press.

Brock, Thomas, Fred Doolittle, Veronica Fellerath, and Michael Wiseman. 1997. *Creating New Hope: Implementation of a Program to Reduce Poverty and Reform Welfare.* New York: Manpower Demonstration Research Corporation.

Brodkin, Evelyn Z. 1997. "Inside the Welfare Contract: Discretion and Accountability in State Welfare Administration." *Social Service Review* 71(1):1–29.

Burt, Martha R., Nancy M. Pindus, and Jeffrey Capizzano. 2000. *The Social Safety Net at the Beginning of Federal Welfare Reform: Organization of and Access to Social Services for Low-Income Families.* Washington, D.C.: The Urban Institute. *Assessing the New Federalism* Occasional Paper No. 34.

Connell, James P., and Anne C. Kubisch. 1998. "Applying a Theory of Change Approach to the Evaluation of Comprehensive Community Initiatives: Progress, Prospects, and Problems." In *New Approaches to Evaluating Community Initiatives, vol. 2: Theory, Measurement, and Analysis,* edited by Karen Fulbright-Anderson, Anne C. Kubisch, and James P. Connell. Queenstown, Md.: The Aspen Institute.

Cummins, Jim. 1999. "Alternative Paradigms in Bilingual Education Research: Does Theory Have a Place?" *Educational Researcher* 28(7):26–32.

Devers, Kelly J. 1999. "How Will We Know 'Good' Qualitative Research When We See It? Beginning the Dialogue in Health Services Research." *Health Services Research* 34(5):1153–88.

Holcomb, Pamela A., LaDonna Pavetti, Caroline Ratcliffe, and Susan Riedinger. 1998. *Building an Employment Focused Welfare System: Work First and Other Work-Oriented Strategies in Five States.* Prepared for the Assistant Secretary of Planning and Evaluation, U.S. Department of Health and Human Services. Washington, D.C.: The Urban Institute.

Lynn, Laurence E., Jr. 1999a. "A Place at the Table: Policy Analysis, Its Postpositivist Critics, and the Future of the Practice." *Journal of Policy Analysis and Management* 18(3):411–24.

———. 1999b. "The Making and Analysis of Public Policy: A Perspective on the Role of Social Science." *The 50th Anniversary Celebration of the Institute for Social Research, University of Michigan, Ann Arbor.* Discussion Paper.

Mead, Lawrence M. 1996. "Welfare Policy: The Administrative Frontier." *Journal of Policy Analysis and Management* 15(4):587–600.

Mitchell, John J., Mark L. Chadwin, and Demetra S. Nightingale. 1980. *Implementing Welfare-Employment Programs: An Institutional Analysis of the Work Incentive (WIN) program.* Washington, D.C.: U.S. Department of Labor Monograph 78.

Patton, Michael Quinn. 1997. *Utilization-Focused Evaluation: The New Century Text,* 3d ed. Thousand Oaks, Calif.: Sage Publications.

Yin, Robert K. 1994. *Case Study Research: Design and Methods,* 2d ed. *Applied Social Research Design and Methods Series,* vol. 5. Thousand Oaks, Calif.: Sage Publications.

4

Three Generations of Implementation Research

Looking for the Keys to Implementation "Success"

Thomas Kaplan and Thomas Corbett

Although implementation studies have been part of the public policy and management literature for only the past three decades or so, concerns about program implementation were voiced much earlier. As early as 1912, for example, Charles Francis Adams, progressive reformer and journalist, published a book about mismanagement, patronage, corruption, and waste in the U.S. government's first major income transfer effort—the Civil War pensions program.[1] The book received wide public discussion (Orloff 1988; Skocpol 1992). With this negative example before them, managers who worked on President Franklin Roosevelt's new public pension program—Old Age and Survivors Insurance, better known as Social Security—devoted much attention to administrative detail, as the impressive record of that complex, nationwide program attests (Derthick 1979; McKinley and Frase 1970).

Issues of program implementation had not been wholly ignored among the social science community either. Wilbur Cohen, an administrator of Social Security as a young man and subsequently secretary of the Department of Health, Education, and Welfare in the 1960s, recalled his major professor at the University of Wisconsin in the early 1930s, John R. Commons, giving this advice to students: "If you ever have a choice between a good law that will be badly administered and a less desirable law that will be well administered, always choose the latter" (Cohen 1986, 163). Until the 1970s, however, implementation details were left mostly to bureaucrats and rarely studied. Commentators and analysts alike typically treated passage of a law as the total solution to transforming programs on the ground.

The War on Poverty created the impetus for change—stimulating a burst of monographs on issues of program implementation for reasons that, in retrospect, are not hard to understand. First, there was little evidence that poverty among the nonelderly poor was falling. Second, unlike the purely federal nature of Social Security, the largest and most enduring social program of the New Deal, many War on Poverty programs worked through state and local governments or—still more challenging—through organizations such as community action or model city agencies, which were created deliberately to be independent of local government influence. Adding to these inherent complexities was a president who was conspicuously unconcerned about any administrative challenges that the programs he proposed might present. As James Sundquist, a member of the War on Poverty Task Force, later recalled, President Lyndon Johnson believed the administration of the War on Poverty "would take care of itself" (Gillette 1996, 149). This combination of circumstances led to what has been called the first (of three) generation(s)[2] of implementation studies.

First Generation

With the rapid enactment of new War on Poverty programs and little evidence of poverty reduction among the nonelderly, a variety of social scientists began to ask why and to point to failure of implementation as a plausible suspect. Stephen Bailey and Edith Mosher (1968), Martha Derthick (1972), and Jeffrey Pressman and Aaron Wildavsky (1973) produced the initial implementation studies of the new programs, using the case study method. Bailey and Mosher considered the early (1964–66) implementation of the Elementary and Secondary Education Act. They found a harassed set of overburdened Office of Education officials who had less than nine months to spend a large infusion of federal funds for new educational programs which were, in some cases, only weakly supported by the local school staff who received the monies. The predominant pattern of implementation, said Bailey and Mosher, constituted "an administrative dialectic—a series of promulgations from [the U.S. Office of Education] which were preceded, accompanied, and followed by inputs and feedbacks from affected clientele. The process was cumbersome, and involved both under-prescriptions and over-prescriptions from Washington" (Bailey and Mosher 1968, 159). Students of government should not be surprised, Bailey and Mosher argued, that "feedback, bargaining, and compromise are as much a part of administrative as of legislative activity (208)," but the time available for this process in implementing the Elementary and Secondary Education Act was so short that the "harried reciprocities, counter-pressures, and adjustments" left many parties dissatisfied.

Derthick, Pressman, and Wildavsky reached still more negative judgments. Derthick examined federal government efforts to create model communities on vacant, federally owned urban land in a Washington, D.C., neighborhood. She judged the efforts to be a failure, frustrated by problems of federal-local coordination and citizen resistance. Pressman and Wildavsky studied a grant and loan program that the U.S. Economic Development Administration tried to implement in Oakland, California, among other cities, in the late 1960s. The program offered funds to public and private employers in return for their commitment to hire low-income African-American workers. Although all parties agreed on the general principles of the initiative, according to the study authors, successful implementation required many more detailed decisions than the process could handle. The initiative involved so many participants and agreements (the authors estimated 30 decision points and 70 agreements) that it foundered on its own complexity. Pressman and Wildavsky, noting that other federal domestic programs were still more complex and involved still more parties, expressed pessimism about prospects for program implementation more generally.

Other authors contributed similarly pessimistic analyses to this literature. Walter Williams (1976) argued that failure to attend to the complexities of implementation had been the major source of problems for the War on Poverty generally. Eugene Bardach (1977) concluded, based primarily on a study of mental health reform in California, that implementation is fundamentally a process of assembling needed contributions from autonomous actors. He argued that resource diversion, goal deflection, resistance to central administrative control, and forms of gaming with attendant energy dissipation inevitably bedevil policy implementation—because actors who must agree on many decisions to make implementation successful inherently mistrust each other and defend their own prerogatives.

Although all these analyses derived from individual case studies, most of the authors sought to add to their descriptive material, often with impressive creativity, assessments of why the particular implementation they described had failed and to find lessons that might be applicable to other implementation instances. Bailey and Mosher judged the implementation problems to lie as much in the nature of the legislation as in the quality of the implementation effort. Derthick, however, found that the implementers themselves often shared the excessive optimism of the statutory formulators.[3] Pressman, Wildavsky, and Bardach wondered about the prospects for successful implementation of any program that had to make its way through the challenges of pluralism and federalism faced by so many domestic policy initiatives.

Not all the new War on Poverty programs experienced major implementation failure, however—even those affecting diverse constituencies and administered across multiple layers of government. Job Corps, for example, and (after a difficult start) Title I of the Elementary and Secondary Education Act, an initiative for educationally disadvantaged students, enjoyed fairly successful implementation compared with the Community Action and Model Cities programs. By the early 1980s, researchers interested in implementation began to view implementation "success" as more complex than a yes/no proposition and to move beyond the complexities introduced by pluralism, federalism, and overly ambitious implementation schedules to find more precise determinants of varying levels of implementation success.[4]

Second Generation

The second generation of implementation researchers criticized two particular aspects of the earlier implementation studies: their heavy reliance on single case studies, and their hierarchical concept of implementation as a process of diffusion (or lack of diffusion) from top policymakers to operational staff. Because the two criticisms were generally distinct, we discuss them separately, starting with those concerned primarily with the single case study focus.

Critics of the single case study approach argued that—if a key purpose of implementation research is the accumulation of knowledge that allows predictions of what is likely to be successful and what is not—implementation researchers need to examine more than one case study at a time, and to give more consideration to explicit conceptual frameworks and precise definitions of explanatory variables (Sabatier and Mazmanian

1979, 1980; Van Meter and Van Horn 1975). Several first-generation researchers had developed plausible hypotheses to explain the implementation failures they observed, according to these critics, but a sufficiently deep understanding of the implementation process to allow for predictions would have to derive from broader investigation.

Two of the critics, Daniel Mazmanian and Paul Sabatier, took up their own challenge. In a well-received book (Mazmanian and Sabatier 1983), the authors considered several examples of implementation across multiple types of governmental activity, including implementation of the U.S. Clean Air Act of 1970, the California Coastal Zone Conservation Act of 1972, and Title I of the Elementary and Secondary Education Act. Mazmanian and Sabatier argued that the specificity of the goal embedded in the statute that created the program and the "tractability" of the original policy problem were key variables affecting the quality of implementation. By goal clarity, which Mazmanian and Sabatier at the time considered to be the most important influence on implementation, the authors meant statutory provisions specifying clear objectives, embodying an adequate causal theory connecting the problem and the program response, minimizing the number of veto points available to opponents, providing enough resources to implementers (including sanctions and incentives available to overcome resistance), and clearly designating supportive organizations to take up implementation responsibility. By tractability, the authors meant the availability of a clear and easily accessible technology that could solve the problem without relying on discretion by implementers or behavioral change by clients.[5] Also considered important were depth of committed and skillful implementing officials, continued support of important interests, and stability in overall socioeconomic conditions, although the authors thought of these conditions as frequently outside the control of the original policy designers.

In general, Mazmanian and Sabatier saw more possibilities for successful policy implementation than much of the literature of the 1970s had suggested. They offered examples, such as the Voting Rights Act of 1965 and the regulation of coastal development in California, in which government had specified an outcome and then achieved it. Although their book received wide acclaim (it won an American Political Science Association award 13 years after publication for its enduring influence on policy studies), it has also been the subject of criticism, including self-criticism (Sabatier 1986).

Among its critics were researchers concerned with the top-down concept of implementation, which characterized the first-generation studies and was maintained by Mazmanian and Sabatier. Based in part on the writings of Michael Lipsky (1978, 1980), Richard Weatherley (1979), and Richard Elmore (1978, 1982) on "street-level bureaucrats" and patterns of influence in organizations, several researchers challenged the view that implementation is fundamentally a question of whether policy decisions made at a high level were implemented at a lower level.

For some of these "bottom-uppers" the issue is at least partly normative—a question of whether the presence of substantial control by street-level staff over key policies is more or less desirable than control by elected or appointed elites. Richard Matland (1995) has argued, for example, that bureaucrats protected by civil service laws and their unions are less responsive to the broader public, and perhaps to their clients, than are elected officials or those appointed by elected officials. Lipsky, in contrast, in a series of complex and subtle arguments (1980), suggests that clients can impose modest costs on street-level bureaucrats who ignore their will but are powerless against higher managers.

The more frequent claim of the bottom-uppers is empirical—that the top-down conceptualization of implementation misses much of the real implementation process. The "reality," says Lipsky (1980, 207), is that "street-level bureaucrats primarily determine policy implementation, not their superiors." People who deal with real clients every day inevitably have discretion. Discretion, says Lipsky, "is required by virtue of the need for human interaction" (198) and by the high level of demands on line staff and the limited resources at their disposal. Staff in such situations inevitably establish coping mechanisms, such as limiting information to clients about the full range of services that could be available; giving priority to simple and routine cases at the expense of those likely to be more draining (or to crisis cases at the expense of those needing preventive or follow-up services); or "creaming" (biasing program acceptance to favor those most likely to do well in it).

Richard Elmore (1982) argued that, for programs in which frontline staff exercise great control, analysts who want to help policymakers exert as much control as potentially available to them should follow a practice of "backward mapping." Rather than the more traditional approach—beginning with congressional intent and mapping forward through progressively lower levels of government activity and stating an outcome—backward mapping begins with a precise statement of the new behavior desired at the lowest level of the administrative process. It then "backs up through the structure of implementing agencies, asking at each level two questions: What is the ability of this unit to affect the behavior that is the target of the policy? And what resources does this unit require to have that effect?" (Elmore 1982, 21).

In a subsequent assessment of the bottom-up criticisms of his theory, Sabatier (1986) acknowledged that the critiques had merit. He conceded that at least the European bottom-up investigations, such as those by Hjern (1982), were based on carefully described methodologies likely to yield similar results even if applied by different investigators. Sabatier thought that the most important advantage of the bottom-up investigations might be their broader focus. Because they did not necessarily start with a concern for the attainment of stated policy objectives, they could consider broader influences on agency activity that top-down investigators might miss. But Sabatier also worried that the bottom-up investigations might fail to notice the indirect influences top policymakers could exert (through setting agendas, providing or withholding resources, and establishing appointment and staffing requirements). And he criticized bottom-up research in both the United States and Europe as too lacking in explicit theory. Because bottom-up research "relies very heavily on the perceptions and activities of participants," said Sabatier, "it is their prisoner—and therefore is unlikely to analyze the factors *indirectly* affecting their behavior or even the factors directly affecting the behavior which the participants do not recognize" (Sabatier 1986, 35; emphasis in original). More recent U.S. researchers with a bottom-up orientation have investigated how street-level staff actually experience reforms imposed from top-level policymakers. Evelyn Brodkin, who discusses this approach in chapter 7 of this volume, found in earlier work that

> Caseworkers, like other lower-level bureaucrats, do not do just what they want or what they are told to want. They do what they can. Their capacity depends on their professional skills, agency resources, and access to good training and employment opportunities for clients. Within that context, their practices are shaped by agency incentives and mechanisms that make staff accountable to clients and to the public (Brodkin 1997, 24).

Marcia Meyers, Bonnie Glaser, and Karin MacDonald (1998) examined the implementation of the California Work Pays program in four counties in the early 1990s, following Elmore's (1982) recommendations for backward mapping. The authors identified characteristics of interactions between caseworkers and clients that would have to be present if Work Pays were to be successfully implemented. In particular, the authors posited that caseworkers would have to take two specific steps: suggest that work was desirable and realistic under the new policy, and show concretely how work would affect the income of individual clients. The authors then observed 66 sessions between caseworkers and clients and scored them for the presence or absence of these two characteristics.[6] Under the standards of the backward mapping structure they had created, Meyers, Glaser, and MacDonald found that successful implementation had not occurred because these two types of interaction were seen in only 18 percent of the sessions.

Third Generation

Malcolm Goggin, Ann Bowman, James Lester, and Laurence O'Toole were the first to suggest generational characteristics in implementation research. In a book titled *Implementation Theory and Practice: Toward a Third Generation* (1990a) and a separate chapter in another publication (1990b), the authors argued that 20 years of research on implementation had produced "some middle-range theorizing with substantial potential utility," but primarily propositions with "proverbial rather than scientific characteristics. The need is apparent," the authors said, "for more careful, systematic inquiry" (Goggin et al. 1990b, 183).

The authors proposed a third generation of implementation research that would use a mixed-method, dynamic model with clearly stated, testable hypotheses. An example of a testable hypothesis, the authors wrote, might be that a state agency with a high level of organizational capacity would be more likely, all else equal, to implement a new federal mandate promptly and in conformity with the original policy vision than a state agency lacking that capacity. The authors suggested that researchers could test the hypothesis by following the implementation of mandated programs in a large number of states. This could be accomplished, thought the authors, under reasonable resource constraints through interviews (usually over the phone) with top state officials, mail questionnaires (containing both closed and open response categories) of other people identified by the officials as influencing the implementation of the mandate, and careful and systematic content analysis of agency policy documents and budgets.

The advice to generate clear and testable hypotheses, and then do the multiple-site research necessary to verify or falsify them, has not been followed in most implementation work, although one of the authors did usefully test the hypothesis that certain kinds of organizational structures would best fit particular policy initiatives (O'Toole 1993) and apply formal game theory and rational choice constructs to implementation research (O'Toole 1995). Part of the problem may be with the practical difficulties (including cost) of performing multisite research. But another part of the problem may be the more fundamental difficulty of stating up front hypotheses that are both testable and sufficiently rich to be interesting (that is, more than statements of the seemingly obvious).

Recent writings on implementation have more commonly accompanied impact evaluations (as discussed by Sherwood and Doolittle in chapter 9 of this volume) or taken the form of public management advice to high-level government executives with implementation responsibilities. Some especially interesting advice has come from former government officials who moved into academic positions, such as Laurence Lynn (1981, 1987) and Richard Nathan (1993). Lynn argued that achieving the implementation of key initiatives is ultimately a question of whether public executives "secure reliable behavior from strategically significant subordinate agents within the organization" (Lynn 1987, 230). Executives can best achieve this, according to Lynn, through clearly specifying the behavior they want, creating incentives and disincentives for the appropriate behavior, and monitoring and policing. While a heavy hand is occasionally necessary, "achieving control is a subtle, largely indirect, personal process" (237), often best conducted by executives with practiced political skills.

Nathan offers different, but generally complementary, lessons on implementation: Keep the number of new initiatives manageable; select a core management group of no more than 10 people and forge relationships that allow that group to function well; stay at least five years in the same agency to allow a new initiative to bear fruit; set clear goals and, especially, reward those who meet them, but do not shirk from punishing those who do not; and avoid becoming mired in details. Both Nathan and Lynn suggest that the talents and behaviors of top executives are key variables in the success of program implementation, and that skilled executives can accomplish much.[7]

Do Three Generations of Implementation Research Offer Lessons for the Study of Welfare Reform?

Peter deLeon (1999), noting that the field is losing some of its most original and persuasive investigators (including Eugene Bardach and Paul

Sabatier) to other research interests, calls for implementation analysts to change their expectations about what implementation research should (and can) offer. He suggests the need for a fourth generation of research that would (1) expend as much energy describing implementation success as its failure; (2) accept (following the approach of Deborah Stone [1997]) that implementation of new programs can be "all right" by appropriate standards of government administration, even if it appears flawed under the different standards of the market; and (3) accept, at least for a while longer, simple implementation descriptions without demanding predictive capability.

The fundamental message of the subsequent chapters in this volume suggests that deLeon's third point at least is overly pessimistic, for at least two reasons. First, although the formal predictive capability that comes from establishing causation may be an inappropriate goal for implementation research, such research has much more to offer in illuminating the issues involved in policy and program implementation than "simple description." Second, searching for any single best approach to implementation analysis is both unnecessary and unproductive. Various complementary approaches are now being used, productively, many of which have their roots in the earlier implementation analysis work reviewed in this chapter. Backward mapping, for example, has great potential for helping illuminate the welfare reform implementation process, which is designed explicitly to encourage local staff initiative.[8] Especially if future implementation researchers can persuade agency managers to allow observation of randomly selected staff-client interactions, the backward-mapping effort can supply important clues to what observers should watch for and code. The frontline research discussed by Brodkin in chapter 7 of this volume exemplifies a backward-mapping approach.

The top-down approach may also have new relevance under current welfare reform, as reflected in the field network approach discussed by Lurie in chapter 5 of this volume. In particular, it can offer something like a natural experiment to test the relative importance of goal clarity and problem tractability (the key variables suggested by Mazmanian and Sabatier in their 1983 book) to implementation quality.[9]

Clarity of goals—if not a feature of the Personal Responsibility and Work Opportunity Reconciliation Act of 1996 (PRWORA) as it emerged from Congress—has become a distinguishing characteristic of current state-based welfare reform. PRWORA, as might be expected of such controversial legislation, passed Congress only after compromise and with some potential inconsistencies. The act sought to establish ambitious welfare-to-work policies while also saving money, to provide a flexible block grant to states while also establishing tough outcome standards governing the percentage of the caseload that must work, and to reduce unwed pregnancy without creating a program structure for doing so. Still, PRWORA clearly specified the percentage of state caseloads that must participate in work or work-like activities. It also clearly required the U.S. Department of Health and Human Services to rank states each year on placements in long-term private sector jobs, on the number of children living in poverty, and on reductions in the percentage of out-of-wedlock births. States wanting to score well in the rankings or obtain financial rewards could be certain about the outcomes they would need to achieve.

Within this policy environment, most states have succeeded in establishing a clear vision of what their programs should do. They have largely ignored the adolescent pregnancy reduction goals of PRWORA and, aided by an unexpected drop in caseloads, focused on welfare-to-work strategies (Nathan and Gais 1999). Even some of the largest welfare agencies, in which communication from top managers to frontline staff is most challenging, have managed to create and maintain a clear welfare-to-work focus. Jason Turner, Commissioner of the New York City Human Resources Administration, described the clarity of welfare-to-work goals as a predominant feature of welfare reform in New York City:

> I think that one of the things that we discovered is that the classic management techniques that are written about in the business books are very valuable. That is, to have a vision of where you want to go. To communicate that vision to all employees. You can now go anywhere [in the New York City Human Resources Administration] and talk to any of the staff down to the lowest level and they know that our mission is self-reliance and they know that we have to get everybody who is currently receiving public assistance into private employment or alternatively into 35 hours a week of activities, of which 20 is work and the balance is other activities. . . . What politicians often do, and here I think Mayor Giuliani is a notable exception, is that they define only in some general sense where they want to lead, for instance "I want to be the education president," or something like that, but not something for which they can be measured and held accountable. We have 18,000 people understanding a very detailed and definable objective (Rockefeller Institute of Government 1999, 12).

That the broad goals are reasonably clear in most state and local welfare reform programs, however, in no way implies a uniform set of yardsticks against which to measure the performance of the different programs.[10]

Take the size and characteristics of a TANF caseload. A program like Wisconsin's W-2 initiative, for example, incorporates strong incentives to keep people off the TANF rolls—by providing child care and health benefits to low-income families that are not on TANF, on the one hand, and having no income disregards in the grant calculation for TANF participants who find a job, on the other. This combination will tend to yield a TANF caseload that is small and made up of families in extreme need whose work readiness is low. In contrast, a program that ties child care and health benefits to TANF participation and offers a generous income disregard to persons who combine TANF participation with a job will tend to have a larger caseload that is more job-ready on average.

Problem tractability—Mazmanian and Sabatier's other major criterion—may offer less reason for optimism. In general, the challenge of carrying out welfare-to-work programs is more complex than that of implementing AFDC-type income transfer programs. Program implementers have more discretion. They also face the harder tasks of developing unique plans for (and contracts with) each individual and family, ensuring compliance with those plans through careful coaching and close supervision, and determining whether any failures to comply are excusable. The new programs also depend for their success on behavioral change among program staff and participants.

A recent study by Amihai Glazer and Lawrence Rothenberg (2001) has suggested other program features that render problems harder or easier for government action to address: the credibility of government on the issue (particularly based on its previous experience with similar programs); the rational expectations of those affected by a government program; the ability of the program to be self-reinforcing (so that behavioral change induced by the program itself encourages more change); and the ability to define program success in small increments. By these standards, the prospects for successful implementation of welfare reform may be more favorable. Welfare-to-work programs may be self-reinforcing, in the sense that work by some participants may create a norm that encourages other similarly situated people to work; and the programs allow government, through the specification of performance standards as a percentage of participants who are engaging in work, to define success at multiple points of equilibrium. It is an open question whether the greater clarity of goals in the new reform environment and the presence of some of the features identified by Glazer and Rothenberg will be sufficient to overcome the technical difficulties of the welfare-to-work task.

NOTES

1. The book was titled *The Civil War Pension Lack-of-System.*
2. The "three generations" phrase comes from Goggin et al. (1990a).
3. In a subsequent study, Derthick (1990, 183) suggested that optimism for agency capabilities may be a necessary characteristic of skilled government managers: "One of the ways in which leaders motivate staffs is by articulating high expectations, which with luck are then fulfilled. By setting impossible goals, they seek to stimulate and inspire— and in the end to discover that the goals were not impossible after all. Also, pride and a sense of proprietorship inhibit the identification of organizational incapacities. Psychologically, it is not easy for successful leaders to acknowledge what cannot be done."
4. We thank Lawrence Mead for sharing his notes and thoughts on first-generation implementation research.
5. Nelson (1977, 14) provides a now classic definition of intractable problems as those that are "innate in the particular intransigencies of natural laws or in basic flaws of human nature. . . . It simply may be enormously more difficult to design policies to equalize educational achievement or to eliminate prejudices than to design spacecraft to go to the Moon."
6. The 66 sessions were selected by supervisors, not by random draw, a situation the authors acknowledged "introduced an unknown bias into the sample of clients and workers" (8). The authors also noted that the presence of observers might have influenced the nature of worker-client interactions.
7. Robert Behn offers some of the same insights and lessons from the perspective of a management and policy researcher in his book on the Massachusetts ET program, *Leadership Counts.*
8. Meyers, Glaser, and MacDonald (1998), for example, have usefully demonstrated how Elmore's backward-mapping strategies can be applied to current welfare-to-work programs.
9. Although Sabatier (1986) later rejected the importance of the goal clarity variable, subsequent research by Kenneth Meier and Deborah McFarlane (1995) found through a regression-based model that clarity of goals is a key determinant of implementation quality in publicly funded family planning programs.
10. Reaching agreement on yardsticks is problematic for any policy. Sometimes, as Matland has noted (1995, 155), statutory mandates "are exceedingly vague . . . and they fail to provide reasonable yardsticks with which to measure policy results." Even when clear statutory yardsticks are available, some researchers (Bailey and Mosher 1968; Ferman 1990) celebrate significant gaps between policy intent and actual implementation as a healthy sign of the Madisonian checks and balances deliberately introduced into the U.S. political system.

REFERENCES

Bailey, Stephen K., and Edith K. Mosher. 1968. *ESEA: The Office of Education Administers a Law.* Syracuse, N.Y.: Syracuse University Press.

Bardach, Eugene. 1977. *The Implementation Game: What Happens after a Bill Becomes a Law.* Cambridge, Mass.: MIT Press.

Behn, Robert D. 1994. *Leadership Counts: Lessons for Public Managers from the Massachusetts Welfare Training and Employment Program*. Cambridge, Mass.: Harvard University Press.

Brodkin, Evelyn Z. 1997. "Inside the Welfare Contract: Discretion and Accountability in State Welfare Administration." *Social Service Review*, March: 1–33.

Cohen, Wilbur J. 1986. "Comment." In *The Roosevelt New Deal: A Program Assessment Fifty Years After*, edited by Wilbur J. Cohen. Austin, Texas: Lyndon Baines Johnson School of Public Affairs.

deLeon, Peter. 1999. "The Missing Link Revisited: Contemporary Implementation Research." *Policy Studies Review* 16(3–4):311–38.

Derthick, Martha. 1972. *New Towns In-Town: Why a Federal Program Failed*. Washington, D.C.: Urban Institute Press.

———. 1979. *Policymaking for Social Security*. Washington, D.C.: Brookings Institution.

———. 1990. *Agency under Stress: The Social Security Administration in American Government*. Washington, D.C.: Brookings Institution.

Elmore, Richard F. 1978. "Organizational Models of Social Program Interaction." *Public Policy* 26 (spring):185–228.

———. 1982. "Backward Mapping: Implementation Research and Policy Decisions." In *Studying Implementation: Methodological and Administrative Issues*, edited by Walter Williams. Chatham, N.J.: Chatham House.

Ferman, Barbara. 1990. "When Failure Is Success: Implementation and Madisonian Government." In *Implementation and the Policy Process: Opening Up the Black Box*, edited by Dennis J. Palumbo and Donald J. Calista. New York: Greenwood Press.

Gillette, Michael L. 1996. *Launching the War on Poverty: An Oral History*. New York: Twayne Publishers.

Glazer, Amihai, and Lawrence S. Rothenberg. 2001. *Why Government Succeeds and Why It Fails*. Cambridge, Mass.: Harvard University Press.

Goggin, Malcolm L., Ann O'M. Bowman, James P. Lester, and Laurence J. O'Toole Jr. 1990a. *Implementation Theory and Practice: Toward a Third Generation*. Glenview, Ill.: Scott, Foresman.

———. 1990b. "Studying the Dynamics of Public Policy Implementation: A Third-Generation Approach." In *Implementation and the Policy Process: Opening Up the Black Box*, edited by Dennis J. Palumbo and Donald J. Calista. New York: Greenwood Press.

Hjern, Benny. 1982. "Implementation Research—The Link Gone Missing." *Journal of Public Policy* 2(3):301–8.

Lipsky, Michael. 1978. "Standing the Study of Public Policy Implementation on Its Head." In *American Politics and Public Policy*, edited by Walter Dean Burham and Martha Wagner Weinberg. Cambridge, Mass.: MIT Press.

———. 1980. *Street-Level Bureaucracy: Dilemmas of the Individual in Public Services*. New York: Russell Sage Foundation.

Lynn, Laurence E., Jr. 1981. *Managing the Public's Business: The Job of the Government Executive*. New York: Basic Books.

———. 1987. *Managing Public Policy*. Boston: Little, Brown.

Matland, Richard E. 1995. "Synthesizing the Implementation Literature: The Ambiguity-Conflict Model of Policy Implementation." *Journal of Public Administration Research and Theory* 5(2):145–74.

Mazmanian, Daniel A., and Paul A. Sabatier. 1983. *Implementation and Public Policy*. Glenview, Ill.: Scott, Foresman.

McKinley, Charles, and Robert W. Frase. 1970. *Launching Social Security, 1935–1937.* Madison: University of Wisconsin Press.

Meier, Kenneth J., and Deborah R. McFarlane. 1995. "Statutory Coherence and Policy Implementation: The Case of Family Planning." *Journal of Public Policy* 15(3):281–98.

Meyers, Marcia K., Bonnie Glaser, and Karin MacDonald. 1998. "On the Front Lines of Welfare Delivery: Are Workers Implementing Policy Reforms?" *Journal of Policy Analysis and Management* 17(1):1–22.

Nathan, Richard P. 1993. *Turning Promises into Performance: The Management Challenge of Implementing Workfare.* New York: Columbia University Press.

Nathan, Richard P., and Thomas L. Gais. 1999. *Implementing the Personal Responsibility Act of 1996: A First Look.* Albany: Nelson A. Rockefeller Institute of Government, State University of New York.

Nelson, Richard R. 1977. *The Moon and the Ghetto.* New York: W. W. Norton.

Orloff, Ann Shola. 1988. "The Political Origins of America's Belated Welfare State." In *The Politics of Social Policy in the United States,* edited by Margaret Weir, Ann Shola Orloff, and Theda Skocpol. Princeton, N.J.: Princeton University Press.

O'Toole, Laurence J., Jr. 1993. "Interorganizational Policy Studies: Lessons Drawn from Implementation Research." *Journal of Public Administration Research and Theory* 3(2):232–51.

———. 1995. "Rational Choice and Policy Implementation." *American Review of Public Administration* 25(1):43–57.

Pressman, Jeffrey L., and Aaron Wildavsky. 1973. *Implementation: How Great Expectations in Washington Are Dashed in Oakland; Or, Why It's Amazing That Federal Programs Work At All, This Being a Saga of the Economic Development Administration as Told by Two Sympathetic Observers Who Seek to Build Morals on a Foundation of Ruined Hopes.* Berkeley: University of California Press.

Rockefeller Institute of Government. 1999. *Welfare Reform in New York State: Transcript of a Policymakers Forum Held at the Nelson A. Rockefeller Institute of Government, Albany, New York, on November 17, 1998.* Albany: Rockefeller Institute of Government, State University of New York.

Sabatier, Paul A. 1986. "Top-Down and Bottom-Up Approaches to Implementation Research: A Critical Analysis and Suggested Synthesis." *Journal of Public Policy* 6(1):21–48.

Sabatier, Paul, and Daniel Mazmanian. 1979. "The Conditions of Effective Implementation." *Policy Analysis* 5(fall):481–504.

———. 1980. "A Framework of Analysis." *Policy Studies Journal* 8:538–60.

Skocpol, Theda. 1992. *Protecting Soldiers and Mothers: The Political Origins of Social Policy in the United States.* Cambridge, Mass.: Harvard University Press.

Stone, Deborah. 1997. *Policy Paradox: The Art of Political Decision Making.* New York: W. W. Norton.

Van Meter, Donald, and Carl Van Horn. 1975. "The Policy Implementation Process: A Conceptual Framework." *Administration and Society* 6 (February):445–88.

Weatherley, Richard. 1979. *Reforming Special Education: Policy Implementation from State Level to Street Level.* Cambridge, Mass.: MIT Press.

Williams, Walter. 1976. "Introduction." In *Social Program Implementation,* edited by Walter Williams and Richard F. Elmore. New York: Academic Press.

PART TWO
Using Analysis to Understand Implementation

P art two gives an overview of several methodological approaches to implementation evaluations. The methodological strategies grow out of the underlying research issues being addressed and the units of analysis being examined. Thus the chapters cover analytic strategies and methods appropriate for macro issues about how policy is filtered through large government systems (chapter 5) to methods appropriate for implementation questions at the micro level or interactions at the front line of programs (chapters 7 and 8). This part also covers important considerations for when implementation work complements impact analyses (chapter 9).

Field Network Studies (chapter 5). Irene Lurie's focus is on a method for understanding the responses of states, local governments, and private organizations to specific new, large, nonincremental federal policy changes—in other words, to understand the magnitude and direction of the program changes themselves. Called field network studies, this approach examines institutional rather than personal responses and includes multiple states and multiple local governments within each state—selected to be broadly representative of the nation and also to provide a range of variables of particular relevance to the policy change being studied. Data collection and analysis combine the efforts of two types of teams to examine the effects of the policy per se, and more generally their illustration of the behavior of officials and agencies.

One team, composed of knowledgeable observers close to the scene of action (typically academics from departments of political science, public administration and policy, economics, and social work of universities in the geographic areas under study), works in the field. That team uses a common protocol to report responses to the second team. The second team consists of researchers on a central staff, drawn from the same general disciplines, who analyze the responses within a comparative framework to provide a consistent assessment of the implementation of the program in question. Several rounds of data collection are typical, given that program change comes about slowly.

Lurie ends her discussion by assessing the field network study approach along four criteria commonly used to assess social science methods: construct validity, internal validity, external validity, and reliability. Construct validity and reliability are fostered by use of a single report form to guide research in the field. Reliability is further provided by (1) the specificity of the report form regarding data to be collected and (2) a review of the interpretations by experienced central staff. External validity is increased through comparative study of multiple cases. Lack of a counterfactual makes it impossible for field network studies to achieve internal validity, strictly speaking. However, they can be explanatory to the extent that they reconstruct a sequence of events whose relationship is revealed to be so close as to be uncontroversial.

Performance Analysis (chapter 6). Lawrence Mead's concern is with performance analysis—the branch of implementation evaluation that connects internal program practices to their measurable outcomes. The unit of observation is usually the program. "The question," as Mead puts it, "is whether program units with certain measurable features, including client assessments, perform better on outcome indicators than those with different features, when one controls for differences in the clients and the labor market."

The types of performance analysis recommended by Mead involve statistical modeling combined with field interviewing of program administrators—to gain a deep enough understanding of how the program works to guide and help interpret the statistical analysis. Study sites are chosen to reflect the full range of variation in performance, and respondents are chosen to reflect all levels of program administration. Mead recommends semistructured interview guides administered on a private and confidential basis. The main purposes of the interviews are to solicit (1) descriptions of how clients are processed through the program, (2) explanations of the indicators of program performance and client assignments included in the program's administrative reporting system, and (3) program administrators' views about what factors importantly influence program performance. In addition to a new slant on the research hypotheses generated from the literature, respondents may (as in other aspects of implementation analysis) raise entirely new factors for examination.

The statistical part of the analysis uses multiple regression, developing a model for each performance indicator and assessing the independent contribution of the major expected influences on program performance—including administrative variables (such as administrative capacity and percentage of clients participating), demographic variables, and labor market indicators. Mead addresses several methodological challenges facing users of statistical analysis, not only in a process analysis framework but also more generally. These include (1) whether administrative data really capture how a program operates, (2) whether the different explanatory variables are really independent of one another, and (3) whether any statistical basis for comparison that is not founded on random assignment to program and control groups can be sufficiently free of selection bias (participants differing systematically from the population the program is intended to serve) to be useful.

Street-Level Research: Policy at the Front Lines (chapter 7). Evelyn Brodkin turns attention to a branch of implementation analysis—street-level research—that focuses on the extent to which lower-level bureaucrats effectively make policy (irrespective of explicit program statements). This approach becomes important when formal statutes are ambiguous or when implementation requires discretionary decisionmaking at the point of delivery (as in the new environment of welfare reform).

Street-level research combines the theory and interviewing techniques of organizational and political analysis and ethnography to examine through intensive case studies the relationship between program structure and the practice of policy delivery.

Selection of cases builds on existing bureaucratic and political theory to focus on particular organizations or sets of contextual conditions—building in variation that allows the analyst to distinguish particular from systematic features in organizational practice. Street-level research adopts an ethnographic approach in that it observes workers in their "natural habitat" as well as interviewing them—seeking to make explicit the links among organizational structures, the individuals interacting within them, and their policy product.

As Brodkin notes, the chief strength of the street-level approach is its ability to delineate the logic of street-level implementation on its own terms, enabling analysts to understand and probe the consequences of what occurs "beneath the surface of policy rhetoric and administrative measures." Its chief limitation comes from the potential for observer bias and the limits of the case study approach. These can be guarded against, as in other implementation analysis contexts, by using multiple observations in different settings, multiple data sources, and theory to systematize data collection and analysis.

Client-Based Ethnographic Research As a Tool for Implementation Analysis (chapter 8). Kathryn Edin addresses client-based ethnographic research as a way to understand how various aspects of clients' lives may encourage or interfere with client responses to a program. In sharp contrast to the structured questions used by survey researchers, which are based on preconceived or generalized concepts about the issues that affect people's lives, client-based ethnographic studies let some of the complexity of the social world emerge. These insights can guide hypothesis development, improve the fit of some quantitative approaches, provide insight into possible missing variables, and occasionally even lead to whole new ways of conceptualizing the research "problem."

The fundamental technique is to create sessions that are more like a naturally occurring conversation than an interview, letting clients frame the research problem in their own ways. Typically, the process takes place over more than one in-depth session and is combined with first-hand observation (fieldwork or "hanging out") of the home environment and neighborhood. Repeated interactions build trust. They also increase the likelihood that clients are telling researchers the truth as they see it.

Sampling is obviously an issue here. Some ethnographic researchers advocate randomly selecting respondents within a target group. But when members of stigmatized populations, sensitive issues, or both are involved, concerns over trust and rapport become important, and approaches that establish the potential range of social actors within a group without random sampling per se may be more practicable.

What Lies behind the Impacts? Implementation Research in the Context of Net Impact Studies (chapter 9). Within the context of a net impact study, the primary goal of implementation research is to explain the impact findings (or lack thereof). As authors Kay Sherwood and Fred Doolittle discuss, this goal imposes research complexities on implementation analysts that they do not have to confront in other evaluation settings.

The first is that the data must be specified and collected on the basis of *anticipated* impacts. Thus, there is little room for refining hypotheses and data collection techniques as the project is proceeding. This implies that the inductive method (moving from the specific to the general) typical in other implementation research contexts does not play a significant role. As a result, the implementation study design must rely much more heavily on "existing research findings about similar programs and the theory of change articulated about the program under study. Rarely is there time to develop the research design as you go."

This need to set things more or less in stone early in the project has implications for the demands placed on implementation analysts for early feedback. There is no early feedback, by definition, on net impacts. The crucial early feedback for a net impact study is whether the program is being given a fair test: Is the target group being reached? Is the treatment adequately available and sufficiently intense to be capable of having the hypothesized impact? Is the program service context different enough from that facing the control group to constitute a difference in treatment? This feedback is needed preferably before the evaluation design has been completed and certainly before the multi-million-dollar commitment that impact evaluations typically require has been irretrievably made.

The second constraint particular to the impact-study environment is on the research and data collection methods used. It has several facets. One of the most important is that, inasmuch as the net impact study focuses on the relationship between the intervention and the individual, the implementation study must find ways to attach measures of an intervention's context, characteristics, and service implementation to specific individuals in the sample.

The need to explain net impacts also drives implementation research toward quantifiable measures, in particular to variables that are continuous rather than categorical. Rather than classifying responses as yes or no on some attribute, ranking characteristics of programs, sites, or individuals allows a fuller set of comparisons to be made. In the welfare-to-work context, for example, quantifying the measurement of differential staff commitment to various program goals across sites or participant perceptions of their program enables sites and experimental group members to be categorized by similarity and distributed along key implementation dimensions.

Sherwood and Doolittle end with an important point about the changing role of implementation research as the new policy environment moves net impact studies toward a variety of nonexperimental methods. All these methods, by definition, increase the danger of selection bias. Estimating and correcting for this potential distortion obliges impact analysts to use multiple analytic methods to tease out the truth—with implementation analysts playing increasingly important roles in designing the collection and analysis of the data needed for such efforts.

5

Field Network Studies

Irene Lurie

W hen the federal government reforms welfare programs, the institutions operating them—state and local governments and private institutions—face a new set of rules. Because these institutions have some degree of flexibility in responding to the new rules, their decisions influence whether and how the new policy is realized. One method for examining their responses to federal welfare reform, and for examining the responses of institutions to policy changes in other areas, is field network evaluation.

Field network evaluation is a form of comparative case study that was defined, and continues to be defined, by Richard Nathan (1982; Hall and MacManus 1982; Rawlins and Nathan 1982). It is fitting, therefore, to begin with his Note of Introduction to this type of study:

The conduct of field network evaluations began with the general revenue-sharing law enacted in 1972, when a projected surplus in the federal budget prompted the federal government to give general-purpose cash grants to state and local governments. Because these grants came with few restrictions, the response of state and local governments to this large infusion of money, $80 billion before the program ended in 1986, was difficult to ascertain. Economists were skeptical that learning this was even feasible. At a meeting at the Brookings Institution soon after the law was passed, Arthur Okun, who chaired the Council of Economic Advisers under President Johnson, expressed his doubts. "What would you say," he asked, "if your mother gave you a check for $30

(then a lot of money) for your birthday and asked you what you did with it?"
His point was that fungibility makes it difficult—well-nigh impossible, I
think he said—to know what happens to such a gift.

I responded to Okun that I was confident that studying state and local
political behavior (both for policymaking and implementation) would tell us
a great deal about what different governments (rich, poor, big, little) do with
their shared revenue. However, no one seemed satisfied with my response. It
was that old conversation between economists and political scientists. For-
tunately, Brookings had money from the Ford Foundation to study the effects
of the program and we were able to march ahead anyway.

The conclusion I reached two years later when we were in the midst of the
field evaluation of the revenue-sharing program was that my instinct in
responding to Arthur Okun was correct. We did learn a lot systematically and
inductively about the behavior of recipient governments in their use of shared
revenue. Many recipient jurisdictions, as it turned out, were wary about
adding these funds to their program base—i.e., using the money for ongoing
operating purposes. Capital purposes were a big use. This was especially the
case for smaller, relatively well off, generally conservative local governments.
They feared locking this "found money" into their fiscal base, and later hav-
ing to raise taxes or lay off civil service workers when the "Feds" changed the
rules as they were sure to do, or turned off the spigot, which they eventually
did. The prediction of economists, that the fungibility of federal grants would
lead governments to spend the money as if it were their own ordinary rev-
enues, was not confirmed (Nathan et al. 1975; Nathan, Adams, et al. 1977).

Not satisfied with focusing exclusively on this fiscal substitution question,
the revenue-sharing field evaluation also examined the effects of the pro-
gram in functional areas of spending and in redistributing income among
groups in the population. As a political scientist, I was also interested in
their effects on political processes and on the role and structure of different
types of governments.

With support from foundations and government agencies, we conducted
similar field network evaluations of the effects on state and local govern-
ments of other federal programs: the Community Development Block Grant
program, the public service employment program under the Comprehensive
Employment and Training Act, and the Urban Development Action Grants
(Dommel et al. 1982; Nathan and associates 1979; Nathan and Webman
1980; Nathan, Cook, et al. 1981; Nathan, Dommel, et al. 1977). Later, we
studied the effects of all federal grants on large cities and the effects of Presi-
dent Ronald W. Reagan's (1981–89) "New Federalism" cuts and changes in

federal grants-in-aid programs (Nathan, Doolittle, and associates 1983, 1987). Recently, we have studied the start-up and early implementation of the Urban Empowerment Zone and Enterprise Community program. Last, you and I have used the field network approach to study the implementation of welfare reform.

This has been a rich vein of federalism and implementation research, though not everyone would agree. Although the studies are scientific, using numbers and in this sense quantitative as well as qualitative, critics have said they are impressionistic and lacking in rigor, and worst of all, as far as I am concerned, they write them off as "anecdotal." My own view, and no one will be surprised by this, is that we learned a great deal and maintained our independence over many years in which hundreds of academic social scientists performed critical analytical tasks in the field and centrally for these studies. In the final analysis, the body of work produced and its applications provide the basis for assessing this methodology.[1]

Starting with Nathan's view is fitting because Nathan not only created the field network approach, but also has directed or been an adviser to many of the prominent field network evaluation studies. With the continuing evolution of federalism and intergovernmental relations, he has modified the approach to address questions raised by new programs and to examine the dimensions of state and local responses that are relevant to answering them. Despite changes in the specific questions and responses examined, however, the essential features of the method have remained the same.

Recently, researchers have used the field network approach to analyze the implementation of federal welfare reform legislation by state and local governments. Jan Hagen and I used the field network approach to study the implementation of the Job Opportunities and Basic Skills Training Program (JOBS) created in 1988, the final federal reform of the Aid to Families with Dependent Children program (Hagen and Lurie 1994). Nathan and Thomas Gais (1999) have used the approach to examine the management of state and local welfare programs under the Temporary Assistance for Needy Families (TANF) block grant created in 1996.

Like the other forms of implementation and process studies discussed in this volume, the field network approach is poorly understood by many who have not used it. My purpose here is to describe the process of doing field network research and to assess its strengths and limitations in studying the implementation of welfare reform. To do this, I draw on my experiences as a director of the JOBS study, as a member of the team that designed the TANF study, and as a field researcher in New York for Nathan's study of the effects of Reagan's budget, which gave me first-hand knowledge of that role. Before moving to New York, I was a Washington economist with little interest in the quirks of individual states and no appreciation of the gulf between the enactment of a federal law and its implementation by states. I approach this chapter not as a methodologist but as a public policy scholar who gained an eye-opening education about the workings of government, especially the welfare system, by using this research approach.

The first section places field network research in the genre of the comparative case study and gives examples of comparative case studies of welfare policies. Subsequent sections discuss the field network analyses of the implementation of the JOBS program and of the management systems for operating the TANF program. The analyses include purposes of the field network method, unit of analysis, analytical framework and research design, staffing and management of the study, data collection, and data analysis. The final section is a critique of the method.

Comparative Case Studies

Sitting in Washington, neither Okun nor Nathan knew how the states were using the federal funds distributed by the general revenue-sharing program. Even if states were to report how they spent the federal money, they might spend less of their own money on those same items—in other words, substitute federal money for state money. To learn whether states were substituting federal money for their own, it would be necessary to examine how states were spending their own money. Someone with savvy about each state government's ability to move money from one purpose to another would need to watch the changes unfold. Nathan could then compare the states' behavior to assess the amount of substitution and the factors that explain variation among the states.

Watching and examining the responses of states to federal initiatives was the original purpose of field network research and remains the purpose today. Nathan has used a variety of terms for this—evaluating, assessing, monitoring, and tracking—but the aim of them all is to answer questions about the responses of state and local governments to a federal initiative. The essence of field network research is that knowledgeable observers close to the scene of the action analyze and report these responses using a common protocol and that analysts in the central staff compare the responses to answer the questions posed by the study. It is a team effort. The researchers in the field constitute a network to gather and analyze information that the central staff then analyze further to evaluate the consequences of the federal initiative—hence the term *field network evaluation.*

Agranoff and Radin cite Nathan's field network research as an example of the comparative case study approach. As they describe it, this approach consists of multiple case studies designed and analyzed to answer a common set of questions:

> The comparative case study differs from the traditional single case study in that it examines multiple situations within an overall framework. Generally, the research proceeds from a common design, involving the same hypotheses or research questions to be investigated in each case. Cases are built individually by careful research design through a combination of methods. After cases are researched and developed, they are analyzed comparatively. Similar to other methods, the approach is designed to look for unique and common experiences, patterning of variables and relationships (Agranoff and Radin 1991, 204).

As Yin does in his book on case study research (1994), Agranoff and Radin offer guidance for increasing the rigor of comparative case study research. They cite notable studies that employ this approach and describe the method by laying out a sequence of research steps. The process of doing a field network study to examine the implementation of welfare policy, which is discussed below, generally parallels this sequence of steps.

In addition to field network studies of welfare policy, comparative case studies of welfare policy have been done by other organizations such as the U.S. General Accounting Office (GAO), Mathematica Policy Research, and the Urban Institute. The GAO routinely examines and compares the ways that states or localities put federal laws and regulations into operation, often doing this in response to requests by members of Congress or congressional committees (e.g., GAO 1995, 1997, 1998). Mathematica Policy Research compared the projects in the Minority Female Single Parent Demonstration, which consisted of four different employment and training programs for single mothers operated by community-based organizations in the 1980s (Burghardt and Gordon 1990). During the period before TANF, when many states operated welfare reform demonstrations under waivers, the Urban Institute examined five state projects to identify their strategies for increasing participation in work-related activities (Pavetti et al. 1995).

What distinguishes field network research from these other studies of welfare policy is not so much the research method as the people performing the study, the audience for the study's findings, and the source of funding to support the study. From the beginning, Nathan's network of field researchers was composed primarily of academics teaching in the states and localities under study. This approach to staffing both enabled and required a broadening of the focus of the research from substantive questions about programs and policies to the types of questions about the political process itself that are addressed primarily by academic social scientists. The imperative for academics to publish in books and journals gives an additional social science slant to field network research, as authors frame their findings with more general or abstract questions. Finally, the funding for field network studies has come from both private foundations and government. The Ford Foundation supported Nathan's first study, the Pew Charitable Trusts provided the initial funding for the JOBS study, and the Kellogg Foundation provided the initial funding for the TANF study. Researchers supported by a grant from a private foundation have the time and flexibility not normally available to those working under contract with a specified set of deliverables. Yet the questions posed by field network studies are sufficiently relevant to policymakers that the federal government supported several of Nathan's studies of the responses of local governments to federal initiatives and supplemented the private funding for both the JOBS and TANF studies.

These sources of staff and funds mean that field network research addresses two audiences, the officials and agencies concerned with the effects of the policy per se and the academic scholars concerned not only with these effects but also with what they illustrate more generally about the behavior of officials and agencies. With this second audience in mind, field network studies are more broadly drawn than the multiple case studies of the GAO, Mathematica Policy Research, and the Urban Institute by including questions about institutional and political context. Yet they are less motivated by issues of administrative processes and institutional forms than some of the studies reviewed by Agranoff and Radin. Field network studies examine these, but the primary motivation for the studies is to understand responses of states, local governments, and private organizations to specific new, large, nonincremental federal policy changes.

Purposes

The field network method is particularly well-suited to examining the effects of large changes in federal grant programs to state and local governments: new sources of federal money, cuts in federal money, or changes in the rules for distributing federal money. The purpose is to learn how states, localities, and other institutions respond to the changes, responses that may be programmatic, budgetary, organizational, regulatory, managerial, and so forth. A study begins by examining the earliest and most apparent responses by these institutions and then looks for responses that are more gradual and subtle. Implicit in the whole exercise is the idea that change is mediated through various political cultures and structures as it is realized in different jurisdictional settings.

Exactly what is examined depends on the federal policy and what the study director and funders think is worth learning about the states' response or lack of response. Two types of knowledge come from the studies. Foremost is an understanding of the programmatic consequences of the federal initiatives: What changes were made by state and local governments and private organizations? Second is an understanding of the process of change, including more general knowledge about the structure and behavior of governments and other institutions: How and why did it happen this way? The purpose of the research is neither to evaluate the effectiveness of the federal policy itself in cost-benefit terms nor to suggest most effective best practices at the state or local level.

In the studies of welfare reform, the primary question was the extent of programmatic and institutional change in local welfare agencies. Both the JOBS program and the TANF block grant were enacted with dramatic rhetoric about giving welfare agencies a mission to reduce welfare dependence by moving recipients into the labor force. But the chain of events between new federal laws and reforms in the programs of local agencies is complex, involving many actors with divergent interests. The history of federal welfare reforms that failed to change the behavior of local agencies made it difficult to predict their response to JOBS and TANF. Like general revenue sharing, it was necessary to go out and look.

Unit of Analysis

Because the purpose of field network studies is to understand the response of state and local governments to federal policy changes, the unit of analysis is an institution rather than a person. Because the studies follow the policy change down to the lowest level of government affected, the local government may be a county, city, or town, depending on the particular study. Increasingly, as governments contract out for services, the analysis includes nonprofit organizations and, in a few cases, for-profit companies. Because the expectation is that the response of governments will vary, the sample includes multiple states and multiple local governments within each state. The study of federal revenue sharing, for example, examined 19 states and 46 local jurisdictions; the Reagan study included 14 states and three levels of government within a state; the JOBS study included 10 states and three counties within each state; and the TANF study includes 20 states and two counties within each state.

With the goal of selecting states that are broadly representative of the nation as a whole, selection criteria typically include variables such as state per capita income, poverty rate, fiscal stress, dominant political party, degree of urbanization, and geographic region. Selection criteria also included variables of particular relevance to the policy change being studied, such as the level of government responsible for welfare administration in the JOBS study or the strategy for welfare management adopted by government in the TANF study. The criteria for selecting localities depend on the purposes of the particular study. For example, in the study of Reagan's New Federalism, which focused on intergovernmental relations, the sample of local governments consisted of a single county in each state, the largest city within the county, and a town or village within the county. In the JOBS study, where we expected the size of the community to influence implementation, the sample consisted of a large urban area, a medium-sized urban area, and a rural area.

Field network studies are mounted to examine federal policy changes that are big, and governments' responses to big changes play out over time. Program start-up might be slow. Initial reactions might differ from longer-term solutions. Because responses to a federal initiative are often gradual, most studies have been longitudinal, involving more than one round of field observation. In some cases, they involved three or four rounds of field data collection taking place over several years. Field research to study Reagan's 1981 budget initiatives, which made immediate changes in federal grant-in-aid programs, took place in 1981, 1982, and 1984, whereas the field research on the JOBS program created in 1988, but not mandatory for the states until 1990, occurred in 1990, 1991, and 1992.

In the early phases of a study, data reported from the sample of governments permit the central staff to make cross-site comparisons of the responses to the federal initiative. In later phases of the study, when longitudinal data become available, the analysis can also make comparisons over time. This broad perspective, with both geographic spread and multiple waves of data collection, is a primary strength of the approach. It provides a big picture of what happened, or didn't happen, and why it happened that way.

With this wide lens, the individuals and families affected by the federal initiative are not examined directly. All of the programs examined by the field network approach have consequences for their clients and affect the well-being of groups in the population. The purpose of the research, however, is not to evaluate the impact of the program changes on them. Rather, it is to understand the magnitude and direction of the program changes themselves. Information about the effects of the changes on the population may be gathered from secondary sources, but primarily for the purpose of understanding the political pressures for and against the changes.

Analytical Framework and Research Design

The analytical framework varies from one study to another depending on the policy change and the questions of interest. In the early Nathan studies, the framework was designed to examine whether the states would use new federal funds to increase total state spending or whether the states would substitute federal funds for state funds. Similarly, the study of federal grants to stimulate state and local public service employment examined whether the new jobs created were an addition to existing jobs or a substitute for them. The same framework was used for the Reagan study, this time to examine how states responded to decreases in federal funding and whether the states would use their own funds to replace cuts in federal funds. These studies also included and, in some cases, featured other dependent variables such as the uses, distribution, and political effects of the funds, as in the study of revenue sharing and community development block grants.

The common feature of the analytical frameworks is the view of implementation from the top down. This top-down view begins by enumerating the federal policy changes and then examining whether and how lower levels of government respond to them. In this sense, field network research is a method for studying implementation that examines multiple jurisdictions and compares their responses in an effort to learn whether and how the purposes articulated in the federal law are realized by the implementing institutions.

The mission of the JOBS program was to promote employment by offering education, training, and employment services, together with child care, transportation, and other services needed to support work effort. In the JOBS implementation study, the first round of research examined the initial state-level choices in implementing the program (Hagen and Lurie 1992). The research was organized around the provisions of the legislation and the tasks involved in building a capacity to meet the provisions. The framework is shown in figure 5.1, which lists the topics investigated by the researchers. The second round of research examined the implementation of the JOBS program by local welfare agencies (Lurie and Hagen 1993). Because those agencies have direct contact with clients, this round distinguished between the design and structure of the system and the processing of clients through the system. The design and structure of the system, and local strategies for shaping this system to create the JOBS program, received more attention than client processing, as seen from figure 5.1. With a few modifications, the third round of research repeated the work of the earlier rounds (Hagen and Lurie 1994).

The TANF study focuses on management systems and goals for the new welfare system: Have states structured their management systems around discernible goals? What are those goals? What institutional structures and management strategies have states used to accomplish the goals? Are the state goals and management systems being adopted and used by local welfare systems? The analytical framework for the first round of research, which examined both state and local responses to TANF, comprised the elements of policy and management listed in figure 5.2. Like the JOBS study, the framework examines structure more than client processing (Nathan and Gais 1999).

The research design consists of a list of descriptive and analytical questions about each element of the framework. The task of the field researcher is to write a report, or case study, that answers these questions. An instrument called a report form lists the questions and gives the field researcher some instructions for answering them. Importantly, the report form is not an interview schedule but a set of questions that requires the field researcher to do research, to both collect and analyze information. The researcher is asked to gather data and, based on the data, use his or her judgment in formulating an answer to the questions posed in the report form.

Figure 5.1. Analytical Framework for the JOBS Implementation Study

State level	Local level
1. Historical context and political response	1. Implementation context
2. Interagency relationships and program planning	2. Intraorganizational leadership and management strategies
3. Strategies for implementing education, employment, and training programs	3. Interorganizational linkages and coordination
4. Response to the JOBS program by other state agencies	4. Content of selected JOBS components
5. Effects on supportive services	5. Availability of education, training, and employment services
6. Organizational structure and management strategies	6. Availability of child care
7. JOBS and client/agency relations	7. Availability of supportive services other than child care
8. Meeting federal mandates for participation and targeting	8. Models of client flow
9. Summary considerations	9. Delivery mechanisms
	10. Client processing
	11. Measures of institutional outputs
	12. Analysis of institutional outputs
	13. Analysis of factors influencing program design and implementation
	14. Meeting current and future goals

Note: JOBS = Job Opportunities and Basic Skills Training Program.

Figure 5.2. Analytical Framework for the TANF Study

State level	Local level
1. Program status and description	1. Description of local agency and its environment
2. Institutional roles and structures	2. Workload
3. Budgeting and staff	3. Program design and service mix
4. Control, oversight, and accountability	4. Staffing and training
5. Management information systems	5. Mandates and incentives
6. Overview analysis	6. Observation and description of activities and processes
	7. Data systems and reports
	8. Analysis of state-local relations

Note: TANF = Temporary Assistance for Needy Families.

The reports of the field researchers form the primary knowledge base for the subsequent comparative analysis by the central staff. They are written to inform the central staff, not to be the final products released to the public. The report forms, in contrast, have been published as an appendix to the analysis by the central staff so that readers can understand the research design. This practice, which is a good one, was not followed for the second and third rounds of research on the JOBS program. In the first round of research on TANF, the report form was released as a stand-alone document (State Capacity Study Field Research Report Form 1997).

Staffing and Managing the Study

Relying on the judgment of the field researchers requires the study directors to pay close attention to the selection and management of the research team. The field researchers must be familiar with their state's politics and institutions and have some knowledge of the policy area. Established contacts with government officials that enable the researchers to obtain rapid access to information are also helpful, because access can be particularly difficult in the start-up phase of a program. At the same time, the field researchers must be willing and able to report with objectivity. The dilemma here is that most people who go through the trouble of learning the arcane details of institutions and policies either work for government or are advocates on the outside. Because the researchers must be able to act as disinterested analysts, the best solution is to select academics with some expertise and interest in the area of the study. Most commonly, the field researchers are faculty from departments of political science, public administration and policy, economics, and social work. In some instances, independent consultants and journalists have also served as field researchers. The central staff consists of the study director or directors; one or two senior staff, who are often former field researchers; one or two research assistants; and a secretary.

Managing a group of academics who like their freedom requires some team building, which involves creating relationships between the central staff and the field researchers that are collegial as well as contractual. This is done by involving the field researchers in the research design and giving them access to the data for their own research and publications. After the director and central staff build the analytical framework and draft the questions for each element, they hold a conference with field researchers to refine the questions and reduce the inevitable ambiguities in them. Drawing on their expertise encourages field researchers to "buy in" to the study methodology. Equally important, field researchers can use their substantive knowledge about programs or state institutions to sharpen the research questions. The conference also serves to inform the researchers about the methodology, which is frequently unfamiliar to them.

A second way to encourage academics to participate in the study and to continue participating over multiple rounds of research is to invite them to present their findings at scholarly meetings and to permit them to publish articles or book chapters based on their own research, thereby giving them a stake in the enterprise beyond the financial payment for their report. After the central staff releases the findings from the study, the field researchers are free to publish the information contained in their own reports. Field researchers have also contributed to volumes edited by the central staff. In some instances, field researchers have been given access to the data collected by other field researchers to pursue a particular topic or have become members of the central staff.

At the beginning of the study, the central staff must familiarize the researchers with the details of the federal legislation being examined. Early in the study of President Reagan's budget, the central staff prepared a catalogue of the numerous cuts and changes in grant-in-aid programs made by the budget, which not only instructed the field researchers but became the project's first published volume (Ellwood 1982). To inform the researchers about the JOBS program, Hagen and I wrote a background paper about the features of the program that raised issues to be investigated by the study. Nathan and Gais sent the researchers for the TANF study copies of the federal legislation and a selection of the numerous analyses that had already been prepared by other organizations.

Once the data collection is under way, the study director and central staff members visit the states at least once to accompany the field researchers on their interviews and meet some of the key actors. This is an opportunity to monitor the field researchers and, if necessary, suggest adjustments in their approach. Even more important, getting into the field gives the central staff a "feel" for the states. When the time comes for the central staff to analyze the field researchers' reports, having a visual image of the place brings the information to life.

In most of the studies, the study director did not solicit the coopera-tion of the state and local governments that are the object of the research. Because the field researchers were familiar with their states, they had the ability to make informal contacts with government officials, who were sometimes also friends, neighbors, former colleagues, and former students. The JOBS study solicited the approval of the state welfare agency because we planned to supplement the field network research with surveys of frontline workers. The TANF study, on the other hand, relied on the con-tacts and ingenuity of the field researchers to gain access to government agencies.

Data Collection

The report forms instructed the field researchers to collect both qualita-tive and quantitative information for each of the elements in figures 5.1 and 5.2. Examples of quantitative data collected for the JOBS study are

- Allocation of JOBS funds among program components
- Allocation of JOBS funds among jurisdictions
- Percentage of JOBS funds used by the welfare agency to purchase services from other organizations
- Changes in the allocation of staff
- Number of participants in each JOBS service
- Percentage of Job Training Partnership Act (JTPA) participants who are AFDC recipients

Other information requested by the report form was qualitative. For instance, the first JOBS reporting form asked questions such as

"Describe the design of the state's JOBS program, including the sequence of JOBS services and activities, the state's choice of mandatory and optional components, and the degree to which JOBS is tailored to the needs and choices of individual par-ticipants. Provide a flowchart showing the sequence of events and describe any devi-ations that are expected to occur commonly. How uniform is the program expected to be across local jurisdictions in the state? Compared to WIN or the WIN Demon-stration program, did JOBS require significant changes? Are new or different types of educational, employment, and training programs being offered to AFDC recipients?"

"What case management services, if any, will be provided to JOBS participants? Are case management services expected to alter the delivery of services to clients? Have case managers been designated for JOBS and, if so, what is their role? Does this represent a significant change from the predecessor to JOBS?"

The second and third rounds of field research were able to ask more focused questions and to employ forms and checklists. Forms and checklists proved most useful, however, when they did not stand alone but rather summarized text. Forms and checklists without text seemed to convey an incomplete picture of the situation and were, of course, unable to capture unexpected arrangements.

Indigenous field researchers were particularly able to provide information about political and fiscal factors influencing welfare reform. To examine political leadership, the first JOBS reporting form included this section:

> "How aggressive were state leaders in making JOBS, or its immediate predecessor, a prominent issue? Who have been the main political actors and what arguments have they made for the need to implement work/welfare programs? For example, has the rhetoric focused on opportunities, obligations, or both? Is there a specific strategy for 'marketing' the state's employment and training programs? If so, what is the 'message' and to whom is it being delivered—recipients, the public, legislators, other state agencies, client advocacy and other citizens' groups, employers? What methods are being used?"

The TANF study sought to learn whether policymaking differed from previous welfare reforms:

> "Please describe the policy formulation or planning process behind the state's welfare reforms. Please indicate who was involved (including interest groups, state agencies, local government officials). Also, put the process into historical context by indicating whether and how the people, groups, and agencies that developed the reforms differed from the usual persons and organizations involved in state welfare issues."

In addition to answering quantitative and qualitative questions, field associates collected documents such as laws, regulations, budgets, organization charts, plans, contracts and interagency agreements, administrative letters, flowcharts, procedures manuals, forms, and agency reports. They also collected newspaper articles and, in a few instances, videotaped speeches by the governor or welfare administrator.

The report form for the JOBS study strongly encouraged the field researchers to interview a range of people involved in JOBS implementation, including state welfare administrators and policymakers and personnel from other state agencies, such as the JTPA, state education, and the state budget office. Other than asking for diverse perspectives on the implementation of JOBS, we did not give them specific guidance about the job titles of the people to be interviewed; we left the selection of respondents to their judgment. The one exception to this minimal guidance was sending the field researchers a list of welfare advocacy organizations to be contacted, thereby ensuring that we had their perspective on the implementation of the JOBS program.

Because the report form is a set of questions posed to the field researcher, not an interview protocol, the researchers also had leeway to frame the interview questions. To draw candid responses from respondents, we asked the field researchers to assure them of anonymity, to explain that the report would not be used for compliance or audit purposes, and to avoid using a tape recorder. Although the researchers were encouraged to quote the people they interviewed, they were asked to suppress the source of the quotes. They did, however, attach to their report a list of people interviewed, with their title and organization, so we could learn whom they spoke with. Interviewing without a tape recorder had advantages and disadvantages. The one researcher who used a tape recorder gave us quotes that enriched our own report, but state officials did not tell him about a glitch in the management information system that inflated their participation rate. Maybe they were unaware of this weakness at the time of the interviews, but maybe not.

To supplement the data gathered from the states and localities by the field researchers, the central staff use information gathered by the federal agency administering the program. When we studied the JOBS program, HHS was a source of information about federal and state expenditures on the JOBS program and child care, expenditures on the JOBS target groups, participation rates, and participation of recipients in individual JOBS activities. Expenditure data from HHS was more uniform among states than data in the states' budgets, where different fiscal years and biennial budgeting complicate efforts to compare states. Similarly, HHS required states to report participation data using uniform definitions, which enabled the central staff to make more reliable cross-state comparisons of these variables.

Data Analysis

Like the multiple case study approach described by Agranoff and Radin, the field network methodology requires both the field researchers and the central staff to analyze and interpret information. After the field researchers gather and report information from their jurisdiction, they use it to answer a set of analytical questions. The final sections of the report form for the JOBS study, for instance, asked them to analyze institutional outputs and the factors influencing program design and implementation:

"Does the mix of services and the participation rate vary significantly among the local sites? Are there other significant differences among the sites? If so, which of the many factors discussed above (for example, environmental conditions, intraorganizational and interorganizational structure, etc.) explain this variation? If some local agencies are more effective than others in providing services to their clients, what factors appear to promote or hinder success?"

"To what extent has JOBS increased or introduced different education, employment, and training opportunities for AFDC recipients? Which changes have been the most significant? Has JOBS been a repackaging of prior work-welfare programs or is it something more, something different?"

"What are the critical issues or major constraints facing the local welfare agencies at this point in their implementation of the JOBS program? What is being done to address these issues or constraints?"

Concluding the state-level section of the report form for the TANF study was a broad analytical question:

"Based on your analysis of the state as a whole, on which types of goals does its TANF/AFDC program place the most emphasis? What, in other words, is the overall state system really trying to do? As emphasized throughout this Report Form, we want you to consider not only official policies relating to families and individuals, but also the goals revealed in management decisions about the allocation of staff, budgets, and other resources; the types of organizations and people assigned to operate TANF/AFDC; the program's reporting and incentive systems; the nature and degree of control exercised by state administrators over service delivery organizations; the capabilities of its management information system; and other aspects of the state's management system."

Based on the reports of the field researchers, the central staff then writes a report that answers the study's primary questions. This report is not simply a summary of the reports of the field associates, but is a comparative analysis that generalizes about the responses of the states and localities to federal legislation and documents and explains variation in these responses. The analysis varies, however, depending on the questions addressed and the disciplines of the analysts.

The studies of JOBS and TANF were both about the magnitude and direction of change in complex systems. The JOBS study sought to learn whether and how welfare systems were requiring employment and preparation for employment. The TANF study focused on management, the capacity of state governments to create management systems and imbue them with purposes that they then fulfill. Neither of these research questions has a quantitative answer. Unlike Nathan's earlier studies that measured the substitution of federal money for state money, or the replacement of federal money with state money, the studies of welfare reform were fundamentally qualitative. Quantitative data such as changes in expenditures and staff for employment programs were collected, but they were only a few of the many variables indicative of a change in purpose for welfare agencies.

The earlier Nathan studies used a more specific evaluation criterion—the extent of fiscal substitution or replacement—than the welfare reform studies. Although the JOBS and TANF studies were looking for change, the changes were along multiple dimensions. Some of these dimensions were expressed in the legislation and provided implicit evaluation criteria—a higher rate of participation in work activities was "better" than a lower one—but others did not. For example, neither the JOBS legislation nor economic analysis said that job search programs were preferable to education and training. We therefore presented data on the number of participants in each component and discussed the factors that explained the variation among states.

With the information in the state reports on the JOBS program arranged in sections according to the elements in figure 5.1, much of the analysis within sections consisted of looking for similarities and differences among jurisdictions and developing categories for grouping together similar responses. For some of the elements, we identified models that states were using, for example, models of case management. We developed prototype client flow models that illustrated distinctions among the treatment of clients. We also tried, without much success, to develop typologies that would relate one element to another in an insightful way.

My approach to analyzing the state reports was both detailed and holistic. Years of studying welfare have convinced me that reform lies in changes in the fine details of policy and administration, with the smallest nuances acting like seeds for progress or snags for inertia. Yet, I began my analysis by writing descriptive profiles of the JOBS program of each state so I could see the big picture. I assumed that each state had a strategy for implementing the JOBS program whereby it would invest resources in areas it expected to have the greatest return in meeting the participation rate. By examining the fine details in light of the big picture, I hoped to discover that efficient strategy. In hindsight, I see the economist's mind-set asserting itself.

In other words, the analysis of welfare reform was primarily inductive. We made sense of what we saw through the lens of our various disciplines. The constructs I used to interpret the data were different from those used by Hagen, who is a social worker, whereas Nathan and Gais, who are political scientists, used yet another set of constructs to interpret their data. When I read the report on TANF written by Nathan and Gais, I was not surprised to learn that political scientists have a vocabulary for phenomena that I saw and struggled to describe. Although some people may disagree, I believe these different lenses are a strength of the field research method, not a weakness. No discipline has a monopoly on policy research.

The JOBS study and the TANF study asked essentially the same question: Did federal welfare reform legislation make a big difference in state welfare programs, or did states continue pretty much with business as usual? The JOBS study found only incremental change in employment programs, whereas the TANF study found profound change in the goals, programs, and institutional arrangements of the welfare system. Caseload data tell the same story. The increase in caseloads in the early 1990s shows that the JOBS program did not amount to a sweeping change in programs to encourage employment, whereas the sharp decrease in welfare caseloads after 1994 is proof that the precursors to TANF, and TANF itself, were a sharp break with the past. But caseload data tell us only that something is different. The field network studies tell a more complex story about the numerous actions taken by states, local governments, and other institutions as they reacted to the federal legislation within their own political and economic environments. They tell us what these institutions actually did that was different.

Critique

We have all heard a piece of research being dismissed as "just a case study," reflecting the low regard for the case study methodology among many social scientists. Agranoff and Radin acknowledge that comparative case studies are similarly demeaned, and Nathan notes above that field network research has been criticized as impressionistic and lacking in rigor. How then can consumers assess the quality of a particular example of field network research, and what guidelines can be offered to help researchers produce high-quality work using this approach? The suggestions made by Yin for judging case studies and increasing their rigor apply to comparative case studies as well. To judge the quality of research designs for case studies, he applies four criteria that are commonly used to assess social science methods: construct validity, internal validity, external validity, and reliability (Yin 1994, 32–33).

Yin points out that case studies are frequently criticized for poor construct validity, meaning that the data about the concepts being studied are collected using subjective judgments or impressions rather than a well-developed set of operational measures. To ensure construct validity, the investigator must select the specific concept to be investigated and then justify why the operational measures reflect this concept. Internal validity is necessary when the research seeks to establish a cause and effect relationship between variables. To ensure internal validity, the investigator must demonstrate that the relationship between variables is causal and not the result of some unidentified other factors. External validity is the generalizability of the research findings beyond the case examined in the particular study, or the range of situations and places to which the findings can be generalized. Research consisting of a single case is particularly susceptible to the criticism of limited external validity. Finally, the reliability of the study is the extent to which it can be replicated, using the same procedures to repeat the study, to produce the same findings.

Judged by these criteria, field network research has much to commend it. To ensure construct validity and reliability, the single most important procedure is the use of the report form to guide the research of the field analysts. The report form describes the constructs and operationalizes them by specifying a framework for collecting the data that will measure the construct. For example, the primary construct for the JOBS study was the extent to which a state's JOBS program was promoting employment among welfare recipients. In the TANF study, the primary construct is the state's institutional capacity to manage TANF programs so that they achieve the state's goals for welfare reform. Both of these constructs have multiple dimensions, requiring the extensive data collection called for in figures 5.1 and 5.2. Although critics can of course disagree with the particular measures chosen to operationalize the construct, the report form specifies the measures clearly and requires all field researchers to use the same ones.

Because the report form is specific about much of the quantitative and qualitative data to be collected, it also promotes reliability, so that researchers replicating the study would be highly likely to collect the same information. It instructs the field researchers to obtain data on expenditures of specific types, to gather and distill the meaning of laws, regulations, and contracts, to describe the structure and organization of government programs and operations, and to observe the political debate in the media. Yin suggests that in addition to following specific procedures in collecting data, case study research should be conducted "as if someone were always looking over your shoulder" (Yin 1994, 37). In field network research, the central staff is there to look over the shoulder of each field researcher. The initial conference to discuss the report form is to ensure that everyone tries to collect the same information, and the field visits by the central staff during the data collection phase are opportunities to reinforce the process. When the central staff members analyze the reports from the field, they can question the field researchers when data are unclear or inconsistent. Finally, whenever possible, a draft of the report of the central staff is sent to the field researchers so they can offer general comments and check that the data from their sites were used appropriately.

The use of a network of researchers to do a comparative case study naturally raises the issue of inter-rater reliability, or the comparability of data collection and analysis among the researchers. This is certainly a concern that must be addressed by the study director and central staff. In designing the report form, attention must be given to the definition of terms, and indeed thrashing out definitions consumes a considerable portion of the conference with the field researchers. The report form should also request information that is redundant to some extent, giving the field researcher and the central staff the opportunity to check for internal consistency. In addition, the field researchers use their data to answer analytical questions, which encourages them to look critically at their own information. There is no denying, however, that some field researchers dig deeper than others when collecting information and have a better understanding of what they find. Finally, if data are available from the federal government, the central staff can check the consistency of the data with the data collected by the field researchers and try to resolve any large discrepancies.

Like the multiple case study method described by Agranoff and Radin, the field researchers do not simply gather information but also analyze and interpret the information they collect. Because they are asked to make judgments about what they observe, and reasonable people may reach different conclusions, reliability may be lower for the questions in the report form that ask the field researchers for analysis and interpretation. The report form instructs the field researchers to base their conclusions on the data they have presented and thus provide a check on their interpretations, but different interpretations of the data are possible. In fact, one of the strengths of the method is that it incorporates the interpretations of seasoned researchers and brings a diversity of perspectives and insights.

Problems of external validity are generally less at issue in a comparative case study examining multiple cases than in a study examining a single case. In field network research, the study directors make an effort to choose a sample of states that is representative of the nation as a whole by selecting states that vary along dimensions expected to influence the constructs under investigation, dimensions such as income level, poverty rate, racial composition, urbanization, region, and political culture. In selecting samples of local governments, the size of the population or the type of government (county, city, or town) is generally a factor, with an effort to include jurisdictions that are systematically different or similar. External validity, or the ability to generalize beyond the particular study, is enhanced as the sample becomes more representative of the universe and includes a larger percent of the cases in the universe. With 10 states in the sample for the JOBS study and 20 states in the sample for the TANF study, the variation among states is sufficient such that it is possible to establish categories of features of welfare programs that can meaningfully describe programs in states outside the sample.

Although a research design with multiple cases enhances externality validity, it does not solve problems of internal validity or the ability to establish cause and effect. Because case studies by their very nature cannot make comparisons with a counterfactual, or what would have happened in the absence of the hypothesized cause, they are generally considered to lack internal validity. Yin argues that this is not a concern when case studies are descriptive and do not seek to establish causality; field network research avoids this pitfall to the extent that it is descriptive. Mohr (1996), after discussing the concept of causation and its implications for social science methodology, concludes that internal validity does not require a counterfactual. He broadens the definition of internal validity by arguing that causal arguments can be made without a counterfactual by what he calls "physical causal reasoning." For example, when you push a switch and a light goes on, you do not need a counterfactual to reason that the switch caused the light to go on. Mohr argues that physical causal reasoning, rather than factual causal reasoning, can give internal validity to case study research. Using this definition, field network research is explanatory when it reconstructs a sequence of events whose relationship is so close as to be uncontroversial. Process and implementation studies that seek to understand not only what happened but also why it happened can find methodological support in Mohr's distinction between these types of reasoning.

When is the field network method an appropriate research approach? Although it is a flexible approach that can be used in a variety of policy contexts, the types of questions it can answer are limited. The scope of the research questions must be limited to those that the field researchers can answer reliably by the methods they use to collect information. Field network research does not collect primary data on the individuals served by a program, nor do the field researchers do extensive observations of program operations. Institutions are the unit of analysis, not individuals. Although the JOBS and TANF studies included questions about the processing of clients through programs, the method is better suited to examine the institutional structure of programs than to examine client processing. Structural features of programs are revealed in budgets, plans, contracts and interagency agreements, flowcharts, procedure manuals, and other public documents. Obtaining this information requires some cooperation by individuals in the agencies operating the program, but not a high level of effort on their part. But learning about client processing requires data about individual clients and hence either analysis of agency data, observations of clients, or both. Field researchers can interview people in the agencies to gain their impressions, but the results are, well, impressionistic.

The strength of the approach is its ability to get an in-depth understanding of the response of institutions, including states, localities, nonprofit agencies and, increasingly, for-profit firms, to new federal initiatives. We can understand their motivations, their strategies, the ramifications of their choices for other programs and populations, and the unintended consequences those may produce. The researchers can get into the field quickly, which makes the approach particularly useful for providing timely feedback about responses to new programs. Also, although the report form structures the data collection, it is sufficiently open-ended to be exploratory. Our report forms always asked, "Are there important issues or aspects of JOBS implementation not explored elsewhere that are emerging in the state?" Having scholars in the field who are capable of using their judgment to report important but unexpected developments is an advantage of the field network approach, especially when big program changes are occurring. This means that field network research is well suited to studying new programs or large changes in existing programs, particularly when the nature and direction of the responses by lower levels of government are difficult to predict.

NOTES

The author thanks Thomas L. Gais, Mary Clare Lennon, Richard P. Nathan, and Beryl A. Radin for their excellent suggestions.

1. This statement was prepared especially for this chapter by Richard P. Nathan.

REFERENCES

Agranoff, Robert, and Beryl A. Radin. 1991. "The Comparative Case Study Approach in Public Administration." In *Research in Public Administration,* vol. 1, no. 1, edited by James Perry. Greenwich, Conn.: JAI Press.

Burghardt, John, and Anne Gordon. 1990. *More Jobs and Higher Pay, How an Integrated Program Compares with Traditional Programs.* The Minority Female Single Parent Demonstration. New York: Rockefeller Foundation.

Dommel, Paul R., John Stuart Hall, Victor E. Bach, Leonard Rubinowitz, Leon L. Haley, and John S. Jackson III. 1982. *Decentralizing Urban Policy: Case Studies in Community Development.* Washington, D.C.: Brookings Institution.

Ellwood, John William, ed. 1982. *Reductions in U.S. Domestic Spending: How They Affect State and Local Governments.* New Brunswick, N.J.: Transaction Books.

GAO. See U.S. General Accounting Office.

Hagen, Jan L., and Irene Lurie. 1992. *Implementing JOBS: Initial State Choices.* Albany: Rockefeller Institute of Government, State University of New York.

———. 1994. *Implementing JOBS: Progress and Promise.* Albany: Rockefeller Institute of Government, State University of New York.

Hall, John Stuart, and Susan A. MacManus. 1982. "Tracking Decisions and Consequences: The Field Network Evaluation Approach." In *Studying Implementation: Methodological and Administrative Issues,* edited by Walter Williams. Chatham, N.J.: Chatham House.

Lurie, Irene, and Jan L. Hagen. 1993. *Implementing JOBS: The Initial Design and Structure of Local Programs.* Albany: Rockefeller Institute of Government, State University of New York.

Mohr, Lawrence B. 1996. *The Causes of Human Behavior: Implications for Theory and Method in the Social Sciences.* Ann Arbor: University of Michigan Press.

Nathan, Richard P. 1982. "The Methodology for Field Network Evaluation Studies." In *Studying Implementation: Methodological and Administrative Issues,* edited by Walter Williams. Chatham, N.J.: Chatham House.

Nathan, Richard P., and Thomas L. Gais. 1999. *Implementing the Personal Responsibility Act of 1996: A First Look.* Albany: Rockefeller Institute of Government, State University of New York.

Nathan, Richard P., and Jerry A. Webman, eds. 1980. *The Urban Development Action Grant Program: Papers and Conference Proceedings on Its First Two Years of Operation.* Princeton, N.J.: Princeton Urban and Regional Research Center.

Nathan, Richard P., and associates. 1979. *Monitoring the Public Service Employment Program: The Second Round: A Special Report of the National Commission for Manpower Policy.* Washington, D.C.: National Commission for Manpower Policy.

Nathan, Richard P., Charles F. Adams Jr., and associates. 1977. *Revenue Sharing: The Second Round.* Washington, D.C.: Brookings Institution.

Nathan, Richard P., Fred C. Doolittle, and associates. 1983. *The Consequences of Cuts: The Effects of the Reagan Domestic Program on State and Local Governments.* Princeton, N.J.: Princeton Urban and Regional Research Center.

————. 1987. *Reagan and the States.* Princeton, N.J.: Princeton University Press.

Nathan, Richard P., Robert F. Cook, V. Lane Rawlins, and associates. 1981. *Public Service Employment: A Field Evaluation.* Washington, D.C.: Brookings Institution.

Nathan, Richard P., Allen D. Manvel, Susannah E. Calkins, and associates. 1975. *Monitoring Revenue Sharing.* Washington, D.C.: Brookings Institution.

Nathan, Richard P., Paul R. Dommel, Sarah F. Liebschutz, Milton D. Morris, and associates. 1977. *Block Grants for Community Development.* Washington, D.C.: U.S. Department of Housing and Urban Development.

Pavetti, LaDonna, Pamela A. Holcomb, Amy-Ellen Duke, Clemencia Cosentino de Cohen, and Sharon K. Long. 1995. *Increasing Participation in Work and Work-Related Activities: Lessons from Five State Welfare Reform Demonstration Projects, Final Report, Volume 1, Summary Report.* Washington, D.C.: Urban Institute.

Rawlins, V. Lane, and Richard P. Nathan. 1982. "The Field Network Evaluation Studies of Intergovernmental Grants: A Contrast with the Orthodox Economic Approach." *American Economic Review* 72(2):98–102.

State Capacity Study Field Research Report Form. 1997. Albany: Rockefeller Institute of Government, State University of New York.

U.S. General Accounting Office. 1995. *Welfare to Work: Most AFDC Training Programs Not Emphasizing Job Placement.* GAO/HEHS-95-113. Washington, D.C.: U.S. General Accounting Office.

————. 1997. *Welfare Reform: States' Early Experiences with Benefit Termination.* GAO/HEHS-97-74. Washington, D.C.: U.S. General Accounting Office.

————. 1998. *Welfare Reform: States Are Restructuring Programs to Reduce Welfare Dependence.* GAO/HEHS-98-109. Washington, D.C.: U.S. General Accounting Office.

Yin, Robert K. 1994. *Case Study Research: Design and Methods,* 2d ed. Thousand Oaks, Calif.: Sage Publications.

6

Performance Analysis

Lawrence M. Mead

R ecent research on social policy has been dominated by impact evaluation studies. Especially, experimental evaluations done by the Manpower Demonstration Research Corporation (MDRC) showed that mandatory welfare work programs had positive effects, and this has helped to make the expansion of these programs the main theme of recent welfare reform.[1]

But impact evaluation assesses whether a program obtains its goals. It presumes that the program was first carried out as designed. That premise is questionable during an age of turmoil and transition, such as we now experience in social policy. The responsibility for welfare and other antipoverty programs is being devolved to lower levels of government. Washington has given states more say about how to organize and run these programs than previously, and they in turn have delegated heavily to cities and counties. Localities now largely determine who gets some forms of aid, and programs giving assistance and education and training are also being recombined in novel ways.[2] For researchers, therefore, the first concern must now be simply to understand what local programs are doing. What benefits and services are being delivered to which clients, and how? We have to learn "what is going on down there" before the evaluator's question about effectiveness is even meaningful.

The goals of programming have also changed, now that the aim of welfare reform is largely to ensure that adult recipients of aid discharge certain responsibilities as a condition of support. The main demands are to work and cooperate in enforcing child support payment on absent parents, with some localities also requiring that recipients keep their children in school or get them vaccinated. Do clients in fact work or participate in work programs as a condition of aid? That question has more to do with implementation than with the sorts of economic effects that impact evaluations typically measure for welfare programs.

Amid systemic change, it is also difficult to do impact evaluations. An experiment presumes that only a small group of clients gets the tested program. The setting around them is supposed to remain unchanged. That status quo, embodied in the experiences of the control group, provides the counterfactual against which the new program is measured. But if the whole system is changing, everyone is affected, not just the experimental clients. It is now difficult to find recipients who can be "held harmless" to serve as controls. In a way, the controls become the experimentals, because their experience is now the exceptional one.

All forms of process research seek in some way to *describe* how government administers its programs. Performance analysis seeks, in addition, to *relate* the practices of programs to measures of their performance. Statistical connections are drawn between administration and outcomes. The inferences rest on program data, not only on interviews or the researcher's impressions, so they have a degree of rigor. On the other hand, the assessment is confined to quantifiable variables, so it may be less comprehensive than the findings of other process approaches that are more oriented to observation. And inasmuch as the assessment of effects is statistical, it cannot be as definitive as the findings of an experimental evaluation.

Past Research

Performance analysis has focused mainly on national employment programs, some of them connected to welfare. These include the Employment Service (ES), now known as the Job Service, a labor exchange run by federal and state labor departments that helps the unemployed find jobs on a voluntary basis. The Job Training Partnership Act (JTPA) funds voluntary training programs for disadvantaged workers. The Work Incentive program (WIN), established in 1967, was a mandatory program that placed employable recipients of Aid to Families with Dependent Children (AFDC), the principal national family aid program, in work or training.

WIN lacked enough funding and authority to make much impact on the caseload. During the 1980s, it was increasingly replaced by more demanding programs, some of them based on waivers of normal rules granted by Washington.

In 1988, in the Family Support Act (FSA), Congress replaced WIN with the Job Opportunities and Basic Skills Training Program (JOBS), which was better funded and tougher about enforcing participation. JOBS took varying forms around the states, often displaced by further waiver programs. Then in 1996, in the Personal Responsibility and Work Opportunity Reconciliation Act (PRWORA), Congress folded both AFDC and JOBS into Temporary Assistance for Needy Families (TANF), a new block grant to states for family welfare. JOBS is no longer mandated, but states have to meet stiff new work participation standards for TANF recipients, so most continue to run JOBS-like programs.

Performance analysis developed around these work programs largely because they possessed the outcome measures and the other administrative data needed for statistical analyses of performance. WIN had an elaborate reporting system based on the Employment Security Automated Reporting System (ESARS), used by the Employment Service. State and local WIN programs reported data in a consistent format nationwide. The WIN system measured program performance using several indicators, including the number of job entries achieved by the program, the proportion of clients placed in jobs who retained them for at least 30 days, the average wage they earned on job entry, and the average reduction in their welfare resulting from the job. ESARS also gathered data on the demographics of the clients. Later welfare work structures had less adequate reporting, as I discuss below. JTPA has performance measures recording the employment, earnings, and some other outcomes of all adults, welfare adults, and youth.

The performance analysis literature is part of the much larger body of research on public management or public administration.[3] What distinguishes performance research from the rest is that the administrative features of agencies or programs are associated in some statistical manner with measurable indicators of performance. This performance literature has four main parts:

- Studies of the Employment Service and WIN done at the Urban Institute in the late 1970s. This research asked chiefly how the organization and management of these programs affected their performance. Comparisons were drawn among a sample of states and—in the WIN study—also among local offices from those states. Some influence was found for the bureaucratic factors, but secondary to the demographics of the clients and the labor market (Chadwin et al. 1977; Mitchell, Chadwin, and Nightingale 1980).[4]

- Later studies of WIN and JOBS performance, based on comparing programs within states and states within the nation. That research focuses on clients' participation and assignment in the program rather than on organization. Job entry performance was strongly and positively influenced by the percentages of clients who participated and who looked for work, as against entering education and training, even while controlling for demographic and labor market factors. Job quality performance was less affected (Mead 1983, 1985, 1988, 1997a; Provencher 1989).
- Studies of welfare caseload change, with reduction in dependency treated as a performance measure. Results show that caseloads in AFDC and General Assistance (a locally funded aid program) are depressed by the institution of demanding work requirements, including workfare (required unpaid work in government jobs), again controlling for other factors (Brasher 1994; Englander and Englander 1985; Mead 1999, 2000a; Schiller and Brasher 1990, 1993).
- Studies of JTPA that explore the influence of its incentive funding system and other administrative features on its performance. The main interest has been in whether the funding system creates incentives to "cream" (serve the most advantaged clients) and thus undercut the programs impact (Dickinson and West 1988; Heckman, Heinrich, and Smith 1997; Heinrich 2000; Jennings and Ewalt 1998).

In evaluation research, the unit of analysis is typically the individual client. The question is whether a person who experiences a tested program has better outcomes than an equivalent person who does not. "Better outcomes" usually means higher employment or earnings or lower welfare receipt. In performance analysis, in contrast, the unit of observation is usually the program. The question is whether program units with certain measurable features, including client assignments, perform better on outcome indicators than those with different features, when one controls for differences in the clients and the labor market.[5]

Studies differ in the type of variation they investigate. A few offer time series analyses of a welfare caseload in one jurisdiction. They look at the trajectory of the caseload over time and ask whether the institution of a new work policy, such as workfare, affects the trend (Englander and Englander 1985; Mead 1999). Statistically, this amounts to assuming that the program is different in different time periods, usually months or quarters of the year, and then comparing the periods. Econometric problems complicate the use of time series to explain welfare dynamics.[6]

More often, however, the variation is cross-sectional or geographical. That is, programs are compared in different states, or in different counties within a state, within the same time period. Cross-sectional analysis raises fewer econometric problems. Because cross-sections usually use annual rather than monthly or quarterly data, more variables can be measured, permitting more fully specified models. Cross-sections make sense, because there is reason to think that most of the variation that affects work program performance is geographical rather than chronological. That is, performance and its determinants vary more systematically across the subunits at any given time than they vary in all the units over time. Differing outcomes mainly reflect local differences in politics, policy, and bureaucratic capacity, and these change more slowly than economic conditions.[7]

Finally, some studies use pooled models where there is variation over both time and space. Data are gathered across the subunits, not just in one time period, but in several. This permits both the chronological and cross-sectional determinants of performance to be estimated but, as in time series, the time dimension tends to limit the variables that can be measured.[8]

All performance studies involve statistical modeling where performance measures are associated with program features, usually alongside control variables. Some also involve field interviewing of program administrators, the better to understand the meaning of numerical indicators and the forces behind performance. In the following discussion, I concentrate mostly on performance analyses of the type I know best—cross-sectional studies of welfare work programs employing both field research and statistical modeling.

Field Interviewing

Performance analysis preferably should rest on field interviewing of the administrators who run the program of interest. The goal is to grasp how the program operates in enough depth to guide and complement the statistical analysis. Interviewing generates many of the hypotheses about "what works" that are then tested by the numbers. Currently, there is a vogue to use administrative data to study poverty or welfare as if such data, like academic databases, could simply be taken home and analyzed at one's computer. But when administrative data are wrenched from their settings, they may be misinterpreted. Hands-on contact with the program is essential to learn what the numbers mean, and to place them in context.[9]

Researchers typically select interview sites in collaboration with program managers. In national studies, one selects states; in studies within a state, counties or other local offices are selected. If states are initially chosen, localities must then be selected within them. Researchers should visit all the subunits if possible. If that is not possible, they should select a sample that reflects the full range of variation in measured performance and in the program features that are thought to affect it. In the Urban Institute studies, researchers chose states that, controlling for their environments, performed both well and poorly by program measures and that exhibited a range of organizational arrangements, as these were the program features of interest. A random sample could in theory capture all this variation, but with low N the chances of an unrepresentative outcome are too great, or practical constraints limit the sites really available. So a constructed sample is best.

A set of recommendations follows.

1. On arrival at each local program, select a sample of staff to be interviewed. Respondents should include the office director, a preponderance of service-level staff, and some intermediate managers. It is best to interview staff privately and individually; their responses are then more candid and independent. Focus groups of staff may also be used, but only after the individual interviews. Whereas the program director will usually speak on the record, staff below that level should be given confidentiality; that is, promise not to use their opinions in a form in which they or their offices could be identified. Stress that this is an academic study, not an evaluation or audit. Program executives have provided entrée, but researchers are not working for them. Confidentiality is vital for staff to speak openly. Respondents will sometimes mention instances of improper behavior. Ignore that—the purpose is not to uncover "dirt" but to understand the program.

2. The best way to interview is to use a semi-structured interview guide. Merely talking to respondents about the program risks leaving important subjects uncovered. On the other hand, using a pre-formed questionnaire presumes too much knowledge about the program and is too rigid to elicit the unexpected. Rather, use a list of questions that cover the main concerns. Get the respondent talking and steer him or her around to cover all the topics, not necessarily in the order listed. If some questions yield little insight, cut them; if important new subjects arise, add them. Some interviewers tape-record sessions. I prefer written notes and avoid taping, because it may make respondents reticent and because of the time demands of transcribing.

3. Interviews have three main purposes. First, get the respondents simply to describe how clients are processed in the program. Here performance analysis verges closest to other approaches to process research that stress description. Second, get respondents to explain the reporting indicators that are used to measure performance in the program and client assignments. What do the indicators mean, and how are they compiled? These explanations can sometimes come from state-level officials who run the reporting system, assuming it is constant across the state.

   Third, get respondents' views about "what works"—what features of a program tend to make it perform well or poorly. If the interviewing is exploratory, this question may be asked in a general way. More often, researchers have their own hypotheses, and both the interviewing and the data analysis are aimed at verifying these. The Urban Institute studies focused on the influence of management and organization. My studies have focused on the role of authority, meaning demands on clients to participate and to work, and on paternalism, or the supervisory structure meant to oversee compliance.

4. Ask staff about the influence and importance of the factors that you think affect performance. To keep people from parroting what they think you want to hear, do not mention the specific purposes of the study. Ask questions neutrally to permit a range of answers. Respondents told me, as hypothesized, that the more clients were obligated to participate and the more who went into job search, as against education or training, the more entered jobs. However, contrary to expectations, they did not say that the formal sanctioning

of clients (that is, grant reduction for noncooperation) was clearly linked to performance.

But this interpretative material is lower priority than getting down a thorough account of the administrative process. Make sure the description is "in the can" before asking for opinions, or the descriptive picture you get of the program may be distorted. In the main, as in other research, it is respondents who give facts and the researchers who do the interpreting.

5. Be alert for serendipity. Respondents may confirm or disconfirm your hypotheses, but they may also mention new and unexpected determinants of program performance. My interest in enforcing work arose from staff members I interviewed for the Urban Institute projects who said their main problem was lack of authority over the clients, even though those studies did not focus on this. I then designed my own studies to investigate the role of obligation. It was during these, in turn, that the importance of supervision emerged. That became a focus of later studies. In one recent study, respondents said child support enforcement was a force for reducing caseloads, and the statistics confirmed this. And so on. Fieldwork is a source of more new ideas than can ever be gleaned just from the examination of past research or the reanalysis of existing databases.

Should one also interview the clients of the program? Not to do so might seem to bias conclusions, inasmuch as those served by a program may view it differently from the administrators. I have not done this myself. Programs often forbid interviews as contrary to preserving the confidentiality of clients. Even if interviewing is allowed, obtaining representative respondents is difficult. The caseload must first be sampled, and then the sample must be located for questioning, which is expensive and time-consuming. I also found the attitudes and behavior of recipients to be adequately accounted for by other research. I was more interested in the behavior of programs. I judged that staff would be best able to generalize about the nature and effects of the administrative process, whereas recipients could speak mainly about their individual experience. In research on Wisconsin, however, I interviewed community groups. They are more hostile to welfare work programs than the administrators are, but they describe how they work in quite similar terms.

Statistical Analysis

The next step is to confirm hypotheses about program influences by statistical analysis of the performance indicators. The question is whether the features of programs have the ties to outcomes that the study supposes or respondents say. Perhaps there is no association; or, if there is, it may be spurious. Does a program generate many job entries, or unusually high-paying jobs? Perhaps this is due to having employable clients or a good labor market, rather than to anything the program does. Program features may seem connected to performance only because both policy and performance are the joint product of a favorable environment.

Testing these possibilities requires a statistical model in which all the main influences on performance are accounted for. If administration still matters with the environment controlled, one is surer it has independent influence. One builds a regression model of each performance indicator. The question is what explains the variation in this indicator across the units of observation, which may be time periods, program subunits, or (for a pooled analysis) both. The assumed model is

$$P = \alpha + \beta A + \gamma D + \psi L + \varepsilon \tag{6.1}$$

where

$P =$ The performance measure being modeled, for instance, percentage of clients entering jobs.

$\alpha =$ The intercept, or the mean value of P when the explainers are zero.

$A =$ A vector of administrative variables. For example, measures of organization or administrative capacity, or the percentages of clients that participate, are assigned to various activities, or are sanctioned for noncooperation.

$D =$ A vector of demographic terms describing the caseloads, for instance, the percentage of clients who are female, black, high school graduates, and so on. These terms should come from administrative data or, if unavailable there, from census data for the locality.

$L =$ A vector of labor market variables, for instance, the unemployment rate or the growth in employment in the locality. These come from the U.S. Bureau of Labor Statistics.

β, γ, φ = Regression coefficients for each variable chosen to minimize errors, that is, the difference between actual and predicted performance for each unit of observation.

ε = The error term, which is assumed to be uncorrelated with the explainers and to meet other assumptions usual in regression.

The A, D, and L terms are assumed to be independent, or exogenous, that is, not caused by each other or by other possible explainers of P. When this assumption is questioned, as I note below, a more complex model is needed.

All these variables have to be specified for each unit of observation. In a cross-sectional study, interviewing may cover only some subunits, but the statistical analysis should include all of them, unless some are excluded as atypical of the program. Inasmuch as local programs typically differ in caseload size, I normalize terms where necessary by expressing them as rates or as percentages of the caseload. Variables denominated in percentage have the advantage that the regression coefficients are easily interpretable: Each coefficient expresses an elasticity, or the amount by which performance changes when that variable shifts by one percentage point.

The degree to which administrative terms are quantified varies. In the Urban Institute studies, judgments were made during fieldwork about bureaucratic features such as management patterns and reporting capacities. Those variables were associated with performance on a bivariate basis, judgmentally at the state level and quantitatively at the local office level. In later WIN and JOBS studies, administrative dimensions were quantified in percentages of caseload. In time-series models of caseload change, new programs enter as dummy variables alongside control terms at the time they are implemented. The JTPA studies use both metric and dummy variables to capture administrative variations.

To build the models, one first examines the variables individually to see whether their distributions are strange, or to detect outliers (extreme values) that may require investigation. One then correlates each performance term with its possible explainers one at a time, inspecting scattergrams to determine if relationships are reasonably linear; otherwise, terms may have to be transformed. Finally, one assembles multivariate regression models using several explainers.

Ideally, in such modeling, one should include all explainers that theory or previous research suggests are important, whether or not they prove to be statistically significant (that is, to have clear influence on the performance term). But doing this assumes one has enough guidance to specify the model in detail, and enough degrees of freedom (that is, observations) to estimate the coefficients of all variables. In individual-level analyses with hundreds of observations, these conditions are often met. Researchers can justify and estimate models with many terms.

In performance research, guidance is less precise, in part because the literature is still small. And studies often suffer from a "low N" problem because the unit of analysis is usually the program rather than the client. This means there are not enough observations to test all possible explainers. A cross-sectional, state-based study of a national work program, for instance, will have at most 51 cases—the 50 states plus the District of Columbia. A study based on counties or regions within a state might have fewer still. Accordingly, one must collapse the number of explainers or pick among them somewhat arbitrarily. In one study I combined terms using two-stage least squares (2SLS) and factor analysis (Mead 1985), whereas in others I simply included in the model only terms that were statistically significant, eliminating the others. In deference to low N, I often use an alpha level of .10 rather than the more usual .05 to determine whether terms are significant.

As one example, table 6.1 shows the model for the percentage of JOBS clients entering jobs among counties in Wisconsin in 1993. Results show that each percentage of clients that enrolled in the program and was assigned to job readiness (a workshop in motivation and job search skills) was associated with more than a quarter-point more clients entering jobs.

Table 6.1. Regression Model of Percentage of JOBS Clients Entering Jobs, Wisconsin Counties, 1993

Variable	Coefficient	Standard error	Significance
Percentage of clients enrolled in JOBS	.274	.096	.006
Percentage of clients in job readiness activities	.296	.062	.000
Percentage of black clients	−.361	.102	.001
Percentage growth in employment	−.382	.204	.066
Population density	.004	.002	.053
Proportion of variation explained (R^2)	.54	—	—

Source: Mead 1997a.
Note: JOBS = Job Opportunities and Basic Skills Training Program.

This corroborated the views of staff that such activities were important for job-entry performance. Alongside these policy variables, several control terms were significant. A county tended to have lower performance if its caseload was heavily black, and higher performance if it had high population density. It is not clear why employment growth has a negative and not a positive sign; the findings of performance models are occasionally anomalous.[10]

Typically, such analyses explain measures of job placement performance quite successfully. The given model is strong—accounting for over half the variation in job placements with only five terms. Similar models also explain well other measures of job placement performance, such as the proportion of clients working while still on welfare and the proportion whose JOBS cases were closed. The models for measures of job quality, such as retention rate or job entry wage, are less potent. In them, the human capital of the caseloads—education and training—counts for more, although participation rates and administrative assignments still matter.

Performance Standards

In the preceding model, as in most performance analyses, policy variables as well as environmental variables are included. The point is to understand what works, with both policy and environmental factors in the picture. However, one can also use statistical analysis of outcome measures to appraise how well individual programs are doing relative to their settings.

One way to do this is to model the performance measure *without* policy variables—that is, using just controls for the demographics of the caseload and economic conditions. Such a model will predict what a particular program's performance *should be* based simply on its surroundings. If it performs better or worse than this, the difference must be due to factors not controlled, including the effectiveness of that program. In statistical language, programs that show a large positive residual from such a model are performing above their expectation, whereas those with negative residuals are performing below it.

Figure 6.1, for example, shows the actual versus predicted performance of the Wisconsin counties in the percentage of JOBS cases that they closed in 1993, usually due to getting the recipients jobs. The predicted values were generated by regressing actual performance on several features of the recipients and economic conditions that were significantly related to that performance term.[11] The middle diagonal line across the

Figure 6.1. Actual versus Predicted Percentage of Cases Closed in JOBS, Wisconsin Counties, 1993

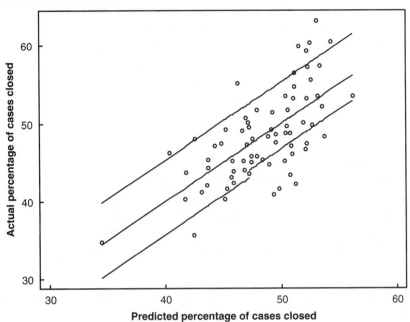

Note: The middle diagonal line separates counties that exceeded their predicted performance from those that fell short of it. The other diagonals are one standard deviation of the errors above and below the middle diagonal.

graph separates counties whose actual performance exceeded their prediction (above the line) from counties where predicted performance exceeded the actual (below the line). The other diagonals are drawn at a distance from the middle line of plus or minus one standard deviation of the residuals. Counties outside these lines probably are over- or underperforming for internal reasons that go beyond chance.

In the Urban Institute studies of the Employment Service and Work Incentive program, this sort of analysis was done at the outset to identify which state programs seemed to be high and low performers relative to their environment. The states chosen for fieldwork were then selected to have a range of variation in performance defined this way, as were (for the WIN study) the local offices chosen within the states (Chadwin et al. 1977, app. 1; Mitchell, Chadwin, and Nightingale 1980, ch. 2). The bureaucratic features under study were then associated with high- and low-performing state and local programs on a bivariate basis.

Another use of such models is to adjust the performance standards that programs may be held to by managers in light of the conditions they face. The most elaborate adjustment has occurred under the Job Training Partnership Act. The performance of local JTPA programs, known as Service Delivery Areas (SDAs), is rated on a number of measures, for example the percentage of adults who are employed following the program and their earnings. The U.S. Department of Labor sets standards on each measure at a level where 75 percent of local programs can meet them, based on past experience. However, the criteria are then adjusted to be fair to programs that face more or less difficult environments. This is done using regression models that relate the variations in each performance measure to conditions beyond the control of the programs (Barnow 1992).

Table 6.2 summarizes the procedure used to adjust one of JTPA's performance measures—the employment rate of adult welfare recipients—in 1995. This example uses a national adjustment model, but states are also able to substitute their own models. The first column lists several demographic and economic factors that affect the likelihood that clients on

Table 6.2. Adjustment of JTPA Welfare Employment Standard, 1995

Adjustment factors (% of caseload except for unemployment)	SDA factor values[a]	National averages on factors	SDA value less national average[a]	Weights (regression coefficients)	Change in performance expectation[b]
Female		82.3		−.144	
High school dropout		25.7		−.062	
Post–high school		23.7		.073	
Black		30.9		−.048	
Ex-offender		6.1		−.088	
Lacking work history		40.9		−.070	
Unemployed 15 weeks or more		46.3		−.103	
Not in labor force		36.1		−.100	
Long-term AFDC		40.4		−.150	
On general assistance		10.7		−.140	
Unemployment rate		7.3		−.514	

Source: Bartik 1995, figure 1.

Notes: JTPA = Job Training Partnership Act; SDA = Service Delivery Area; AFDC = Aid to Families with Dependent Children.

a. SDAs can insert their own values here.

b. Results depend on individual values inserted by SDAs.

welfare will find jobs. The SDAs insert their own values for these factors (column 2) and compare them with national averages (column 3). They then multiply the difference (column 4) by the weights (column 5), which are the regression coefficients from the adjustment model.

By this means, the performance expectation for each SDA is adjusted for the ways in which its environment is better or worse than average. In this instance, the national standard for the welfare employment measure was 47 percent. However, if an SDA had an unemployment rate 10 points above average, for example, its predicted performance would be 5.1 percent lower than average ($10 \times -.514$). So its target on this performance measure would be cut by 5.1 points, or to 41.9 percent. Analogous adjustments up or down would result from the other terms in the table (Bartik 1995, 6–8).

Practical Problems

Performance analysis can help us understand social programs and improve their performance, but it faces two important difficulties.

Clearance

The first is obtaining clearance to do research. Much other research on poverty or welfare can be done entirely at one's computer, using academic databases such as the Panel Study of Income Dynamics (PSID) or government surveys such as the Current Population Survey (CPS) or the Survey of Income and Program Participation (SIPP). To do performance analysis, however, one must directly study programs' administration and reporting, and that requires the cooperation of program officials. It is sensitive to interview inside programs or to analyze program data. Officials typically have three concerns. One, already mentioned, is compromising the confidentiality of recipients. A second is that interviewing or data collection imposes burdens on staff and takes them away from their normal tasks. Yet the results may be of academic interest only, without value to managers in improving the program.

A third concern is the tension that has arisen in recent years between government and most academicians who study poverty. Welfare reform largely means demands by government that welfare recipients work and otherwise function in return for support. Although academic experts on poverty also would like more poor adults to work, most disapprove of enforcing work as a condition of aid. They would prefer to promote employment through new services or work incentives for the clients, rather than by threatening to deny support to them and their children (Mead 1997b). In view of this impasse, officials hesitate to allow outside researchers to study their programs, lest the results be used to embarrass them. (See chapter 2 of this volume for further discussion of this potential problem.)

Performance analysis can address these concerns, perhaps, more easily than other forms of process research. The performance method seeks to optimize programs using outcome indicators that the program has defined, not different values entertained by researchers.[12] If analysis can reveal how best to run a program for its own goals, management will gain. This is one reason why program executives have permitted past performance studies. Indeed, the Urban Institute studies of the Employment Service and WIN were commissioned and published by the U.S. Department of Labor. Researchers who approach programs on their own initiative must be ready to promise feedback useful to the agency. In both New York City and Wisconsin, I gave presentations based on my findings to program personnel. Also, managers will be readier to accept the burdens of research if they can help choose the offices to be visited and schedule the interviews to minimize the disruption of normal operations.

On the other hand, the contribution to management is still limited. Performance research is not, strictly speaking, an evaluation of the program. The question is how and why performance varies across subunits, not whether the program as a whole is worthwhile. Nor can the study—for reasons of confidentiality—be used to hold individual staff or subunits accountable to superiors. When performance analysis is used to set standards for individual programs, as explained above, the work is done by in-house analysts or consultants. For academics, the point is to learn "how to do it" in general terms.

For the larger tension between government and academia, the best solution may be a buffer institution. In Wisconsin, the state welfare department set up a Management and Evaluation Project (MEP) to oversee research on the radical state welfare reform. MEP's executive committee reviews requests for access by outside researchers. It asks whether the projects are methodologically sound and consistent with state goals, and whether they would produce feedback useful to the agency. The committee members include senior welfare officials, with a power to take decisions without further review; in-house research personnel, who would have to prepare data for the researchers; and two outside experts on welfare research.[13] MEP also has a technical advisory committee, including other experts, to address methodological issues.

MEP has substantially depoliticized welfare research in Wisconsin. It has approved most proposals presented to it, and it has sponsored projects of its own. Although some proposals are disapproved, the reasons are usually methodological rather than the politics of the research. Several MEP-sponsored studies are currently under way. They should yield information useful for fine-tuning the state's new work-based welfare system. Officials in Wisconsin have a tradition of seeking guidance from researchers, and their own reform has gone smoothly enough to limit fears of outside criticism. The reform also commands consensus within the state (Mead 2000b).

In more polarized settings, the potential to bridge the government/academic divide is smaller. In New York City, the question of research on welfare or other social programs is highly politicized. Since 1996, the city has instituted Wisconsin-like welfare reforms designed to divert some applicants from aid (that is, to help them in ways other than putting them on the rolls) and to require more adult recipients to work and look for work as a condition of aid. Opposition from local politicians, academics, and advocates is stiff. Accordingly, City Hall has disapproved most outside research and made little data available to academics or the press. In early 1999, opponents obtained a court injunction against the new diversion procedures on grounds that applicants were being denied access to food stamps. Plaintiffs' lawyers obtained an internal study done by the welfare department that had revealed this and other implementation problems, and they used it against the agency in court (Swarns 1999). Such an outcome is bound to discourage official cooperation with process research.

Data Availability

Performance analysis also assumes that data are available to measure the outcomes of programs and their possible determinants. As mentioned, national employment programs have been the chief arena for performance analysis because they have had the required reporting. Those systems have weakened, however, because of the devolution of social policy to lower levels of government since the origins of performance research in the 1970s.

WIN had uniform reporting that provided most of the data needed to measure and analyze its outcomes. But because the WIN system was based on the Employment Service, it was available only as long as federal and state labor departments, which run the ES, continued to have the main responsibility for WIN.[14] When many states instituted alternative programs in the 1980s, Congress allowed them to shift control to the welfare department. The argument was that labor had generally run WIN poorly, because it did not care much about serving welfare recipients. Welfare departments would do a better job. That shift was mandated for JOBS. A cost, however, was the loss of the WIN reporting system. This unnoticed death in the bureaucracy meant the end of a comprehensive national performance assessment system in welfare employment.

JOBS never developed comparable reporting of its own. The new program, like WIN, collected data from states on the demographics of its clients and the activities to which they were assigned. The data, however, were meant only for Washington and did not rest on comparable reporting at the state or local level. States were allowed to submit a sample of cases rather than the universe. As for performance measures, the only goal the law defined for state JOBS programs was meeting specified participation rates, and this was all that most states focused on. Wisconsin was able to transfer its old WIN performance indicators to JOBS, but many states did not.

JOBS was supposed to develop more WIN-like performance measures, but it never did. One reason was that federal planners preferred to await the results of a national evaluation of JOBS before recommending how to measure its results (Mead 1997a, 114, 121). Another reason was that no sooner was a task force convened to frame the new measures, in 1992, than the Clinton administration won office and shifted focus toward a new stage of welfare reform. The new administration's proposals, in turn, were overtaken by the Republican conquest of Congress in the 1994 elections and the ensuing enactment of PRWORA.

TANF has elaborate reporting, but the data are less comprehensive than earlier. JOBS is disestablished, although most states continue such programs. TANF has performance measures that resemble WIN's, in the form of the criteria used to allocate bonuses to states for "high performance," but data on these measures do not cover all states because not all apply for the awards. States report on numbers of cases in various statuses within work programs—such as job search or community jobs—but those data cover only families that are meeting the participation standards. The U.S.

Administration for Children and Families may produce data on work activities by all families in future. TANF reporting also includes data, comparable to AFDC/JOBS, on the demographics of caseloads. Some states are technically outside JOBS or TANF due to waivers, so their reporting may not be comparable to that of other states.

All these problems may make it most feasible to conduct performance analysis in future at the local level, using state or local reporting. Welfare agencies have their own reporting systems. At present, these are oriented mainly to accuracy of claims payment. The question they address is whether individual recipients are eligible for aid and receiving the correct benefit, not whether they are complying with the work and other requirements that welfare has recently imposed. Wisconsin is one of the few states that have managed to build a single computer system covering both claims payment and employment activity. Welfare agencies must now develop afresh the kinds of employment outcome and activity measures that WIN had 30 years ago. Often, the problem is not that an agency lacks all data, but that reporting is not used systematically for analytic or management purposes. In New York City, the welfare department designed a performance management system based substantially on existing data.

Although JTPA still has a national reporting system, it may be affected by the reorganization mandated by the Workforce Investment Act. And these data are not sufficient to support persuasive performance analyses by themselves. In the existing studies, much of the information about administrative variations comes from special surveys done by researchers, or it is available only on the 16 local JTPA sites that participated in the national evaluation of the program (Heinrich 2000; Jennings and Ewalt 1998). There has also been less field research on JTPA to clarify the meaning of the data than in the case of welfare work programs.

A further difficulty is the control variables needed to capture the nonpolicy determinants of performance. Although the WIN reporting system included demographic data describing the entire welfare work caseload, JOBS and now TANF allow states to report data to Washington on only a sample of clients. For my recent studies of JOBS performance in Wisconsin, I needed demographic profiles of the caseloads by county. Fortunately, I was able to persuade the state welfare department to generate these for me. Few other states, probably, would be willing or able to do this. In New York City, demographic data on the local welfare centers that are now enforcing work are not available because case records are not fully computerized. The alternative is to use census data on the demographics of census tracts or county populations, but these data are available only for census years, and they capture the characteristics of program caseloads only very roughly.

For economic control terms, the situation is better. The U.S. Bureau of Labor Statistics generates state- and county-level estimates for most of the required variables. Data on employment, unemployment, and the labor force come from the Current Population Survey, although estimates for small jurisdictions also make use of census data. Estimates for years are more reliable than for months, and this is another reason to prefer cross-sectional analyses using annual data. Data on employment and wages, by industry and overall, come from Unemployment Insurance reporting.

Thus, recent developments in social policy make process analysis more important, but the same developments have damaged the reporting needed to do performance research. Reporting systems will no doubt recover and improve. There will still be programs and localities where the data will support performance analysis. But with weaker national reporting systems, researchers will have to locate those programs on their own.

Statistical Problems

A number of more technical objections may be raised about appraising program performance using statistical models. An initial question is about the validity of the data. Can measures of administrative assignment, such as rates of clients who participate or are sanctioned, really capture how a program operates? At the local level, I find that participation is a strong positive influence on job entry performance, whereas sanctioning rates tend to be *negatively* linked to performance. What does this mean?

I rely on interviews to tell me. Program staff typically interpret participation and sanctioning as exertions of authority. In a mandatory program, clients participate mostly because they have to, whereas those who do not participate are sanctioned. Staff members say that participation promotes performance by requiring recipients to organize their lives for work. They also suggest that sanctioning occurs mainly when staff fail to make expectations clear to clients informally. Programs perform best when they credibly *threaten* to sanction, and clients comply. That is why a high incidence of actual sanctioning is linked to lower performance. For me, such feedback makes enough sense of the numbers to take administrative assignments as meaningful indicators of the demands made on clients.

But even if the data are valid, are they reliable? Students of street-level bureaucracy (see chapter 7 of this volume) emphasize the discretion that service-level staff have in deciding how to treat their clients. They suspect that staff may cover up what they do when they record actions in the computer or case files. So reporting data may not indicate how a program really operates. Again, fieldwork is a safeguard. Even in confidential interviews, respondents have not told me that the reporting is systematically deceptive, although one does need to understand what the categories mean. It is enough that the variation on an indicator reflects real differences among units, even if there is some noise or inaccuracy in the data. As long as interviews tend to corroborate the data, I am inclined to trust them.

Performance analysis presumes that the various forces that influence an outcome measure can be tested side by side in the same model. This assumes that the different variables are distinct. But what if there is high multicollinearity among them? That is, what if the performance, administrative, demographic, or labor market terms are highly interrelated? This means that subunits that have high performance also have high levels of client participation and work activities, and also have favorable client demographics and labor market conditions, compared with other subunits. The overlap of the variables means that it is difficult to separate their effects. Perhaps they are all measuring the same, rather than different, things.

This implies that high performance as measured by outcome indicators may not be distinct from the administrative assignments that appear to promote it. Maybe clients are made to participate only because they are about to be placed in jobs, not because participation really enables job entries.[15] More important, performance that appears to result from obligating clients to participate and look for work may really result from a favorable environment outside the program.

One safeguard is, again, interviews. Program staff members do not suggest that job placement follows automatically from participation in the program; rather, they say participation is essential to get clients to focus on work. Respondents generally tell me that the level of obligation in a program reflects local policy rather than the environment. So there is reason to regard the administrative determinants as important forces in their own right, even if they are correlated with the control terms. Another solution is to widen the variation within the data set. Multicollinearity was a problem mainly in my studies of WIN in New York City and New York State, which had few cases (Mead 1983, 1985). In later studies of WIN nationwide and JOBS in Wisconsin, I had more observations and intercorrelation declined. But administrative variables retained their causal importance (Mead 1988, 1997a).

Explanatory variables may be not only intercorrelated, but also causally related. Performance models combine explainers of various kinds as if they were all independent. But maybe some of them are really products of the others. As statisticians say, they may be endogenous to the model, not exogenous. Again, maybe the administrative terms that seem so potent are really reflections of the environmental variables. It may appear that programs that obligate a lot of clients and put them in job search achieve high performance. But perhaps these programs are willing and able to do this only because they have relatively employable clients and many jobs available. Thus, it is really the external opportunity structure that drives the results and not the way clients are treated inside the program.[16]

A further objection is that the administrative factors might reflect other forces not included in the model at all. Perhaps a work program's power to obligate recipients to participate and look for jobs stems from its funding or administrative resources. Some programs simply have more money or staff to help people find work than others. If that were true, then the interpretation of participation rates or assignment to job search as expressions of authority would be in doubt. Maybe all these indicators really capture is how fully the caseload is being served. It is difficult to get data on staffing or administrative resources, in part because agencies cannot always allocate their money and personnel among different programs or among subunits. In studies where I could measure resources, I found them in two cases to be significant predictors of performance, but in another case not.[17] In all these cases, administrative terms expressing activity levels retained their importance.

These last two points raise what statisticians call identification issues. In the performance literature to date, explanatory models have generally been simple. A performance measure is made the dependent term, and administrative differences and social or economic controls are all treated equally as independent, or exogenous, variables that predict this term. But if some explainers are endogenous, that is, influenced by other variables in the model, or even by the dependent term, they are no longer strictly independent. A way must be found to "identify" them, that is, to estimate what they would be if they were independent.

Statisticians try to do this by what is called instrumental variables (IV). They find one or more variables that plausibly predict the endogenous term but not the main dependent term (here, the performance measure). The endogenous explainer is regressed on these "instruments," and its predicted value from this equation is then used to estimate it in the structural, or primary, model.

In a common form of IV, called two-stage least square (2SLS), the endogenous term is regressed on the instruments and on all other variables in the system that are judged to be independent. If there is one endogenous term to instrument, then equation 6.1, the basic structural model for performance analysis, becomes

$$X_i = \lambda + \theta I + \beta A + \gamma D + \psi L + \omega \tag{6.2a}$$

$$P = \alpha + \eta \hat{X}, \beta A + \gamma D + \psi L + \varepsilon \tag{6.2b}$$

In equation 6.2a, X_i is an administrative explainer that is judged to be endogenous. It is regressed on I, a vector of one or more instrumental variables, and on other administrative, demographic, or labor market terms that are judged to be exogenous; θ is the coefficient of I, λ is the intercept, and ω is the error term. This equation generates a predicted value of X_i, or $\hat{X}$. Then $\hat{X}$ is used as an estimate for X in equation 6.2b, which is parallel to the original equation 6.1. Inasmuch as all the antecedents of $\hat{X}$ are variables assumed to be independent, $\hat{X}$ is also independent and the endogeneity problem is solved.

However, IV depends on the availability of instrumental variables—terms, in this case, that plausibly cause X, but not P, and hence can be excluded from the structural equation 6.2b. If instruments cannot be found, then the independence of the explainers has to be established on theoretical grounds or by using other evidence, such as interviews with program staff. That is one reason that interviews are vital to convincing performance analysis.[18] Statistical modeling like this will be one of the frontiers of performance analysis in future.

Selection Bias

The most serious objection to performance analysis questions the very idea of assessing programs using statistics. Since the early 1980s, the orthodoxy among evaluators has been that only an experimental trial, involving the random allocation of clients between experimental and control groups, can really determine whether a program achieves any impact. Here, impact means the improvement that occurs in the clients' average employment, earnings, or dependence, compared with the averages for equivalent clients who do not receive the benefit.

One might attempt to estimate impact statistically. That is, build a model where clients' employment or earnings after a program is related to whether they received a certain treatment, as well as to a string of control variables for demographic features or other exogenous conditions. The coefficient for the treatment variable supposedly captures the benefit of receiving the program. The orthodoxy says that such models are invalid due to "selection bias." The reason is that clients' success after a program may be due heavily to psychological factors that one cannot measure and control, including their willingness to participate in the program in the first place. Thus, any statistical estimate of the benefit of participation will tend to overestimate it, attributing to the program gains that are really due to the unmeasured features of the clients.

The only solution to selection bias is to abandon statistical modeling in favor of an experimental trial, where the clients to be served are allocated by chance to either an experimental or a control group. Random assignment eliminates any serious chance that the clients getting and not getting the treatment will differ systematically in any dimension, whether measured or unmeasured. Only then does the experimental-control difference in outcome become a trustworthy measure of program impact (Burtless and Orr 1986).[19]

Performance analysis can easily appear to be a throwback to non-experimental evaluation, inasmuch as it professes to appraise programs using statistical models. Statistical associations, by themselves, do not establish causation. And how do we know that the endorsement of mandatory participation and job search that emerges from many of these studies does not really rest on selection bias? Perhaps programs that appear to perform well due to these methods really owe their results to intangible advantages in client motivation, or perhaps to agency leadership or staff quality or something else unmeasurable. The objection here is not, as above, that relationships among the explainers are unexplored or that obvious explainers have been omitted, but rather that diffuse differences that could never be controlled are driving the findings.

The response is that in performance analysis, statistics should not stand alone. Hypotheses about what causes what are derived initially from prior studies and from staff interviews. Statistical analysis is then intellectually justified as a reasonable way of testing those expectations. Performance analysis also makes no pretense of judging impact. The point is to discover what influences the program's performance measures and how these determinants can be changed, not to decide how much difference the program makes in impact terms. Comparisons are made among units all of which are part of the program, not between one clientele that receives a program and another that does not. The assessment is meant to guide program management and administration, not to decide the program's overall effectiveness, efficiency, or value. The question is "what works" in this rough and ready sense, not impact in the evaluator's more precise sense.

If one insists on regarding performance analysis as evaluation, however, several features of it are reassuring. First, as explained above, interview findings in performance studies generally run parallel to the statistical conclusions. Respondents do not suggest that intangible factors not captured in the models are responsible for the higher performance of more demanding programs.[20] Staff impressions include the intangible dimensions omitted from the statistical models, so if the findings run parallel, concerns over selection bias should not invalidate the procedure.

Second, the concern about selection bias arose in evaluation studies where the unit of analysis was the individual client. Statistical models that predict outcomes for individuals are typically weak. That is, they explain very little of the variation in results across clients. The reason is that individual-level data contain a lot of "noise"—random variation. That weakness abets the worry about selection bias, for if little of the variation is explained by the variables in the model, more may reflect unmeasured influences.[21]

In performance analyses, however, the unit of analysis is commonly the program. The data are aggregates for program units. Such data are produced by averaging over many individual clients within each program, and this removes a lot of the noise. The variation across programs then tends to be systematic. As a result, explanatory models using these data tend to be strong, often accounting for well over half the variation in the performance term across the units. Models for the job-entry measures, where administrative terms are most important, are particularly strong.[22] Correct specification of the model is still essential. But with most variation accounted for, it becomes less reasonable to worry about unmeasurable influences.[23]

Finally, the policy implications of performance analysis usually run parallel to those from the experimental literature. The MDRC evaluations, although diverse, mostly support a conclusion that welfare work programs that enforce participation and stress actual work outperform those that are voluntary or stress education or training. The highest-performing programs MDRC has studied—in Riverside and San Diego, California, and in Portland, Oregon—all had these features, although they did not exclude all remediation (Hamilton and Friedlander 1989; Riccio, Friedlander, and Freedman 1994; Scrivener et al. 1998). In the recent National Evaluation of Welfare-to-Work Strategies, MDRC has directly compared programs stressing "work first" with others with an education and training emphasis. "Work first" emerges as superior on most counts, although both approaches achieve worthwhile impacts (Freedman et al. 2000). The fact that these findings run parallel to those from performance analyses of welfare work programs suggests that the two literatures are tapping a common reality, although they do so with different methods and assumptions.

With JTPA, admittedly, the correspondence is weaker. Studies here find only a limited association between programs that performed well on the JTPA performance measures and those that had greatest impact in the national JTPA evaluation (Barnow 2000; Heckman et al. 1997). The reason is unclear. It is apparently not that programs "cream," inasmuch as higher-skilled clients actually gain more from this program than do the more disadvantaged (Heckman et al. 1997, 391–92). It may be that JTPA is a voluntary program, so that the enforcement methods that look good in welfare work programs cannot be used. To put this differently, it may be that welfare work evaluations parallel the performance results because impacts vary with implementation, and performance analysis measures implementation (see further below). With a fully implemented, voluntary program such as JTPA, more divergence between evaluation and performance must be expected. Research on JTPA (both performance and evaluation studies) is also less developed than on welfare work, and further inquiry may hold the answers.

Standards for Studies

How does one distinguish a strong performance analysis from a weak one? I have already indicated the basics: First, derive hypotheses about the determinants of performance from the existing literature on the program in question, and from interviews with administrators. Then test the hypotheses with quantitative models where terms expressing policy or administrative differences operate alongside environmental controls for demographic or economic conditions. Administrative and demographic variables should come, to the extent possible, from the program's own data.

When I read performance analyses with weak or unconvincing results, the reason is usually

- Lack of interviews in the program: The author has derived hypotheses a priori based on his or her own reasoning, or on the existing literature, but without talking with administrators. That is particularly dangerous when the program in question is a new one or operating in a changed policy or social environment, such as current welfare reform programs.
- Lack of program data on how clients are treated: Some studies gauge the policy of local units using preformed surveys that are administered to managers by mail or phone. These data are less valid and reliable than the program's own reporting. In the case of welfare reform programs, some studies use dummy variables for whether a state has a federal "waiver" or not. These measure the demands clients face very crudely.
- Lack of adequate demographic controls: Studies often lack data from the program describing its clients. They use census data in place of it, which is a poor substitute, or none at all. But inasmuch as these terms usually compete with policy variables in explaining outcomes, models become invalid or implausible.
- Lack of adequate economic controls: Some studies use statewide unemployment rates for local offices when they could get jobless rates by county. They may omit other economic controls that are also available, such as labor force participation rates or employment levels.

The internal validity of a study is established largely by the consistency of its data sources. When interviews and statistical analysis give the same message about what generates performance, findings can be trusted. Interviews, other outside information, or statistical modeling should be used to deal with identification issues and establish the autonomy of the policy terms of interest. External validity hinges on whether the findings are consistent with other performance analyses, or with other evidence about the results of programs, such as evaluation findings. Large discrepancies, when they arise, are usually due to one of the above weaknesses.

The performance literature shows steady advances toward rigor. In the Urban Institute studies, the first systematic effort was made to connect the program structures to outcomes, although with limited quantification. In the WIN and JOBS studies, program policies are more fully quantified and controlled, using program data. In some recent JTPA studies, a statistical tie is shown between performance and macro features, such as which agency runs the program (Heinrich 2000; Jennings and Ewalt 1998). In the later studies, identification and modeling issues are dealt with more fully.

Pros and Cons

The advantages and disadvantages of performance analysis are best grasped by comparing this method first with impact evaluation experiments and then with other approaches to process research.[24]

Performance Analysis versus Impact Evaluation

As mentioned already, performance analysis does not establish that a program has impact or is worthwhile in some overall sense. That is the task of evaluation. On the other hand, evaluations do not establish whether or how a program is implemented before it is assessed. Indeed, evaluation may obfuscate the extent of implementation. To ensure the comparability of their experimental and control groups, randomized trials must compare average outcomes for all experimental clients with the same averages for all control clients, without being sure how many people in either group were served or unserved. Not all experimental clients may actually participate in the tested program, and on the other hand some members of the control group may obtain equivalent services from other sources. Both these tendencies bias downward the estimates of the treatment effect.

Evaluators may document the extent of implementation to clarify what the impacts mean (see the Sherwood and Doolittle discussion in chapter 9 in this volume). But this assessment is usually detached from

the impact analysis and, typically, gets little attention. Evaluators sometimes try to adjust impacts for the proportion of experimental clients that
claimed their benefit, and these calculations have some resemblance to
performance analysis. In contrast, rather than assume implementation,
performance research examines it. The same administrative terms that
embody much of the method's policy implications area are also measures
of implementation. Does the program reach the entire caseload or only
part of it? The trend in welfare employment evaluations has been for
impacts to grow over time, and one reason probably is that implementation improved.

Performance analysis also helps solve the "black box" problem with
impact evaluation. Net impact experiments may establish that a program
as a whole has good effects, but they seldom say how. Social programs are
typically composed of several services or benefits, and it is seldom clear
which aspect generated the effects. In theory, separate experiments can be
run to test the effects of subelements of a program. That is, clients can be
randomly assigned not to one but to several experimental groups, each
receiving some particular combination of treatments, and all of them
compared with a control group. The National Evaluation of Welfare-to-
Work Strategies has attempted this more widely than any previous
research. This study contrasts "labor market attachment" and "human
capital development" approaches to welfare employment, and also different approaches to case management (Brock and Harknett 1997). Experimentation remains cumbersome, however, and the packages of services
tested remain too complex for the meaning of impacts, if any, to be clear.[25]

With performance analysis, one is less sure of the effect on performance but more sure of what the treatment means. The proportions of
clients assigned to particular activities become explicit variables. The
treatment can be taken apart into its separate elements, so to speak, and
the influence of each on performance can be measured, even if the
results cannot be interpreted as impacts. The black box is not totally pen-
etrated. The program remains too complicated to present only one reality. But the combination of interviewing and administrative measurement captures more of what is going on internally than experimentation
usually can.

Finally, performance analysis can speak to the relative efficacy of programs in widely different settings. Evaluations tend to be local. The random allocation of clients to experimental and control groups occurs at a
particular site. Demographic influences bearing on the groups are equal-

ized by random assignment, and economic influences are ignored because it is assumed that both groups experience the same labor market. This leaves unclear what the performance of the program would be with a different clientele or in a different labor market. To get a sense of the general efficacy of the program, findings from many sites must be aggregated. That requires some form of meta-analysis, and every approach is contestable.[26] MDRC is notably cautious about concluding which of the programs it evaluates are better and worse, in part due to this aggregation problem (Gueron and Pauly 1991; Riccio et al. 1994). Just as experimentation could in principle probe the black box, so it could in principle be done across many sites (Greenberg, Meyer, and Wiseman 1994). But the practical problems would again be very difficult.

Performance analysis may determine program effects less surely than an experiment at each site, but it also permits easier aggregation across sites. All local programs are part of a single analysis. Demographic and labor market differences are not assumed away but included explicitly as controls. We then learn something about what works in general, without the need for a separate meta-analysis.

Performance Analysis versus Other Process Methodologies

Performance analysis is the most quantitative of the process research methodologies. That makes it, in one sense, the most rigorous. Other approaches depend more on qualitative methods, and lack the check that statistical measures and analyses provide. Street-level analyses (see chapter 7 of this volume) question the reliability of program reporting, but they rely on interviews with staff and clients that may be subjective. The same is true of ethnographic studies of program clienteles (see chapter 8). The field analysis/monitoring approach depends heavily on interviews for information about higher-level state or local policies and structures; the influence of these choices on performance is not directly tested. Implementation analysis, as mentioned, may be an adjunct of evaluation studies, but the findings are separate from the impact finding and thus are not connected systematically to performance.

On the other hand, performance analysis presumes that a program is in being before it is analyzed. Implementation is a variable, not an assumption as in impact evaluation, but for performance analysis to work, meaningful service delivery must be occurring and recorded in every subunit of the program. In that gross sense, implementation is assumed. Performance analysis, thus, does not contemplate a complete breakdown in implementation.[27]

The performance method also assumes that the major policy influences on outcomes can be quantified. That presumes that the administrative features subject to reporting, such as the assignment of clients, capture the relevant policy influences on outcomes. But some features of a program are too high-level, too structural in nature to be easily reduced to numbers. These include which agency runs a program, the overall organization of the agency, or the degree of intervention by state and local politicians. Existing performance analyses have been able to appraise these factors only to a limited extent.

There may even be less tangible influences that escape any statistical model. For example, the current rapid decline in the national TANF caseload seems driven by an anti-welfare atmosphere in the country as well as by welfare reform. Many needy families are leaving the rolls, or failing to apply for aid, even in states that have not yet implemented serious work requirements. That diffuse, atmospheric suasion on clients is not reducible to any concrete feature of a program. In one early study, I was able to explain some of the residual in performance not accounted for by the performance models by judging during interviews whether staff in the offices interacted with clients in a demanding or undemanding way (Mead 1985, 244–47). Today, measures of stigma in welfare might help explain variations in movement off the rolls. Less systematic but more catholic process methodologies, such as field monitoring or street-level analysis, may be more able to capture these influences.

Audiences

The direct audience for performance analysis is policymakers and managers interested in improving existing social programs. On the assumption that a program is in being and has reporting on its outcomes and administration, this method probably tells more about how to optimize those outcomes than any other. Academic performance studies can help reveal "what works" in general terms, and management systems that allow for the local environment can hold subunits fairly accountable for results. Performance analysis is part of the larger movement toward the "reinvention of government," which has emphasized the breakup of large bureaucratic agencies into smaller delivery organizations, some public and some private. The latter are then held accountable for results through various forms of performance assessment (Osborne and Gaebler 1992).

Performance analysis can also inform the broader public debate about social problems because it captures more of the forces that bear on these conditions than other forms of policy research. Most academic studies of poverty use nonprogram databases that cover many of the social and economic forces bearing on the poor but lack measures of the enforcement pressures that are now transforming welfare. We know from the Panel Study of Income Dynamics, the Current Population Study, or the Study of Income and Program Participation what benefits respondents receive from social programs, but not whether they have been required to work, cooperate with child support enforcement, and so on. And, as mentioned above, conventional evaluation focuses on the program treatment while saying little about nonprogram influences because they are taken out of the picture by random assignment and the local nature of the experiment.

In performance models, by contrast, programmatic influences on outcomes appear alongside demographic and economic determinants. The coefficients on the different variables are not strictly comparable because the terms are measured in different units, but one can glean some sense of the relative importance of all the forces. Especially if the internal practices of programs show influence on outcomes even with the environment controlled, they become plausible levers for change. A broader case can then be made for strengthening those levers. And the more performance analysis learns to model administrative determinants, the more it will teach about how to do that.

It was evidence that work enforcement in welfare could be effective that largely motivated the nation's drive toward work requirements since the Family Support Act. MDRC's studies showing the positive impacts of mandatory work programs provided the main technical basis for the Family Support Act and the creation of JOBS. Another support came from research by Bane and Ellwood and others showing that long-term dependence was a serious problem (Baum 1991; Haskins 1991). Meanwhile, the idea of refounding welfare on "reciprocity" or "social contract" provided a larger political rationale for the reform (Mead 1986). But the technical and political arguments were connected. The broader case for work enforcement would have been difficult to make if it had not been shown that requiring work improved client outcomes. New policy goals tend never to come on the agenda unless a way to achieve them has appeared (Kingdon 1995).

The main audiences not served by performance assessment are those who disagree with the goals embodied in the performance measures. Some will dissent from the narrow focus of the current performance systems on employment. Should the only goal of welfare or training programs be to move the poor and dependent into jobs? Even if these goals are accepted, some will dissent from the mandatory nature of current welfare work programs. They may prefer a program like JTPA, where a performance measurement system guides a voluntary training program for the disadvantaged. Some others may object to the whole idea of setting goals for programs outside the poor themselves. Any such structure must treat the clients as objects of a production process that program staffs, in the end, control. If one wants to solve social problems in the terms the clients understand, even a voluntary structure may seem too directive.

But as long as society still claims the authority to set program goals and pursue them, performance analysis can tell it a great deal about how to do that. Along with impact evaluation and other forms of process research, it can help guide the current rebuilding of the welfare state.

NOTES

I am indebted for comments on earlier drafts of this chapter from Eugene Bardach, Tom Corbett, Mary Clare Lennon, Charles Metcalf, Howard Rolston, and several authors of other chapters in this volume.

1. For a summary of most of these studies, see Gueron and Pauly (1991).

2. The changes were triggered chiefly by welfare reform and also by the Workforce Investment Act of 1998, which mandates the reorganization of federal training programs. See Nathan and Gais (1999).

3. For a critical overview, see Lynn, Heinrich, and Hill (2001).

4. An accessible summary of the WIN study appears in Chadwin, Mitchell, and Nightingale (1981).

5. Unusually, Heinrich (2000) models performance with both individual-level and program-level determinants by using a hierarchical estimation technique.

6. One problem is "unit root," or the tendency of some chronological series to trend continuously up or down, without a clear mean. To avoid this, researchers must transform the series into something that is "stationary." Typically, one examines not changes in the raw caseload but the percent change in the caseload from month to month. Another problem, arising from underspecified models, is serial correlation in the error term.

7. Among the studies referenced above, the following are cross-sectional: Chadwin et al. (1977); Chadwin, Mitchell, and Nightingale (1981); Mead (1983, 1985, 1988, 1997a); Mitchell, Chadwin, and Nightingale (1980); Provencher (1989).

8. Pooled studies include Brasher (1994); Heinrich (2000); and Schiller and Brasher (1990, 1993).

9. The presumption, mentioned above, that most of the variation in program performance and determinants is cross-sectional, not temporal, facilitates fieldwork. It implies that the policy and administrative styles of local programs are not likely to change quickly, so interviewing need not be precisely contemporaneous with the reporting data used for the statistical analysis. A gap of a year or two is acceptable.

10. One interpretation might be that, in counties with high employment growth, most employable recipients are already working, so that the remaining cases are less placeable.

11. These terms included the percentages of the caseload that were defined as disadvantaged under JOBS rules, under age 25, high school graduates, black, and Asian, plus the labor force participation rate in the county.

12. However, researchers may have to work with administrators to decide the priority and weighting of official goals, if this is unclear. The Urban Institute studies carried out elaborate consultations and analyses for this purpose.

13. The outside experts are myself and Michael Wiseman, formerly of the University of Wisconsin–Madison and currently a consultant in Washington, D.C.

14. Officially, WIN was run jointly by the labor and welfare departments at the federal and state levels. In practice, the Employment Service was chiefly responsible because it provided most of the local office structure.

15. Michael R. Sosin (1987) made this and other technical criticisms in a review of Mead (1986). My reply appeared in Mead (1987).

16. Michael Wiseman (1988) suggests this objection.

17. In Mead (1985), a measure of staff resources for caseload did affect performance, but administrative assignment was still important. In Mead (1997a), I constructed a measure of administrative funding for caseload, but it had hardly any influence once activity levels were controlled. In Mead (2000a), spending variables were significant and negative explainers of caseload change, but I omitted them from the final model on theoretical grounds and also so I could use them as instruments to test the independence of one of the administrative terms.

18. In Mead (2000a), I was able to test the independence of one administrative term using 2SLS but not another.

19. Statistical models are still used to adjust impact estimates for small experimental-control differences that may have occurred, and also to improve the power of the estimate, but this is valid because random assignment has broken any probable correlation between the errors and the explainers.

The experimental orthodoxy is not uncontested. James Heckman (1992) argues that experimentation has its own biases and that, for many questions, statistical modeling is superior. There are some means of dealing with selection issues in individual-level models without experimentation. These include Heckman corrections, fixed-effect models, and instrumental variables. It is my sense that most experts in this area still doubt the efficacy of any but experimental methods.

20. I note below that differences in program atmosphere not captured by measurable administrative differences do appear to have some influence on performance, but their influence is marginal once the measurable differences are controlled.

21. As one example, R^2 for the models used to estimate impacts in Hamilton and Friedlander (1989) ranged from .10 to .22. This means that most of the variation in out-

comes is accounted for by the error term. This enhances the danger that the errors are correlated with the explainers, which biases their coefficients.

22. R^2 for the control analyses in the Urban Institute studies, which used only non-program terms, ranged from .20 to .67. R^2 for the six Wisconsin performance models in Mead (1997a), which included policy plus environmental variables, ranged from .22 to .61. The figures for the models for job-entry performance (that is, for the percents of clients entering jobs, working while on welfare, and with cases closed) in this study were, respectively, .54, .61, and .59. In Mead (1985), R^2 for five performance models ranged even higher, from .62 to .93, because the use of composites as explainers removed even more noise. In Mead (1999), R^2 for the main cross-sectional model explaining caseload decline in Wisconsin was .76; in Mead (2000a), it was .81.

23. In technical terms, when the error term explains little of the variation in the dependent term, its capacity to bias the parameter estimates is reduced, at least mathematically. In the bivariate case, if the standard regression model is $Y = \alpha + \beta X + \varepsilon$, it can be shown that $\beta = \dfrac{S_{xy}}{S_{xx}} - \dfrac{S_{x\varepsilon}}{S_{xx}}$. In this second equation, the first right-hand term is the OLS estimator of β. The second right-hand term estimates the bias in β that results when X and the errors are correlated. The selection bias evaluators worry about results from this correlation. Bias is zero only if $S_{x\varepsilon}$, the covariance of X and the errors, is zero—the standard OLS assumption. But as R^2 rises, the share of variance in P explained by the errors falls, as does the variance of the errors themselves. This means that $S_{x\varepsilon}$ also falls. In theory, bias can always occur if the model is wrongly specified, even if there is no error at all. But in practice, when R^2 is as high as in many performance models using aggregate data, $S_{x\varepsilon}$ becomes so small that there is little mathematical room in which bias could occur. So the fear of it becomes less reasonable. I am indebted for advice on this point from my colleague David Greenberg of New York University.

24. The following draws upon Mead (1996, 1997a, 1998).

25. The "labor market attachment" and "human capital development" programs contrasted in the National Evaluation of Welfare-to-Work Strategies, for example, both have several elements. The first allows some training, whereas the second involves some job search.

26. In the national evaluation of JTPA, random assignment was done separately at 16 local sites. Then all the experimentals and all the controls were pooled to make the overall impact assessment. See Bloom et al. (1992). Another approach is to assess impact separately at the different sites, then average these estimates with weighting for sample size or precision. I am indebted for guidance on this point to Howard Bloom of MDRC. For an introduction to these problems, see Cooper (1989).

27. To diagnose and prescribe for that situation, discrepancy analysis is more appropriate.

REFERENCES

Barnow, Burt S. 1992. "The Effects of Performance Standards on State and Local Programs." In *Evaluating Welfare and Training Programs*, edited by Charles F. Manski and Irwin Garfinkel (chapter 8). Cambridge, Mass.: Harvard University Press.

———. 2000. "Exploring the Relationship between Performance Management and Program Impact: A Case Study of the Job Training Partnership Act." *Journal of Policy Analysis and Management* 19(1):118–41.

Bartik, Timothy J. 1995. "Using Performance Indicators to Improve the Effectiveness of Welfare-to-Work Programs." Kalamazoo, Mich.: W. E. Upjohn Institute for Employment Research.

Baum, Erica B. 1991. "When the Witch Doctors Agree: The Family Support Act and Social Science Research." *Journal of Policy Analysis and Management* 10(4):603–15.

Bloom, Howard S., Larry L. Orr, George Cave, Stephen H. Bell, and Fred Doolittle. 1992. "The National JTPA Study: Title II-A Impacts on Earnings and Employment at 18 Months." Bethesda, Md.: Abt Associates.

Brasher, C. Nielsen. 1994. "Workfare in Ohio: Political and Socioeconomic Climate and Program Impact." *Policy Studies Journal* 22(3):514–27.

Brock, Thomas, and Kristen Harknett. 1997. *Separation versus Integration of Income Maintenance and Employment Services: What Model Is Best? Findings from a Case Management Experiment in Columbus, Ohio.* New York: Manpower Demonstration Research Corporation.

Burtless, Gary, and Larry L. Orr. 1986. "Are Classical Experiments Needed for Manpower Policy?" *Journal of Human Resources* 21(4):606–39.

Chadwin, Mark Lincoln, John J. Mitchell, and Demetra Smith Nightingale. 1981. "Reforming Welfare: Lessons from the WIN Experience." *Public Administration Review* 41(3):372–80.

Chadwin, Mark Lincoln, John J. Mitchell, Erwin C. Hargrove, and Lawrence M. Mead. 1977. *The Employment Service: An Institutional Analysis.* U.S. Department of Labor, R&D Monograph 51. Washington, D.C.: U.S. Government Printing Office.

Cooper, Harris M. 1989. *Integrating Research: A Guide for Literature Reviews,* 2d ed. Newbury Park, Calif.: Sage Publications.

Dickinson, Katherine P., and Richard W. West. 1988. *Evaluation of the Effects of JTPA Performance Standards on Clients, Services, and Costs.* Washington, D.C.: National Commission for Employment Policy.

Englander, Valerie, and Fred Englander. 1985. "Workfare in New Jersey: A Five Year Assessment." *Policy Studies Review* 5(1):33–41.

Freedman, Stephen, Daniel Friedlander, Gayle Hamilton, JoAnn Rock, Morisa Mitchell, Jodi Nudelman, Amanda Schweder, and Laura Storto. 2000. *National Evaluation of Welfare-to-Work Strategies: Evaluating Alternative Welfare-to-Work Approaches: Two-Year Impacts for Eleven Programs.* New York: Manpower Demonstration Research Corporation.

Greenberg, David, Robert Meyer, and Michael Wiseman. 1994. "When One Demonstration Site Is Not Enough." *Focus* 16(1):15–20.

Gueron, Judith M., and Edward Pauly, with Cameran M. Lougy. 1991. *From Welfare to Work.* New York: Russell Sage Foundation.

Hamilton, Gayle, and Daniel Friedlander. 1989. *Final Report on the Saturation Work Initiative Model in San Diego.* New York: Manpower Demonstration Research Corporation.

Haskins, Ron. 1991. "Congress Writes a Law: Research and Welfare Reform." *Journal of Policy Analysis and Management* 10(4):616–32.

Heckman, James. 1992. "Randomization and Social Policy Evaluation." In *Evaluating Welfare and Training Programs,* edited by Charles F. Manski and Irwin Garfinkel (chapter 5). Cambridge, Mass.: Harvard University Press.

Heckman, James, Carolyn Heinrich, and Jeffrey Smith. 1997. "Assessing the Performance of Performance Standards in Public Bureaucracies." *American Economic Review* 87(2):389–95.

Heinrich, Carolyn J. 2000. "Organizational Form and Performance: An Empirical Investigation of Nonprofit and For-Profit Job-Training Service Providers." *Journal of Policy Analysis and Management* 19(2):233–61.

Jennings, Edward T., and Jo Ann G. Ewalt. 1998. "Interorganizational Coordination, Administrative Consolidation, and Policy Performance." *Public Administration Review* 58(5):417–28.

Kingdon, John W. 1995. *Agendas, Alternatives, and Public Policies,* 2d ed. New York: Longman.

Lynn, Laurence E., Jr., Carolyn J. Heinrich, and Carolyn J. Hill. 2001. *Improving Governance: A New Logic for Empirical Research.* Washington, D.C.: Georgetown University Press.

Mead, Lawrence M. 1983. "Expectations and Welfare Work: WIN in New York City." *Policy Studies Review* 2(4):648–62.

———. 1985. "Expectations and Welfare Work: WIN in New York State." *Polity* 18(2):224–52.

———. 1986. *Beyond Entitlement: The Social Obligations of Citizenship.* New York: Free Press.

———. 1987. "Author's Response to Reviewer." *Social Service Review* 61(2):373–77.

———. 1988. "The Potential for Work Enforcement: A Study of WIN." *Journal of Policy Analysis and Management* 7(2):264–88.

———. 1996. "Welfare Policy: The Administrative Frontier." *Journal of Policy Analysis and Management* 15(4):587–600.

———. 1997a. "Optimizing JOBS: Evaluation versus Administration." *Public Administration Review* 57(2):113–23.

———. 1997b. "Conflicting Worlds of Welfare Reform." *First Things* 75:15–17.

———. 1998. "Are Welfare Employment Programs Effective?" In *Social Programs That Work,* edited by Jonathan Crane (chapter 11). New York: Russell Sage Foundation.

———. 1999. "The Decline of Welfare in Wisconsin." *Journal of Public Administration Research and Theory* 9(4):597–622.

———. 2000a. "Caseload Change: An Exploratory Study." *Journal of Policy Analysis and Management* 19(3):465–72.

———. 2000b. "The Politics of Welfare Reform in Wisconsin." *Policy* 32(4):533–59.

Mitchell, John J., Mark L. Chadwin, and Demetra S. Nightingale. 1980. *Implementing Welfare-Employment Programs: An Institutional Analysis of the Work Incentive (WIN) Program.* U.S. Department of Labor R&D Monograph 78. Washington, D.C.: U.S. Government Printing Office.

Nathan, Richard P., and Thomas L. Gais. 1999. *Implementing the Personal Responsibility Act of 1996: A First Look.* Albany: Rockefeller Institute of Government, State University of New York.

Osborne, David E., and Ted Gaebler. 1992. *Reinventing Government: How the Entrepreneurial Spirit Is Transforming the Public Sector.* Reading, Mass.: Addison-Wesley.

Provencher, Paul J. 1989. "Welfare Recipients and Employment: The Influence of the Attitudes of Case Managers and Other Factors on Program Performance in Local Welfare Offices." Ph.D. diss., Brandeis University, Waltham, Mass.

Riccio, James, Daniel Friedlander, and Stephen Freedman. 1994. *GAIN: Benefits, Costs, and Three-Year Impacts of a Welfare-to-Work Program.* New York: Manpower Demonstration Research Corporation.

Schiller, Bradley R., and C. Nielson Brasher. 1990. "Workfare in the 1980s: Successes and Limits." *Policy Studies Review* 9(4):665–80.

———. 1993. "Effects of Workfare Saturation on AFDC Caseloads." *Contemporary Policy Issues* (January): 39–49.

Scrivener, Susan, Gayle Hamilton, Mary Farrell, Stephen Freedman, Daniel Friedlander, Marisa Mitchell, Jodi Nudelman, and Christine Schwartz. 1998. *National Evaluation of Welfare-to-Work Strategies: Implementation, Participation Patterns, Costs, and Two-Year Impacts of the Portland (Oregon) Welfare-to-Work Program.* Washington, D.C.: U.S. Department of Health and Human Services and U.S. Department of Education.

Sosin, Michael R. 1987. "Beyond Entitlement" (book review). *Social Service Review* 61(1):156–59.

Swarns, Rachel L. 1999. "Judge Delays Giuliani Plan on Welfare." *New York Times,* 26 January: B1, B4.

Wiseman, Michael. 1988. "Obligation and Social Policy." *Policy Sciences* 21:100–101.

7

Street-Level Research
Policy at the Front Lines

Evelyn Z. Brodkin

Acrucial challenge for the analysis of welfare policy in the post-reform era is to understand how it is being created in a newly devolved and increasingly discretionary environment. There, street-level workers produce policy in public, quasi-public, and private agencies, extending even into the private workplace. This challenge impels the development of research methods that permit what I sometimes call "deep dish analysis," that is, analysis that reaches beyond visible policy constructs to see what occurs beneath the surface of policy and examines how it reaches into everyday life.

The street-level approach is grounded in a theoretical logic designed to extend understanding of how street-level practice and, ultimately, social politics is structured within specific organizational settings.[1] In a more practical sense, it aims to address critical gaps in our understanding of policies and how they work. This approach is most valuable when policy implementation involves change in organizational practice, discretion by frontline workers, and complex decision-making in a context of formal policy ambiguity and uncertainty. By focusing on specific institutions and the informal, lower-level routines through which they create policy at the point of delivery, it is possible to give greater transparency to policies that are otherwise opaque and provide a fuller picture of how policy is produced and experienced in everyday life.

The first section of this chapter offers an overview of the analytic foundations of implementation research and the evolution of the street-level perspective as an alternative to hierarchical analytical models. The latter sections discuss the application of the street-level approach to research on welfare policy.

From the Old to the New: Evolving Approaches to Implementation Research

The field of implementation research developed out of two related concerns. The first was normative, grounded in the constitutional notion of policymaking as the province of the legislative branch. The underlying assumption was that legislators, as policymakers, should authoritatively determine the "big" questions of national goals, and the bureaucracy should devise the means to put policy goals into practice. Bureaucratic failure to do its job constituted, in effect, a failure of democratic authority. Second, implementation research responded to a fundamentally practical concern. It seemed that good policy ideas often foundered on the rocky shoals of administration. How to prevent administrative shipwrecks?

The programs of the War on Poverty and the Great Society, as discussed in chapter 2 of this volume, offered rich research fodder for analysts seeking examples of good ideas gone astray. Who was to blame? All too often, the finger pointed to public bureaucracies—federal, state, and local—as the graveyard of good intentions. This perspective was vividly expressed in Pressman and Wildavsky's seminal volume *Implementation* (1973), notably subtitled: *How great expectations in Washington are dashed in Oakland; Or, why it's amazing that federal programs work at all, this being a saga of the Economic Development Administration as told by two sympathetic observers who seek to build morals on a foundation of ruined hopes.* Between "great expectations" and "ruined hopes" lay the uncharted terrain of implementation, the so-called "black box" into which policy ideas disappeared only to re-emerge in unrecognizable form, if at all.

The issues raised in this literature were revealing. The translation of policy ideas into practical action could not simply be referred to subunits of government and administrative agencies with orders given and fingers crossed. It required deeper understanding of implementing agencies and how they worked. The central problem for analysis was to determine how public bureaucracies could be made to comply with legislative intent and put policy ideas into action. Underlying the quest for understanding was the normative assumption of a policy hierarchy that demanded bureaucratic allegiance to legislative aims. The bureaucracy's job was to bring "neutral competence" to the task of policy delivery. But that vision did not square with ample evidence of bureaucratic autonomy and discretion often operating at cross-purposes to political authority. The *compliance model* that informed the first wave of implementation research generally sought to identify what interfered with the linear progress of policy as it made its way from legislation to realization.

A rich and varied set of studies applying this model began to shine light into the black box, creating a picture of implementation processes that were highly complex, subject to the idiosyncrasies of leaders and "the moment," and confounding to those who would attempt to assert authority over far-flung bureaucracies (Bardach 1977; Bullock and Lamb 1984; Derthick 1972, 1975; Murphy 1971; Pressman and Wildavsky 1973; Sabatier and Mazmanian 1979; Van Meter and Van Horn 1974). Some of the studies produced commonsense—if politically improbable—advice; for example, to keep policy simple, set clear objectives, or avoid "complex joint action." Other advice was hopeful but difficult to follow, suggesting, for example, that implementation would benefit from good leadership and problem fixers.

These studies, and the advice they produced, were consistent with normative notions of an authoritative policy hierarchy and directed toward achieving greater allegiance between policymaking and policy delivery. However, the assumptions embedded in the compliance model seemed increasingly doubtful. Perhaps legislated policy *should* be authoritative, but what if it wasn't? What justified the great expectations of policy protagonists and their corresponding dismay at the bureaucracies that dashed their hopes? If bureaucracies were the graveyard of good intentions, were they the *cause* of death or simply its *location?*

These doubts pointed to two critical problems with the compliance model as a guide to research. First, the hierarchical premise of the model requires some degree of policy definitiveness. Yet, both the literature on legislative policymaking and ordinary experience indicate that policy is often replete with ambiguity, conflicting objectives, and uncertainty. Paradoxically, while the emerging field of implementation searched for bureaucratic deviance from legislative authority, political scientists were documenting and, at times, bemoaning the failure of authority in lawmaking (Arnold 1990; Lowi 1979; Mayhew 1974; Price 1978). Analyses of legislative policymaking reveal how, in a pluralist policy system, it is strategic to oversimplify problems, overstate solutions, and mask competing objectives to build a legislative majority. Unfortunately, successful coalition-building strategies often produce policies better geared to claiming political credit and avoiding blame than to successful implementation (see Rabb and Winstead, chapter 2 of this volume, for a discussion of this reality). Those policies that survive the legislative fray tend to be creatures of compromise in which policy inconsistencies, ambiguities, and silences constitute a necessary price for passage.

From this perspective, it is too great an analytic leap to impute authority to legislated policy. Instead, it becomes apparent that implementation difficulties emerge, in part, out of the dilemmas of policymaking. As I have discussed more fully elsewhere,

> The strategic imperatives of social policymaking present difficult dilemmas. . . . First, constructions of "the problem" that advance the issue onto the policy agenda . . . may mobilize groups with competing views of and interests in the matter that are difficult to reconcile at the policymaking stage. Then, too, constructions of policy solutions that enable coalitions to form around specific proposals and potentially permit political credit-claiming at low cost may produce policies containing ambiguous or contradictory objectives and resources insufficient to deal meaningfully with problems. . . . Third, strategies used to overcome indifference to social problems and political stalemate, by overstating problems and understating the resources needed to address them, may lead to disappointment and backlash (Brodkin 1992, 171).

This suggests a second problem with the compliance model, namely, that implementation problems cannot readily be separated from problems of legislative politics. As Lowi has pointedly observed, "Typical American politicians displace and defer and delegate conflict where possible," preferring to delegate resolution "as far down the line as possible" (Lowi 1979, 55). The task of implementing bureaucracies may be manifestly one of compliance, but functionally the burden is far greater. In the course of converting policy into administrative practices, implementing agencies must, in a practical sense, choose among conflicting objectives and specify abstract policy elements. Consequently, implementation must be understood as far more than a technical administrative enterprise. It also must be understood as the continuation of policy politics by other means (Brodkin 1987–88, 1990).

This phenomenon is not limited to the case of welfare policy, but is well illustrated by it. Gilbert Steiner (1971) has somewhat wryly observed that welfare raises issues of race, class, and gender—issues that politicians normally would prefer to avoid. These contested issues are precisely the type that politicians generally prefer to elide in policymaking and "delegate down," imparting discretion to states, localities, and street-level bureaucracies. The difficulty occurs when the political logic of policymaking confronts the administrative logic of implementation. Ambiguous, complex, and discretionary policies are unlikely vehicles for producing consistency, certainty, and transparency in policy implementation.

A second wave of implementation research emerged out of the gap between the normative assumptions of the compliance model and growing evidence of policy indeterminacy and bureaucratic autonomy. If formal policy did not account for the actions of implementing organizations, what did? Researchers employed a variety of analytic perspectives to examine policy implementation as structured within complex organizational systems[2] (e.g., Berman 1980; Brodkin and Lipsky 1983; Edelman 1964; Goodsell 1981; Hagen 1987; Handler 1986; Handler and Hollingsworth 1971; Hasenfeld and Brock 1991; Ingram 1977; Majone and Wildavsky 1984; McCleary 1978; Miller 1983; Prottas 1979; Rein and Rabinovitz 1978; Simon 1983; Weatherly and Lipsky 1977).

A major contribution to this second wave was Michael Lipsky's seminal book *Street-Level Bureaucracy* (1980), which provided the theoretical template for a new approach to implementation research that embraced the ambiguities and inconsistencies of legislated social policy, creating an environment in which bureaucratic discretion could flourish. Lipsky's approach virtually reversed the normative premises of a policy hierarchy. He contended that under certain circumstances, it was analytically useful to regard those bureaucrats at the bottom of the ladder as policymakers. According to Lipsky, lower-level bureaucrats effectively make policy when formal statutes are ambiguous or internally contradictory, policy implementation requires discretionary decisionmaking at the point of delivery, and the routine activities of frontline workers cannot be fully monitored or controlled. Lipsky took particular interest in large, public bureaucracies and the mass production of human services under conditions of limited resources and virtually unlimited demand.

The street-level bureaucracy model directed attention to the ways in which policy deliverers actually worked. It sought to understand the world of the lower-level bureaucrat as one in which tensions between management objectives, client demands, and bureaucratic interests were played out. It offered a different view of the policy process, one created from inside the agencies charged with policy delivery. The analytic challenge was to investigate the nature of "policy-as-produced" and the factors shaping its production. Liberated from the deeply held myth of hierarchy, analysts could reevaluate practices that might seem on their face to be deviant and the product of willful obstruction, indifference, or sheer incompetence to understand how lower-level bureaucrats responded to the structural logic of street-level conditions.

One practical implication of this second wave of implementation research was that recommendations to improve "command and control" seemed both less likely to succeed and, in some measure, undesirable. If policy couldn't be made simpler, or certainly simple enough to be regimented, then it made sense analytically to recognize discretion as intrinsic and necessary to policy delivery. That recognition prompted a search for alternative strategies to create workable policies. Richard Elmore (1979) took up that challenge, offering an ingenious strategy of backward mapping that built implementation plans from the bottom up and sought to marshal lower-level discretion as a constructive element of policy delivery.

Unlike the first wave compliance model, which sought to examine deviation from hierarchically imposed mandates, the second-wave street-level bureaucracy model sought to examine lower-level practice organizationally. Extending that view, a third wave of implementation research has emerged that investigates policy delivery, not only as an organizational phenomenon but also as an extension of policy politics (Brodkin 1987–88, 1990, 1992; Lin 2000; Meyers, Glaser, and MacDonald 1998; Sandifort 1998; Stone 1984). Building on the theory and techniques of street-level bureaucracy research, this analytic model directs attention to the ways that conflicts over the terms and scope of social policy are reconfigured and advanced within the context of implementing institutions. It also extends the range of street-level analysis beyond the large, public bureaucracies featured in second-wave research to incorporate privatized forms of policy delivery.

Street-Level Analysis in Policy Evaluation

As I have attempted to show in this brief review of the field, street-level research is best understood as part of a fundamentally theoretical project. It provides an analytic point of departure for the study of complex organizations and for the study of social politics, and it locates those studies within the variety of institutions that put policy into practice. Beyond its theoretical purposes, street-level research as applied theory can be used to extend the range of policy evaluation and the assessment of social policies in welfare and other areas.

Although street-level research on social welfare policy is hardly new, there is no blueprint for its use in applied research. The research is still in its formative stage, but there is now sufficient experience to begin formulating a rough guide that can help identify when and how to use this approach. The rough guide outlined here is not intended to be a definitive statement of the field, but rather is a work in progress aimed at stimulating its further development. For the simple reason of familiarity and to highlight issues specific to welfare policy, most of the examples used here draw on my own research experience. However, as noted earlier, there is a rich, emerging literature that offers more, and undoubtedly better, examples of street-level policy research.

When Should Street-Level Research Be Used and Why?

Street-level research helps address critical gaps in our understanding of policies and how they work. This approach is most valuable when policy implementation involves change in organizational practice, discretion by frontline workers, and complex decisionmaking in a context of formal policy ambiguity and uncertainty. By focusing on the informal, lower-level routines that create policy at the point of delivery, it is possible to give greater transparency to policies that are otherwise opaque. The analytic challenge is to understand what is produced as policy, how, and, most importantly, why.

At its most basic level, street-level research provides a strategy for separating policy fact from policy fiction. By policy fiction, I refer to the rhetorical or ascribed intent of policy (e.g., to prepare welfare recipients for work) as well as to the administrative constructs used as proxies for program activities (e.g., training, education). Implementation research built on the compliance model began to unravel these distinctions by documenting whether and to what extent any policy-relevant activities occurred at all. Subsequently, most welfare evaluations now use administrative data to monitor participation rates and enrollment in program components as a means of identifying policy's reach—for example, counting the numbers of people enrolled in training or education programs.

But data organized around pro-forma categories cannot reveal whether the "right" people were placed in the "right" programs or what these individuals received as "training" or "education" while in these programs. Take public school education as an example. We hope that children will be placed in the classes and special programs most appropriate to their needs. But we recognize that children may be inappropriately placed or excluded from useful programs. (See Weatherly and Lipsky 1977, for a street-level view.) Although it is possible to keep count of various types of school placements, such accounting hardly takes into consideration the content of the educational experience. Certainly, it is not particularly meaningful to compare hours spent in the overcrowded and ill-equipped classroom of an inner-city public school with hours spent in the stimulating environment of a selective and affluent private school. An advantage of street-level research is that it allows analysis to reach beyond formal administrative categories to uncover the policy experience.

In this sense, street-level research makes a crucial link in the causal chain. If we wish to attribute outcomes to policy, we need to be able to specify the policy intervention, not as imagined or reconstructed in administrative measures, but as experienced. Street-level research directly investigates what implementing organizations produce. Let me briefly offer a case in point from my research on the Family Support Act of 1988, a predecessor to the current welfare reform.

Early findings from MDRC's experimental studies of job programs in California indicated that job clubs, as a policy component, were producing earnings improvements and that the program in Riverside County was an exemplar of this strategy.[3] I had been observing job clubs in Chicago, where no experimental data on outcomes existed, but administrative data generally gave little indication of increasing employment. Nor did my observations lead me to be sanguine about this strategy. Caseworkers were conducting job clubs with little guidance or supervision. Their sessions ranged from no more than a pro-forma sign-in and go-home arrangement to extended, freewheeling group conversations of no particular content.

The notion that job clubs constituted an effective strategy for employment seemed remarkable in that context, and led me to extend my observations to Riverside and two other California counties for purposes of comparison. In practice, the program experience of "job club" in Riverside bore little resemblance to the Chicago experience or to that of other

California counties in which I conducted street-level research. The Riverside program was highly structured (designed by an outside consulting firm), short-term (lasting only several days), and conducted by carefully selected staff specialists. In addition, material supports were abundant: video cameras for recording practice interview sessions, telephone banks for making job calls, and computers and copying machines for preparing resumes. Although there is considerably more to this story, it should at minimum be apparent that to evaluate "job club" as a general welfare-to-work strategy or to generalize from an exceptional operation is apt to mislead (Brodkin 1997).

The more interesting and important questions are how and why policies—as produced—assume the forms they do. This requires more than casual observation. It necessitates a theoretically grounded strategy for detailed and systematic data collection. One such strategy is comparative, selecting multiple sites for investigation that allow the analyst to distinguish the general from the idiosyncratic and explore variation in the production of policy.

For the job club story, the challenge was to account for the differences between "job club A" and "job club B." Riverside County managers, when interviewed, tended to ascribe their results to their ideological values, determination, or office culture. However, a comparative street-level approach guides the analyst to probe beyond such claims. Do the same personal motivations or beliefs produce the same results under different organizational conditions? What organizational conditions account for different modes of street-level practice? In this case, were Chicago's harried caseworkers—who lacked not only computers, consultants, and videos, but pencils, paper, and access to a supply of jobs for their clients—undermined by a failure of belief or a failure of organizational support?

These questions require a deeper and broader understanding of the organizational context within which implementation occurs than interviews alone or even interviews plus casual observation permit. The analyst must be able to trace the links between key organizational features, street-level practice, and the caseworker-client interaction. In this case, my research led me to conclude that neither formal rules nor personal beliefs accounted for differences in the production of "job club." In short, variations in practice were better understood as responses to the organizational conditions within which implementation occurred (Brodkin 1997).

Some Practical Benefits of Street-Level Research

By investigating why and how bureaucratic practices develop, street-level analysis can inform the search for improved implementation and account-ability in policy delivery. Street-level analysis moves beyond the com-mand and control assumptions of the compliance model to take empiri-cal account of factors that actually influence routine practice. Richard Elmore has pointed out that street-level research "forces us to contend with the mundane patterns of bureaucratic life and to think about how new pol-icies affect the daily routines of people who deliver social services. Policy-makers, analysts, and administrators have a tendency to focus on variables that emphasize control and predictability . . . [which] leads to serious mis-perceptions" (Elmore 1978, 207). Beyond the myth of hierarchy lies the possibility of understanding what frontline implementers do, the systemic features of their work life that shape their practices, how routine practices create policy, and the content of policy as they have produced it.

Despite the persistent hopes and preferences of both policymakers and managers, street-level research reveals that "caseworkers . . . do not do just what they want or just what they are told to want. They do what they can" (Brodkin 1997, 24). In studying the implementation of work-oriented programs, a street-level perspective revealed that casework practice is a function of capacity, which, in turn, depends on "profes-sional skills, agency resources, and access to good training and employ-ment opportunities for clients. Within that context, their practices are shaped by agency incentives and mechanisms that make staff accountable to clients and to the public." Perversely, management strategies based on imposing rules and regulations may produce undesirable effects, driving discretion "beneath the radar" where it becomes subject to the logic of street-level practice. Discretion, in itself, is neither good nor bad but the wild card of implementation, likely to produce different results in differ-ent organizational contexts.

This perspective offers a cautionary tale for those searching for simple performance-based solutions to achieving accountability. In the case of job clubs described earlier, I concluded that caseworkers in Chicago wel-fare offices did what they could under adverse conditions, with uncertain technology for advancing employment, and given accountability for making the numbers and not much more. The form that discretion took was circumscribed by measured dimensions of performance, namely, federal participation rates specifying minimum quotas for enrollment and hours, used to determine the disbursement of federal funds to states.

Ironically, these quotas, ostensibly designed to hold states accountable for policy implementation, distorted the implementation process by skewing attention to making the numbers without regard for *how* quotas were achieved. In practice, caseworkers did what they could to fill their job clubs with "participants" and to somehow fill the hours spent in them, for better or worse. Although this counted as successful implementation by federal performance measures, it is hard to support such an assessment except in the most superficial and mechanical sense.

The creation of meaningful accountability measures in welfare continues to constitute a difficult challenge. Certain types of performance quotas, such as participation rates, are easy to measure and enforce; but they do not address the content of practice and may even create incentives that undermine it. Alternatively, broader outcome measures (such as caseload reductions) may hold agencies responsible for things beyond their control, including the adequacy of agency resources and conditions in the external environment, and they, too, neglect to take account of the means through which such outcomes are produced.

Superficial accountability has continued to be a problem since welfare reform. For example, administrators and politicians were eager to declare TANF a success as caseloads dropped 57 percent in the five years following its implementation. But caseload counts reveal little about how caseload reductions were achieved—whether by helping recipients improve well-being through work, by diverting them into problematic lower-wage jobs, or by blocking their access to welfare regardless of the availability of work or income. Clearly, each of these possible explanations has profoundly different implications. Assessing competing claims about reform's broader effects requires a variety of research strategies that go beyond caseload counts and administrative data. Particularly important are strategies that carefully examine the content of agency practices and reveal *how* organizations distribute opportunities and support for work or, alternatively, provide few opportunities but systematically restrict access to assistance. Street-level research offers a lens through which to discover these unmeasured dimensions of implementation—dimensions so critical to understanding reform in practice and its policy outcomes.

Understanding New Modes of Policy Production

Beyond credit claiming or finger pointing, the harder and more important question is how to create policy and organizational structures that are conducive to good street-level work. I recently visited a welfare office where water was dripping down the wall, computers functioned erratically, phones rang incessantly with no workable system for taking messages, the heat could not be regulated to a comfortable level, and manila case files overflowed their stacks on the floor. After a day in that setting, it was hard to blame caseworkers for much of what looks on its face like bureaucratic carelessness, indifference, and error. Street-level research forces the analyst to contend with the realities of policy delivery as they are experienced by those charged with the task and acted out in interactions between case-workers and their clients.

Another important challenge for the analysis of welfare policy in the post-reform era is to understand how it is being created in a newly devolved and increasingly discretionary environment, where street-level workers produce policy in public as well as private nonprofit and for-profit organizations. What are the structural features of policy delivery under these evolving arrangements and how do they influence the street-level production of welfare policy? These are some of the questions that researchers have sought to address through a variety of strategies. They are central concerns for our Project on the Public Economy of Work, which has been investigating how the relationship between welfare and lower-wage work is being restructured in welfare offices, community welfare-to-work organizations, and private workplaces.[4] In developing this project, we, like other researchers, faced difficult methodological issues. The following section highlights some of these issues, with the hope of building methodologies that will advance street-level research.

How Can Street-Level Research Be Done? Methodological Issues

Street-level research combines the techniques of organizational analysis and ethnography to examine the relationship between organizational structure and the practice of policy delivery. It uses intensive case studies to explore complex processes and patterns that cannot be adequately understood through experimental or quantitative research designs (Campbell and Stanley 1966; Yin 1989).

In general, qualitative case study methodology provides a means of searching for patterns of practice and constructing social explanations from situation-specific data. It is commonly used in research that empha-sizes depth and complexity rather than seeking to survey surface patterns.

It uses iterative processes of interviewing and observation to explore possibilities rather than to test hypothesized relationships among known, quantifiable variables. For example, bureaucratic theory indicates that the structure of street-level work affects the exercise of bureaucratic discretion. But this emerging body of theory is insufficiently well developed to fully identify structural elements, ways of operationalizing them, and whatever else may be important. Case study research permits an exploration into these elements and allows for the discovery of other factors that may not have been anticipated. Moreover, it offers a richly descriptive foundation for exploring the dynamic processes through which bureaucratic patterns of practice develop and shape policy.

Case Selection

Cases are selected to extend theory by focusing on a particular organization or set of contextual conditions and by making those conditions transparently observable. This method of theoretical sampling differs from that used in research that seeks to generalize from a sample to a population. For example, in our Project on the Public Economy of Work, case selection criteria were designed to extend theoretical and empirical research on bureaucratic practice and welfare reform in the specific context of urban poverty. Prior work in these fields suggested that policy delivery in the context of concentrated urban poverty and big city welfare administration would be apt to differ from that which would occur under other conditions (e.g., in a small-town agency or low-poverty area). We designed our Chicago study to examine how policy emerges in specific urban neighborhood settings and within specific types of organizations that mediate between the public economy of welfare and the private economy of the market, namely, public welfare agencies, private welfare-to-work contractors, and workplaces. This methodology could be, and I hope will be, used in other settings over time.

Although the validity of case-based analysis is in some respects problematic (the reverse of the problem of abstracted generalization in large-scale quantitative studies), case selection can contribute to validity by incorporating a comparative perspective—in our project, between differently located and differently structured welfare offices, organizations, and workplaces. This strategy builds in variation and allows the analyst to distinguish particular from systematic features of organizational practice.

Research Techniques

The objective of street-level analysis is to reconstruct agency practice in terms of its own internal logic rather than the logic of managerial command and control. This involves a systematic examination of both the conditions of work and the content of practice, moving heuristically between the two in an effort to explain the particular form that implementation takes in specific settings.

In pursuit of that objective, street-level analysis combines interview techniques often used by organization researchers with observation techniques commonly used in ethnography (see Bate 1997). It adopts an ethnographic perspective in the sense that it studies street-level bureaucrats "in their own time and space" and at work in their "natural habitat," seeking to make explicit the links between organizational structures, the individuals interacting within them, and their policy product. Observation permits data on interactions between caseworkers, employers, and recipients to be generated in the specific context in which the interactions occur.

In contrast to organizational studies that rely on interviews and survey data, observation has the considerable advantage of its directness: it does not depend solely on the recall of interviewees or their reconstruction of events. As Michael Burawoy describes it, the advantages of observation "are assumed to lie not just in direct observation of how people act, but also how they understand and experience those acts. It enables us to juxtapose what people say they are up to against what they actually do" (Burawoy 1991, 1).

Interviewing is particularly effective as a method for probing the reasoning and perceptions behind behaviors. It enables researchers to dig beneath administrative categories to probe their content and how they are used. For example, analyzing administrative data on the imposition of sanctions cannot provide insights into how caseworkers use discretion in applying sanctions. Although a caseworker must identify a cause for a sanction in the formal case record, usually selecting a reason from a checklist, administrative records do not reveal the actual reasoning behind the decision of whether or not to apply a sanction. Skilled interviewing can probe the decisionmaking involved in the case and provide a more accurate understanding of how, when, and why an individual's behavior is labeled "noncompliant" and sanctions are used.

However, the analysis is still incomplete at that point. Combining interviews and observation provides a method of searching for the discrepancies between what they say and what they do that raise a red flag for the researcher. What is producing this divergence? This dual strategy was useful in exploring the application of sanctions. In interviews, caseworkers often portrayed themselves as tough or soft in applying the rules. However, my observations showed their practices to be inconsistent with what they preached. Why? Comparing practices across workers and offices and over time, I discovered considerable elasticity in the use of sanctions, with variation unexplained by differences in rules, ideology, or even the behavior of recipients.

Applying an organizational lens that located casework within the institutional structure helped explain the apparent anomaly. It revealed that caseworkers generally sought the path of least resistance, using discretion in ways most consistent with the logic imposed by the organizational pressures and incentives existing at the street level. If sanctions were complicated or time-consuming to apply, other things being equal, they tended not to use them. However, sanctions use increased when caseworkers faced increased risk of being penalized by their managers for failing to catch case errors or when sanctions became easier to apply (Brodkin 1986, 1997). Combining interviewing and observation makes it possible to cross-check alternative explanations of informal bureaucratic practices. Once qualitative research uncovers variations in practice underlying administrative indicators, dimensions of those practices can be further investigated using both qualitative and quantitative methods (see, for example, Hasenfeld and Weaver 1996).

"Deep Dish" Research: Pros, Cons, and Considerations

Implementation research has evolved from first-wave, formalist studies that take a normative view of the policy process to second- and third-wave behavioral studies that bring organizational and political perspectives to bear. Street-level research has constituted an important strategy in the development of these behavior-based studies and, in particular, in directing analytic attention to how policy is produced at the front lines.

Any assessment of the street-level research approach requires a careful weighing of its strengths and limits. The chief limitations of this method come from the potential for observer bias and from the limits of the case study approach itself. Although observer bias is always a risk in this methodology, it is possible to limit that risk by using multiple observations in different settings, by using multiple data sources, and by using theory to systematize the collection and analysis of data. It is also useful to apply a triangulation method to cross-check different forms of data with each other, subjecting inconsistent findings to special scrutiny (Denzin 1989). A second obvious drawback of this method is that it is very labor intensive and difficult to use in projects requiring large-scale data collection. Bate, somewhat tongue-in-cheek, advises: "Rule 1 for aspiring organization researchers surely has to be: keep away from organizations; fieldwork takes too long!" (Bate 1997, 1151).

The chief strength of this approach is that it allows the researcher to get inside street-level practice, understand its logic on its own terms, and explore the policy experience at the ground level. This permits "deep dish analysis," which can reach beyond visible policy constructs to see what occurs beneath the surface of policy rhetoric and administrative measures, seek to explain it, and probe its consequences.

It is worth emphasizing that the approach described here is grounded in a theoretical logic and designed to extend understanding of how street-level practice and, ultimately, social politics is structured within specific organizational settings. Burawoy refers to this strategy as the extended case method, in which "the significance of a case relates to what it tells us about the world in which it is embedded" (Burawoy 1991, 281).

Understandably, evaluation research has more proximate interests. Yet, applying theory to evaluation research enables us to ask better questions and to clarify what we think we see when we conduct evaluations. As applied theory, street-level research can help to guard against the reification of policy categories and constructs that may inhibit our ability to appreciate what actually goes on under the rubric of policy implementation. It offers a lens through which to acquire a fuller picture of how policy is produced and experienced in everyday life.

NOTES

This chapter describes elements of the methodology for the Project on the Public Economy of Work at the University of Chicago. The author acknowledges support for that project from the National Science Foundation (grant #9730821), the Ford Foundation, and the Open Society Institute of the Soros Foundation.

1. It is not possible within the confines of this chapter to do justice to this rich and diverse literature, which addresses, among other things, issues of administrative symbolism, organizational behavior, caseworker-client relations, legal indeterminacy, and policy bargaining.

2. I note that Riverside was highly touted as a "model" program without endorsing that view. Earnings were modest, driven by an increase in hours worked more than wage improvements, and generally insufficient to bring families out of poverty.

3. The Project on the Public Economy of Work at the University of Chicago, which I co-direct with my colleague Susan Lambert, investigates how welfare reform is redefining the relationship between welfare and lower-wage work. It comprises a linked set of organizational studies designed to analyze responses to welfare's work requirements in the context of urban poverty across three institutional domains: neighborhood welfare offices, community agencies, and private workplaces. See http://www.ssa.uchicago.edu/research/pubeconwork.html.

4. Ethnographers often use participant-observation, with participation providing a means of achieving a highly contextualized understanding of individuals through shared experience. Street-level implementation research tends to operate at a different level of analysis, focusing on the context itself, that is, the organization, where observation and interviews (and sometimes survey research) are favored over participant-observation. There is, of course, a natural overlap between these perspectives, which suggests that participant-observation techniques might enrich street-level research. For an insightful discussion of ethnographic methods in organizational anthropology, see Bate (1997).

REFERENCES

Arnold, R. Douglas. 1990. *The Logic of Congressional Action.* New Haven, Conn.: Yale University Press.

Bardach, Eugene. 1977. *The Implementation Game.* Cambridge, Mass.: MIT Press.

Bate, S. P. 1997. "Whatever Happened to Organizational Anthropology? A Review of the Field of Organizational Ethnography and Anthropological Studies." *Human Relations* 50:1147–75.

Berman, Paul. 1980. "Thinking About Programmed and Adaptive Implementation: Matching Strategies to Situations." In *Why Policies Succeed or Fail,* edited by Helen M. Ingram and Dean E. Mann. Beverly Hills, Calif.: Sage Publications.

Brodkin, Evelyn Z. 1986. *The False Promise of Administrative Reform: Implementing Quality Control in Welfare.* Philadelphia: Temple University Press.

———. 1987–88. "Policy Politics: If We Can't Govern, Can We Manage?" *Political Science Quarterly* 102:571–87.

———. 1990. "Implementation as Policy Politics." In *Implementation and the Policy Process: Opening Up the Black Box,* edited by Dennis J. Palumbo and Donald J. Calista. New York: Greenwood Press.

———. 1992. "Teen Pregnancy and the Dilemmas of Social Policymaking." In *Early Parenthood and Coming of Age in the 1990s,* edited by Margaret K. Rosenheim and Mark F. Testa. New Brunswick, N.J.: Rutgers University Press.

————. 1997. "Inside the Welfare Contract: Discretion and Accountability in State Welfare Administration." *Social Service Review* 71:1–33.

Brodkin, Evelyn Z., and Michael Lipsky. 1983. "Quality Control in AFDC as an Administrative Strategy." *Social Service Review* 57:1–34.

Bullock, Charles S., and Charles M. Lamb. 1984. *Implementation of Civil Rights Policy.* Monterey, Calif.: Brooks/Cole.

Burawoy, Michael, ed. 1991. *Ethnography Unbound: Power and Resistance in the Modern Metropolis.* Berkeley: University of California Press.

Campbell, Donald T., and Julian C. Stanley. 1966. *Experimental and Quasi-Experimental Designs for Research.* Boston: Houghton Mifflin.

Denzin, Norman K. 1989. *The Research Act: A Theoretical Introduction to Sociological Methods,* 3d ed. Englewood Cliffs, N.J.: Prentice Hall.

Derthick, Martha. 1972. *New Towns In-Town.* Washington, D.C.: The Urban Institute.

————. 1975. *Uncontrollable Spending for Social Services Grants.* Washington, D.C.: Brookings Institution.

Edelman, Murray. 1964. *The Symbolic Uses of Politics.* Urbana: University of Illinois Press.

Elmore, Richard. 1978. "Organizational Models of Social Program Implementation." *Public Policy* 26:185–228.

————. 1979. "Backward Mapping: Implementation Research and Policy Decisions." *Political Science Quarterly* 94:601–16.

Goodsell, Charles T., ed. 1981. *The Public Encounter: Where State and Citizen Meet.* Bloomington: Indiana University Press.

Hagen, Jan. 1987. "Income Maintenance Workers: Technicians or Service Providers?" *Social Service Review* 61(2):261–71.

Handler, Joel F. 1986. *The Conditions of Discretion: Autonomy, Community, Bureaucracy.* New York: Russell Sage Foundation.

Handler, Joel F., and Ellen Jane Hollingsworth. 1971. *The "Deserving Poor": A Study of Welfare Administration.* New York: Academic Press.

Hasenfeld, Yeheskel, and Thomas Brock. 1991. "Implementation of Social Policy Revisited." *Administration and Society* 22:451–79.

Hasenfeld, Yeheskel, and Dale Weaver. 1996. "Enforcement, Compliance, and Disputes in Welfare-to-Work." *Social Services Review* 70:235–56.

Ingram, Helen. 1977. "Policy Implementation through Bargaining: The Case of Federal Grants-in-Aid." *Public Policy* 25:501–26.

Lin, Ann Chih. 2000. *Reform in the Making: The Implementation of Social Policy in Prison.* Princeton, N.J.: Princeton University Press.

Lipsky, Michael. 1980. *Street-Level Bureaucracy: Dilemmas of Individuals in Public Services.* Cambridge, Mass.: MIT Press.

Lowi, Theodore J. 1979. *The End of Liberalism: The Second Republic of the United States,* 2d ed. New York: W. W. Norton.

Majone, Giandomenico, and Aaron Wildavsky. 1984. "Implementation As Evolution." In *Implementation,* 3d ed., edited by Jeffrey Pressman and Aaron Wildavsky. Berkeley: University of California Press.

Mayhew, David R. 1974. *Congress: The Electoral Connection.* New Haven, Conn.: Yale University Press.

McCleary, Richard. 1978. "On Becoming a Client." *Journal of Social Issues* 34:57–75.

Meyers, Marcia, Bonnie Glaser, and Karin MacDonald. 1998. "On the Front Lines of Welfare Delivery: Are Workers Implementing Policy Reforms?" *Journal of the Association for Public Policy Analysis and Management* 17:1–22.

Miller, Gale. 1983. "Holding Clients Accountable: The Micro-Politics of Trouble in a Work Incentive Program." *Social Problems* 31:139–51.

Murphy, Jerome. 1971. "Title I of ESEA: The Politics of Implementing Federal Education Reform." *Harvard Education Review* 41:35–63.

Pressman, Jeffrey, and Aaron Wildavsky. 1973. *Implementation*. Berkeley: University of California Press.

Price, David. 1978. "Policy Making in Congressional Committees: The Impact of 'Environmental' Factors." *American Political Science Review* 72:548–74.

Prottas, Jeffrey. 1979. *People Processing*. Lexington, Mass.: Lexington Books.

Rein, Martin, and Francine Rabinovitz. 1978. "Implementation: A Theoretical Perspective." In *American Politics and Public Policy*, edited by Walter D. Burnham and Martha Wagner Weinberg. Cambridge, Mass.: MIT Press.

Sabatier, Paul A., and Daniel Mazmanian. 1979. "The Conditions of Effective Implementation: A Guide to Accomplishing Policy Objectives." *Policy Analysis* 5:481–504.

Sandifort, Jodi. 1998. "The Structural Impediments to Front-Line Human Service Collaboration: The Case of Welfare Reform." In *American Political Science Association Annual Meeting*, Boston.

Simon, William. 1983. "Legality, Bureaucracy, and Class in the Welfare System." *Yale Law Journal* 92:1198–269.

Steiner, Gilbert. 1971. *The State of Welfare*. Washington, D.C.: Brookings Institution.

Stone, Deborah. 1984. *The Disabled State*. Philadelphia: Temple University Press.

Van Meter, Donald, and Carl Van Horn. 1974. "The Policy Implementation Process: A Conceptual Framework." *Administration and Society* 6:445–88.

Weatherly, Richard A., and Michael Lipsky. 1977. "Street-Level Bureaucrats and Institutional Innovation: Implementing Special Education Reform." *Harvard Educational Review* 47:171–97.

Yin, Robert K. 1989. *Case Study Research: Design and Methods*. Newbury Park, Calif.: Sage Publications.

8

Client-Based Ethnographic Research As a Tool for Implementation Analysis

Kathryn Edin

Notes on the Research

When policy researchers decide to incorporate a client-based ethnographic study into an evaluation of a given social program, they are often hoping for a powerful set of stories that can sell what might be an otherwise tedious or technical story and make the study's findings memorable and compelling. The close-up lens of what some term ethnography—client-based, semi-structured, in-depth qualitative interviewing combined with some level of observation within an ecological context (a neighborhood, for example)—has practical as well as scientific merits. My colleagues who testify before government bodies sometimes claim that at the end of the day, the best story wins. Reading or hearing about real people's views and behaviors, especially if it is in those people's own words, is somehow more interesting than scanning a statistical table, at least for most. Although policy researchers often hope to use numbers to determine what the main storyline will be, they hope the stories drawn from the ethnographic data will put flesh on the narrative.

If an ethnographic or qualitative in-depth-interview study is executed properly, the resulting data can do much more than provide anecdotal stories, though I do not deny that this is one of its roles. The social world is complicated, and any scientific endeavor to study it necessarily oversimplifies it. Ethnographic and qualitative research sometimes helps by allowing us to look at a small corner of the social world somewhat more holistically than surveys generally allow. Most policy researchers have long acknowledged the "black box" problems a purely quantitative approach (or impact analysis) creates for policy analysis, and for this reason have added implementation components to their studies. Yet those components have generally been program based. Many policy researchers still have little knowledge of the world inhabited by the clients of the social program they seek to evaluate.

Survey researchers often must develop their questions based on preconceived or generalized concepts about the issues that affect peoples' lives and their interrelationships. When the researcher borrows concepts from findings based on subjects who inhabit substantially different social worlds, this can become problematic. Some of the researchers' measures may not fit the client population well. Other factors that these subjects might identify as key could be missing altogether from the survey repertoire of measures. What client-based ethnographic studies allow us to do is to let the complexity of the social world reemerge a bit, and to guide hypothesis development. In the process of data collection and analysis, ethnographic research can identify ways to improve the fit of some measures. It can also provide insight into what the missing variables might be. In some cases, qualitative in-depth-interview research may reveal something new and unexpected—and the new and unexpected findings can lead to a whole new way of conceptualizing the research "problem."

Qualitative researchers tend not to prejudge which variables will turn out to be important in answering the question "What is going on here?" Rather, they look to the social setting and study the population for both relevant questions and answers (Strauss and Corbin 1990). The sheer number of variables that may potentially coalesce within the life of any given program participant, much less their interrelationships, is often beyond the scope of even the best quantitative data collection and analysis techniques. By privileging the subject (the client) and letting the client frame the research problem in her or his own way, the qualitative in-depth-interview study allows researchers to try to identify which variables and which interrelationships might be of greatest importance from the subjective perspective.

Qualitative research's strength is its depth. Qualitative in-depth-interview researchers know their subject matter intimately. The best of them truly achieve the *verstehen* that Max Weber advocated for more than a century ago. Qualitative research's weakness is its breadth. In recent years, some qualitative researchers have teamed up with quantitative researchers to surmount these difficulties, a growing trend in social policy research. Other qualitative researchers have tried to employ more heterogeneous sampling strategies and increase the sample size of their in-depth-interview studies.

Meanwhile, many quantitative social policy researchers are virtually unaware that the qualitative research community shares a number of well-established methodological and analytical traditions. Even those who know that such traditions exist generally have only a vague notion of what they might be. Indeed, many graduate programs in sociology, a field that shares the ethnographic research tradition with anthropology, do not regularly offer courses in qualitative methodology. We who collect and analyze qualitative data are partly to blame for the ignorance surrounding our method, because we are notorious for leaving many of our methodological and analytical techniques out of the write-ups of our work. These factors combine to give outsiders the impression that the qualitative approach is more art than science, and more appropriate for anecdote than for analysis.

In this chapter, my intent is to address two questions on the role of client-based qualitative research in studying the effects of social programs. In the first portion of the chapter, I discuss why I think a qualitative component can be useful for these kinds of studies and describe the unique types of data that can be gathered through these approaches. In the second part, I outline some methodological lessons others and I have learned in actually carrying out the work. In the last portion, I offer some illustrations of how qualitative data has proved useful in studies of program impacts in recent years.

Throughout I draw on examples from my own work as well as the work of others. The reader should be warned that many of the studies I refer to were not part of evaluations of social programs per se, though all are related to the way social programs work and are thus relevant here. In addition, much of the chapter can easily be applied to multimethod research of any kind. Finally, every scientific method has multiple branches. I try to mirror this heterogeneity as much as I can.

Why Is a Client-Centered Qualitative Component Important? What Can It Add?

Ethnographic research techniques can help us understand what is happening on the client side in the context of a program or policy evaluation in at least two ways. First, ethnographic research is good at getting at what clients are hearing and capturing the heterogeneity in the messages that clients perceive. Second, ethnographic research can enable researchers to interpret how the program or policy fits within the larger context of clients' lives. Specifically, this research can flesh out the ecological context (a kin network, a neighborhood, a transportation system, a legal system, a local labor market) of the clients' lives, and can reveal how various aspects of that context may encourage or interfere with client responses to the program or policy.

What Are Clients Hearing?

When I was a graduate student, I interviewed for a job on a project aimed at understanding the effects of a low-end training program on the work efforts of single mothers (in truth, the program had not yet had any measurable effects, and program operators wanted to know why). Their intent was to send an ethnographer to look at what clients thought of the program, as well as to get a sense of the "informal" structure of the training program (how the program really worked) as opposed to the "formal" structure (what was written down in the staff's program manual). In the end, rather than hire me, they told me they had decided to "impute" the informal structure of the program and client responses to it from what they knew about the formal structure (in other words, from the program manual). This logic eludes me as much now as it did then.

Other researchers I have since met are far more sophisticated and incorporate some level of process implementation research in their studies. However, even many process implementation designs that include repeated, systematic observations of program implementation at the program site still fall short, and may sometimes use the data to make improper imputations about client attitudes and behaviors. By relying on on-site observations, even if they include observations of client-staff interactions, such researchers may assume that they know what the clients think the program's "message" is. After all, they've just heard what the client has been told!

My experience with the Manpower Demonstration Research Corporation's four-city study of welfare reform, entitled "Project on Devolution and Urban Change" (which has both a program-based process implementation component and a client-based ethnographic study) has shown me how dangerous this sort of imputation is. Messages from program staff are generally only part of the store of informational resources clients draw upon to form their impressions about a given social program. Clients also read newspapers; watch television; talk with friends, relatives, and neighbors; and engage in other types of information-gathering activities to formulate their view of what the parameters and incentive structure of a particular program are. In Miami, the Haitian community might rely on Haitian newspaper and radio for their information about welfare reform, whereas the Cuban community might rely on other community-specific media sources. In Los Angeles, Spanish or Chinese-language media sources might be important. In addition, many cities with substantial African-American populations, like Philadelphia or Chicago, have press outlets that serve the African-American community. Because welfare reform is complex enough to confuse even the most astute student of social policy, it is hard for anyone, even local media, to get the story completely straight. Thus, clients may misunderstand crucial elements of a program even though program staff members feel they have clearly explained them. It is also true that clients' understanding of program parameters might be much more complex than the message program staff communicate, because an advocate group (take the Kensington Welfare Rights Union in Philadelphia as an example) or a local radio station had spread the word.

Devolution from the federal to the state and local levels introduces special problems in this regard. A given metropolitan area may span several states with different programs and program parameters. The Philadelphia metropolitan area spans three states: Pennsylvania, New Jersey, and Delaware. In Philadelphia, the Urban Change ethnographers have followed a group of welfare recipients for roughly three years. Some of our respondents have close kin just over the New Jersey or Delaware state lines, and several have lived in either New Jersey or Delaware for a time. One client even moved across the state line in the first year of our study (fortunately for our research, she moved back). Though we did not find that client confusion was rampant in Philadelphia, some respondents did report they believed they were subject to rules that reflected another state's welfare regime and not Pennsylvania's. When clients' personal networks span several states, clients often become confused over program parameters regardless of what their caseworkers may be telling them.[1]

For the ethnographic component of the Urban Change project, we chose to follow roughly 30 to 40 families in each of four cities over three years to see how they coped with the changes in welfare. In the program-based implementation component of the Philadelphia study, researchers found that program staff had spent little time explaining a key provision of the new Pennsylvania welfare law—one that state lawmakers thought was a powerful new incentive to find work—a more generous work "disregard" that used a simpler formula than the old.[2] Despite the apparent weaknesses in program staff's presentation of the new work disregards, our qualitative research with clients revealed that client understanding of the disregard was surprisingly clear (about half could name the actual percentage). After talking further with these clients to resolve the apparent discrepancy, we learned that most clients had learned of it through word of mouth, newspapers, or television, and not through program staff. Presumably, inasmuch as the new policy of disregarding 50 percent of one's earnings was so simple (there were no changes from month to month and no complicated formulas, as was true with the old AFDC disregard formula), the word from those who understood the new policy quickly spread to those who did not.

That example makes it clear how important client-based ethnographic information can be. If we had lacked this information, we would have assumed that clients did not clearly understand the disregard and, therefore, that it could not have been a primary incentive for finding work. Instead, the opposite was true among our ethnographic sample in Philadelphia (though not in our other sites).

How Does the Program or Policy Fit within the Context of Clients' Lives?

Another advantage of ethnographic research is that researchers can better understand the place the program has within the context of clients' larger life experiences and day-to-day routines.

Much of economic and sociological theory assumes that people make choices based on their perception of the costs and benefits involved. Social program architects apparently think so too, because they design programs that add carrots or sticks that will presumably shift program participants' cost-benefit analyses. Charles Murray's (1984) provocative "thought experiments" of the early 1980s featuring the mythic couple "Harold" and "Phyllis" showed how perfectly reasonable people might choose not to marry because of the perverse incentives supposedly inherent in the welfare system.

Luckily, ethnographic research offers us the opportunity to do better than thought experiments, which may sometimes fail to correctly specify the costs and benefits as they appear to actual or potential program participants. With detailed ethnographic data, one might be able to more reliably specify the mix of costs and benefits that respondents actually consider, and might better specify both the patterning and heterogeneity of those considerations. Such an approach assumes that clients can and will tell qualitative researchers why they do what they do. The former issue (*Can* clients really tell interviewers why they do what they do?) reflects a long debate between sociology and economics, and I only briefly discuss this issue in the paragraphs that follow. Obviously, I am on the sociological side of this debate. I take up the latter issue (*Will* clients really tell interviewers why they do what they do? or "How do you *know* when clients are telling you the truth?") as part of the last half of the chapter.

My qualitative study with Laura Lein focused on how welfare- and wage-reliant single mothers constructed economic survival strategies and how clients interacted with the pre-TANF welfare system (AFDC) (Edin and Lein 1997a, b). Our analysis of multiple, in-depth interviews with 379 low-income single mothers in four U.S. cities provides evidence that poor people within the U.S. context do seem to be able and willing to tell trained ethnographers how they weigh the costs and benefits of welfare as compared with work. Many mothers said they make decisions largely on the basis of those calculations. The welfare-reliant mothers we studied said they considered not only the trade-offs between staying on welfare and taking a formal-sector job, but also the potential impact that full-time work might have on their ability to pursue other income-generating activities, such as the informal-sector work that had allowed them to survive economically while on welfare. Because low-wage formal-sector employment "costs" more than welfare, mothers who worked in the formal sector generally had more trouble paying their bills than did their welfare counterparts. On average, their monthly deficit (formal sector wages minus expenses) averaged $441, whereas their welfare counterparts averaged a deficit (cash and food stamp benefits minus expenses) of only $311 per month. Mothers who had prior labor market experience (most had some) generally knew that if they moved from welfare to work, they would have to continue to pursue additional income-generating strategies to remain economically solvent. They also knew that full-time work would mean that they would have far less time to devote to these strategies than they had while on welfare. Many said they did not choose to work for precisely those reasons. Others did choose to work, but virtually all of these workers enjoyed a set of special circumstances (free rent, no transportation costs, free child care, generous network-based support) that artificially lowered the costs of working.

This example illustrates why understanding the clients' view of the situation is crucial if we are to understand the incentives and disincentives they are actually responding to. Before this research, the research community was largely unaware of (though many suspected) the fact that welfare recipients had to supplement their benefits with outside income-generating activities. Many of these mothers' activities were time consuming (informal sector jobs, for example) and, consequently, the mothers' ability to move from welfare to a job was impeded. In addition, researchers did not generally recognize how difficult it was for single mothers to meet their expenses at low-wage employment, nor were they aware that many working mothers had larger budget deficits than welfare mothers—deficits that often resulted in real material hardship for working families.

I draw another example from work I conducted in the early 1990s, in Charleston, South Carolina (where I spent 12 months collecting some of the data for the study with Lein detailed above). The state of South Carolina had recently implemented one of the toughest child support enforcement policies in the country, and I was eager to see how mothers were responding (Edin 1995). In Charleston, as in other places across the country, a welfare recipient had to sign her rights to child support over to the state in return for her benefits. In cases where there was a legal father (paternity had been established), the mother was required to cooperate with the local child support enforcement office in finding the father. In cases where there was no legal father, mothers had to cooperate by providing any information they had about the identity and whereabouts of the father. If the father contested paternity, he had to submit to a blood test.

Furthermore, South Carolina was one of the first states in the nation to use the family court to issue bench warrants for fathers who fell behind in their child support payments and actually put them in jail. In the early 1990s, payments for welfare recipients were collected through the family court. Thus, issuing a bench warrant for such a father required no action on the part of the mother (nor could such a mother "forgive" the unpaid child support). This meant that fathers of welfare-reliant children were the most likely group to be pulled in on a bench warrant.

When fathers of welfare-reliant children were brought in to family court, they had to pay the full amount of the arrears owed or be jailed by the judge on contempt-of-court charges. Furthermore, during their time in jail—up to one year—fathers' arrears would mount, leaving them with an even larger debt once they were released from jail. If these fathers still could not make good on their arrears, the same process was repeated. Unemployment was not an acceptable excuse, as even indigent fathers were required to pay the state minimum (about $160 per month for one child).

Despite all these measures, the proportion of welfare-reliant single mothers receiving child support was surprisingly low. I conducted several interviews with a local attorney from the Child Support Enforcement Division (the federally funded child support office) to learn why this was so. The attorney confided that part of the problem was that many of the welfare recipients they dealt with could not name the fathers of their children. According to my source, some mothers told staff members their pregnancies had resulted from a one-night stand with a stranger. Others named several men as possible fathers, and the child support enforcement personnel had to arrange for blood samples to be drawn. Still others named a father, but genetic blood tests disproved this. In other cases, the women claimed they knew who their child's father was, but did not know the father's social security number or his whereabouts.

At the time, I was conducting interviews with welfare-reliant mothers in Charleston, and the story the division was telling me about client behavior did not add up. Only one mother had told me that her pregnancy had been the result of a one-night stand with a stranger. Most of the rest claimed they were certain who the father of their child was, though not all knew his social security number or whereabouts. As I began asking more questions about child support, I soon learned that the key to the mystery was simple. Mothers generally knew how the child support system worked and what benefits would accrue to them if they obtained a child support award. However, most viewed cooperating with the system as a last resort, for several reasons. First, most of their children's fathers were already contributing informally. If the state had collected the money through official channels, all but $50 would go to the state in return for the welfare benefits it paid to each mother. Though this "pass-through" would not have led to a reduction in a mother's cash welfare, it would have reduced the amount of food stamps she received (by about $13) and decreased any housing subsidy she might have received (by about $17). Thus, mothers living in private housing would net about $37, whereas mothers living in subsidized housing would net only about $20 if they cooperated fully with the division and the father paid through the court. Compare this scenario with what would result if the mother collected the money directly without telling the welfare department. She would get to keep all of it, and would suffer no benefit reductions of any kind.

Second, mothers had other motivations for engaging in what I have called "covert noncompliance." Judges set child support orders at fixed amounts, yet fathers' employment situations tended to vary dramatically from month to month. Mothers knew that there were months when the fathers genuinely could not pay, and felt there was little benefit to sending them to jail as a result, since this would mean that she and the child would get even less. Due to the precarious employment situations of fathers, mothers felt that they could negotiate privately with fathers about how much they could reasonably be expected to pay.

A third motivation for covert noncompliance was the value that many mothers placed on child-father contact. Mothers claimed a good father should not have to be "forced to do for his child." Mothers said that fathers who were constantly being "dogged" by the child support system often went underground—or cut off contact with the mother and child—to avoid being pulled in on a bench warrant. Some mothers felt that the child support enforcement system impeded fathers' efforts to maintain contact with their children, and mothers said they quietly subverted it for that reason.

Ironically, part of the reason that mothers' strategies for garnering informal support were so effective was the fact that the child support apparatus in South Carolina was strong. Fathers feared it, so mothers could use it as a powerful threat if informally agreed-upon financial or parental obligations were not met.

Finally, there was a strong norm among many of our mothers (and fathers, if we believe mothers' reports) on what the payment of child support "bought" fathers. Mothers whose child's father had abused the mother or child, who was involved in crime, or who was undesirable in other ways often feared that if the fathers were made to pay, they would expect visitation (and even conjugal relations with the mother in some cases) in return. Thus, mothers who did not want fathers involved in their lives or their children's lives often said they covertly subverted the system.

In sum, I learned that some clients often failed to comply (although they pretended to comply) with the child support enforcement office because they valued the father's ability to have an ongoing relationship with the child more than they valued the $50 a month the welfare department would "pass through" to them if the father paid child support. Others were concerned with trying to keep fathers out of their lives and the lives of their children. Without such information, a researcher might have incorrectly assumed that the child support enforcement system was inept (or that clients' sexual practices were such that they genuinely could not tell officials which man had fathered a given child). Our qualitative research with mothers led to a different conclusion. The child support enforcement office's failure to locate many of these fathers was understandable—mothers were withholding information or giving false leads.

I offer a third example from the Urban Change research I have been conducting in Philadelphia. In Philadelphia, an extensive regional rail system connects the city with its suburbs. It is relatively reliable, but there are no regional rail stops within walking distance of many neighborhoods in which welfare recipients tend to be concentrated. Thus, commuting to the suburbs often means taking a bus and then a train, a 1½- to 2½-hour commute each way.

Although I found several poor single mothers who might be quite willing to spend 3 to 4 hours per day commuting to and from a minimum-wage job, arranging for child supervision during the 11- or 12-hour period they must spend away from home is often difficult. Philadelphia schools begin at 8:30 A.M. and end at 2:30 P.M. The logistical problems of coping with a commute that begins at 7 A.M. and ends at 7 P.M. are enormous for many of the clients we have interviewed in Philadelphia. What does one do with one's child between 7:00 and 8:30 A.M.? What about the hours between 2:30 and 7 P.M.? Because parents are not legally allowed to let their children stay at home alone until they are 12 years old, mothers face the risk of losing their children if a neighbor reports parental absence to the child protection agency (mistrust in poor neighborhoods is generally high).

The reader might correctly observe that some of the barriers to work described above are issues covered by many surveys. However, without adequate qualitative grounding, researchers might fail to specify all the relevant variables or to specify them correctly. Simple measures of child care availability, for example, might fail to capture some of the difficulties outlined above. Such measures may not show up as significant in analysis of survey results, indicating that availability is not an important predictor of work behavior. It might be, however, that child care availability is a real issue, but that a lack of availability before and after school and on evenings and weekends, rather than the availability of traditional day care centers for infants and toddlers, is the problem.

One final example: For research purposes, I volunteered one day a week in 1992 at a nonprofit social service agency (see Edin and Lein 1998). The agency was one of the largest in the metropolitan area it served, and served literally thousands of families each year. Like most nonprofits, however, it operated on a shoestring budget, so the amount of assistance it could offer any given family was limited. Though the agency had rules about how often a given family could receive food, agency staff broke the rules freely unless they suspected that clients were involved in outright fraud.

One of the first things I noticed during my volunteer work was how prevalent stories of client fraud were among volunteers and staff. One father came into the agency claiming he was a single father who had lost his job and was forced to stay home to care for his children. The father was asking for help with his rent so that he could avoid eviction. The agency called the landlord, who revealed that the father was married and that his wife did not work. On another occasion, a woman came in for food assistance, claiming her name was Lorraine Johnson. As I was conducting an intake interview with Ms. Johnson (this was my volunteer job), the agency director walked through the waiting room and greeted the woman by another name. The director later related that during the past few months, the client had claimed benefits under at least three different identities, and had been barred from receiving services for six months as a result. Ms. Johnson was sent on her way (with food) and cautioned not to return for the next six months.

Inasmuch as the agency staff and volunteers generally treated clients with a great deal of respect and compassion, and almost never turned anyone away without at least some groceries, I found it hard to imagine why clients so frequently told lies to agency personnel (if volunteer and staff accounts were true). The mystery was solved when several of the families that used this agency ended up in my in-depth-interview sample. The respondents said that inasmuch as their state's welfare benefits were so low (roughly $200 per month), and the jobs available to them generally seasonal, they often needed assistance from several agencies regularly to meet their basic needs. The families often found that because no one agency offered enough of any one service to get them through the month, they often had to approach several agencies. Furthermore, most of the agencies had rules about how often families could receive services. Potential clients soon learned that if they told "white lies" to agency staff about their situations (making them sound more severe than they truly were), they tended to get more assistance than if they told the truth. They believed that such stories also made it more likely that agency staff and volunteers would bend the rules on how often they could receive assistance.

Understanding how a particular program fits within the context of clients' larger life experiences is crucial for understanding the success or failure of program implementation. Were the clients of this social service agency unusually dishonest? Probably not. Rather, dishonesty was a response to a conflict between the way local agencies defined need (as short-term or "crisis" needs) and the real-life situations of clients (whose low welfare benefits and seasonal employment often meant needs were chronic rather than episodic).

How to Do It: Tricks of the Trade

Ethnographic researchers are a heterogeneous group, drawn from sociology, anthropology, political science, and other applied social science fields, such as education and social work. Their methodological predilections, convictions, and subsequent approaches vary even more widely that this disciplinary array would suggest. This heterogeneity poses problems for the newly initiated, but also has advantages in that different kinds of research projects can mine this range for just the right approach. In this portion of the chapter, I discuss the following questions: How do ethnographic researchers working within the context of a process implementation study address sampling issues? What types of data-gathering tools should be used? What kinds of questions are appropriate for ethnographic studies? How can the ethnographic and quantitative components of a particular study complement one another?

Sampling

Quantitative researchers often criticize their qualitative colleagues for not paying enough attention to sampling issues. Historically, ethnographies have been conducted with small groups limited to a specific locale, and concerns about the reliability of the data they produce have been outweighed by the benefits of knowing a lot about each respondent and the social context. Many of the most widely read ethnographies, such as Whyte's *Street Corner Society* (1955), Anderson's *A Place on the Corner* (1978) and *Streetwise* (1990), Liebow's *Tally's Corner* (1967), and Rainwater's *Behind Ghetto Walls* (1970), have been conducted on a single street corner, neighborhood bar, or housing project. Others, such as Willis's *Learning to Labour* (1977), Becker and colleagues' *Boys in White* (1961), Bosk's *Forgive and Remember* (1981), and Stack's *All Our Kin* (1970), have been conducted with a local gang or neighborhood clique, a cohort of medical residents in a given hospital, the staff of an urban medical center, or members of a kinship group or social network. In those studies, the emphasis is on process, or how things work, and on how the people who are involved in the social scene talk about the process.

More recently, some ethnographic researchers have advocated randomly selecting respondents within a target group, and understandably so, because their aim is different (they seek to generalize more broadly) from that of the ethnographies listed above. Many scholars (myself included) have adopted a middle approach, also often trying to generalize to a somewhat larger population, but not advocating random sampling per se. Researchers using middle-range approaches often argue that in research with members of stigmatized populations or on sensitive issues, concerns over trust and rapport can sometimes render random sampling impractical. In these cases, researchers sometimes will engage in fieldwork as well as use existing representative data (for those populations that are not heavily underrepresented) to attempt to establish the potential range of social actors within a given group. They then try as best they can to sample across that range, still relying on the hallmarks of ethnographic fieldwork (personal introductions from key informants) to generate respondents for the study. The main difference is that they often use multiple rather than single "snowballs" or referral chains. These studies have produced samples that are far more heterogeneous than most classic fieldwork studies. They also have had high response rates. Although quantitative researchers will likely remain skeptical about whether the data they produce are even close to representative (understandably so), they satisfy some.

Another issue is how to draw the sample. Studies assessing the effect of social programs often involve a program that reaches a relatively large group of people scattered across a large metropolitan or rural area. One of the advantages of ethnographic work, however, is its ability to capture contextual variables. Whereas some studies attempt to sample across an entire target group, others choose to nest themselves within particular locales or subgroups that they seek to understand well. Some studies fall in between these approaches. They target several specific locales or subgroups that represent some of the heterogeneity of the target population but do not attempt to be fully representative. In our research on the economic survival strategies of welfare- and wage-reliant single mothers, Laura Lein and I attempted to sample mothers from a variety of neighborhoods across the four metropolitan areas we chose. The reason was that we wanted to generalize to the metropolitan area. In the multimethod Urban Change study, the ethnographic team chose to draw ethnographic samples from three or four neighborhoods in each metropolitan area. We used census data to select tract clusters, and selected neighborhoods of particular "types" as case studies. To assess our "bias," we collected demographic data on the ethnographic respondents that we could compare with the demographic characteristics of our survey sample in each city. Inasmuch as the survey and the qualitative component targeted the same types of neighborhoods (those tracts with at least 30 percent of the population living below the poverty level or those tracts with at least 20 percent welfare usage), we could make such comparisons.

Data-Gathering Techniques

Many researchers who have not had adequate training in ethnographic methods and analysis assume that ethnographic research comes in two forms, cheap and expensive. The focus group is cheap, and in-depth interviews coupled with observations are expensive. Following Robert K. Merton and his colleagues (Merton, Fiske, and Kendall 1952), I believe focus groups are useful in helping pretest a list of interview topics and identify neglected topics that should be included in an interview guide. They may also be useful during the analysis stage, when the researcher is unsure how to interpret some portion of the data and cannot go back to the original research subjects. (I recommend, however, that the researcher gain enough rapport with the subjects to permit returning to at least a subset of original subjects, to do what Strauss and Corbin [1990] call theoretical sampling.) However they are used, the individual responses of focus group participants should never be taken as an inexpensive way of gathering individual-level data about attitudes, practices, and so on. Rather, they are a form of public discourse, and must be treated as such. They also are not truly ethnographic unless they involve some level of observation.

A team of researchers in which I participated conducted four focus groups with groups of 4 to 11 low-income, noncustodial fathers in 1997 and 1998 (see Culhane 2000; Nelson, Edin, and Clampet-Lundquist 1999). Some of the fathers were also the subjects of in-depth interviews.

When we compared the in-depth-interview responses with the focus group responses, we found startling discrepancies. One father, for example, claimed he had just found an $11-per-hour job and that because of his economic status, he was about to marry the mother of his child. When our interviewers went to this respondent's home (he lived with his mother in a public housing project), we discovered the job was only temporary (he had gotten it through a temporary employment service) and would last only one more week (he had already been working at the job for a week). Furthermore, his marriage plans were vague, and he said he would only be able to marry if he was able to find a steady job that paid roughly what he was making at the temporary job. In fact, his relationship with his baby's mother was tenuous.

Another father boasted to focus group participants that he held three jobs—two full-time and one part-time. In the in-depth interview, however, we discovered that for most of the year, he worked only at his main job, and only occasionally found jobs at the other occupations he named. This father was clearly more concerned with impressing the other focus group participants than he was with impressing the interviewer, whom he knew and trusted.

A more general difference was that men in our focus group talked with each other in much more callous ways about the mothers of their children and other women in their lives than they did in one-on-one in-depth interviews. They also tended to describe their own behaviors toward women in much more complex ways during interviews than they did in focus groups. In sharing this story in a workshop of social science faculty, one male participant told me that if I took at face value the way that men in his peer group talked with each other about women, I would be "brutalizing men."

Our interpretation of these discrepancies is that fathers were concerned about losing face with peers, and thus presented themselves in a way that was likely to meet with peer approval (what researchers call social desirability). In the in-depth-interview setting, interviewers were able to promise confidentiality, took great care to establish strong rapport with interview subjects, and interacted with research subjects a number of times (which inevitably wears down a subject's ability to maintain a socially desirable response). Fathers also told us that it helped greatly that we were "outsiders," and that they knew the information they shared would not be subsequently shared with others they knew. In these contexts, fathers said they felt more freedom to discuss their thoughts and actions in a more honest way (much of this is due to the skill and training of our interviewers). Of course, we cannot be certain that our respondents were completely honest with us in the in-depth-interview setting either, but we feel fairly sure that we learned more from the in-depth interviews that we could have gleaned from the focus groups. Although it was certainly useful to observe how men talk to each other about women in groups, this was not primarily what we were after in our study.

Though in-depth-interview studies are superior to focus group studies for most research questions, the nature and quality of ethnographic studies vary tremendously. A one-time interview in an unused office of the welfare department may elicit interesting qualitative data, but is probably far less effective than if the interview took place on the respondent's own territory (i.e., the home). Indeed, such research could not properly be called ethnographic at all, inasmuch as no observation is involved. Multiple interviews are also more effective than single interviews. Repeated interviews over a substantial period are the hallmark of the two largest welfare reform studies I am aware of that include a qualitative component. Ethnographic researchers who seek to defend their studies on the grounds that the data have greater validity than survey data should think carefully about whether one-time interviews with no observational component really reach this standard. In addition, repeated interactions with clients can help to satisfy the criticisms of skeptics who worry about whether subjects are telling researchers the truth.

However, virtually all ethnographic studies combine in-depth interviews with some level of "hanging out"—often called fieldwork. Researchers generally observe the condition of the home environment and of the neighborhood, noting the transportation routes that link the neighborhood with others, noting the presence of nonprofit social service agencies and other social institutions in the neighborhood, and so on. Even a small amount of old-fashioned fieldwork can aid in the formulation and interpretation of in-depth-interview data. I offer an experience I had while living in Camden, New Jersey, my research site for a project focusing on childbearing and marriage in the context of a poor community. (Camden is the poorest small city in America and the fifth poorest city of any size.) While I was having my African-American daughter's hair braided by a local "back-alley beautician" who had participated in the in-depth-interview study I was engaged in, my respondent commented: "Someday, when I get my own [beauty] shop, maybe I'll *plan* my babies like you white women do." When I asked her what she meant, she explained, "You know, like Murphy Brown. You got your house, you got your BMW, you got your career, and then maybe, if you have time, then you'll think about having children." Earlier, my respondent had told me that both her three-year-old son and her unborn baby (she was about six months pregnant) were "unplanned." Seizing the moment, I asked, "When you told me earlier that your babies were unplanned, did you mean your pregnancies were accidental?" "No," she replied, "I meant, like a life plan. I didn't have no life plan, like Murphy Brown. You know, a big life plan." When I pressed, "So were they accidental?" She gave me a rather sly look and responded, "Well, I wasn't exactly using birth control, was I?"

After this spontaneous exchange, I began probing subsequent respondents more carefully about whether or not their pregnancies were planned. Many of the women with whom I spoke also said initially that their pregnancies were unplanned, but as I questioned them further, it became clear that the pregnancies were not accidental.

Asking the Right Questions

When I was a graduate student at Northwestern University, my qualitative methods teacher, Howard S. Becker, taught me a great many useful things. Probably the most useful was his suggestion that I ask *how*, not *what* or *why*, questions. For example, when interviewing welfare recipients about their view of welfare reform, one might be tempted to ask, "Why did you go on welfare?" A far more useful question might be "How was it that you got on welfare?" The why question might be read by the respondent as judgmental, and the respondent might feel obliged to defend herself. The how question is likely to elicit a step-by-step description of the events leading up to the initial spell on welfare.

Becker also taught his students to avoid asking questions that can be answered with a single word, and to learn to formulate questions that elicit a narrative. Instead of asking, "Was your baby planned?" It would be more useful to ask, "How was it that you got pregnant?" The first demands a yes or no answer, and nothing more. The second demands a more extensive account of the events leading up to the pregnancy.

Becker emphasized that probing is also crucial to the qualitative endeavor, and these probes should, in general, be as open-ended as possible. My favorite probe is simple. If I asked, "So, how does the child support system work?" a subject might answer, "It doesn't. I have fully cooperated with child support and have never gotten a cent." The interviewer might be tempted to ask, "Why not?" This is not a bad probe, but a far better one is simply, "Tell me about that." This probe is likely to elicit more narrative than the "Why not?" probe. The former would likely result in a process narrative, whereas the latter could simply be answered, "Because they're incompetent, that's why." In the end, the interviewer is likely to learn far more by encouraging the respondent to tell the story of her interactions with child support from beginning to end.

Probes need not be verbal. Simply leaning toward the respondent, nodding one's head, jotting on a note pad, or even lifting one's eyebrows can express interest and encourage the respondent to talk. One of our interviewers tends to repeat the word "wow!" whenever he wants the respondent to expand on a particular topic. It works. The basic idea is to get the respondent talking and keep the questions and probes to a minimum so that the respondent can tell her story unimpeded. When the transcript comes back, the respondent's answers should take up far more space than the interviewer's questions.

Ethnographic researchers also vary in how structured their interviews are. Those who participate in multimethod research often describe our interviews as "semi-structured," meaning that we have planned a list of topics in advance, but let the ordering and the precise wording of the questions vary according to how the conversation naturally unfolds. They also pursue additional topics if they come up in the course of the conversation. A good interviewer who is well acquainted with his or her topic list can sometimes do without any written list at all (and if there are multiple interactions, interviewers can always go back to get what was missed). In general, ethnographers hold that the more the interview resembles a naturally occurring conversation, the better. Any researcher who has been the subject of a survey can attest to the artificiality of the exchange.

Often, investigators are tempted to use ethnographic research to get a "read" on the community the subject supposedly represents. I view this practice as dangerous and misleading. Ethnographers should remember that hearsay is not evidence. Let me offer the following example. In 1992, the state of New Jersey requested a federal waiver to impose a family cap in several counties. The waiver was granted, and the state chose Camden County as one of the experimental counties. I began to ask interview subjects whether they thought people "around here" had babies "just to get money from welfare." A surprising number of subjects claimed the practice was quite common. When I asked them if they had done so, each replied, "Of course not!" Earlier on in the interviewing process, I had asked respondents to draw up a list of the members of their social networks, including kin, friends, and even "acquaintances" they felt they knew pretty well. Following the question, I reintroduced this list, and asked mothers if they thought that anyone on the list had had a baby to get more in the way of welfare benefits. The overwhelming majority could point to no relative, friend, or casual acquaintance who had done so. When presented with the discrepancy, one woman commented, "Well, I guess it must be just a few apples who spoil it for the whole bunch."

When dealing with stigmatized or disadvantaged groups, one must also remember that members of such groups often internalize the stigma society imposes on them. The eminent ethnographer Gerald Suttles (1968) pointed this out over 30 years ago. If you ask the typical welfare recipient what she thinks ought to be done about welfare, she will tell you that it should be abolished. If you probe deeper, you will find that although she knows no "welfare queens" personally, she has heard the same stories of mothers who purchase expensive steaks with food stamps, who drive Cadillacs to the welfare office, and who receive benefits under 13 different identities. Like most Americans, she assumes these traits characterize a far greater proportion of welfare recipients than they actually do. She also has a clear psychological motivation to distance herself from the stigmatized identity she knows is applied to her. Therefore, she sets herself apart, both in her own mind and for the benefit of others, from the "scum" who get welfare. Reviling others in her status is one way of convincing herself and others that she is aware of the stereotype, but is "not like the rest." Indeed, her disapproval of the welfare system is a powerful demonstration that she is morally superior to others sharing her status. Researchers are often intrigued by the idea that they should get a group of program participants together to devise solutions, assuming that they have unique expertise. I would strongly warn against putting a recipient of a highly stigmatized program in the "street-level policy-maker" role.

Nailing It Down

When welfare recipients began telling me in the late 1980s that nobody could live on a welfare check, my dissertation adviser's response was "Can you prove it?" This led to a large research project in which Laura Lein and I gathered detailed budgets from 214 welfare recipients living in four U.S. cities. When these same mothers told us they were not working because they couldn't afford it, Lein and I decided to get detailed budgets from a comparable group of low-wage working mothers living in the same cities to see how those mothers who did work were making it.

Many have expressed surprise that two ethnographers would be interested in gathering so much quantitative data. However, many of the classic ethnographic studies of the field make meticulous counts of bowling scores (Whyte 1955), grocery store prices (Valentine 1978), and so on. By getting the details down, qualitative researchers can partly justify their claim that they can get more in-depth data than survey researchers can.

Obtaining details might be particularly important with stigmatized populations who have good reason to lie to researchers. In every type of human interaction I can think of, people are motivated to present themselves in particular ways. This problem becomes more intense when admitting a particular behavior can have severe stigma costs or legal implications. Mothers who covertly combine work and welfare can lose their welfare benefits if caught and, in some cases, might even be prosecuted for fraud. Parents who admit to drug use might risk losing custody of their children to the state if the information became known to child protective services. Public housing residents might be evicted, or at the least have their rent raised, if they admit that a working partner is living in the household and the housing authority finds out. A couple who marries might want to hide the fact from outsiders because the marriage of a low-wage worker to another low-wage worker generally means that the couple forfeits several thousands of dollars in their earned income tax credit. Researchers must understand enough about the world of their subjects to anticipate some of these motivations and fears in advance (here is where some participant observation comes in handy), and adjust their technique accordingly.

When interviewing welfare recipients about their budgets, Lein and I made sure to ask mothers about their expenditures first. Then we asked them about their income. We were afraid that if we asked the questions in the reverse order, people would lower their expense estimates to fit within their "official" incomes. When we asked about expenditures first, and then about income, there was a large gap. This is because mothers did not generally reveal all of their income sources (the covert sources) right away. In addition, repeated interactions in welfare recipients' households helped us to gauge the accuracy of expenditure estimates (if we saw a table and chairs that looked new, we asked how much they cost). Unlike survey researchers, we were ultimately able to construct budgets that balanced.

Nevertheless, I would caution against weighing down a qualitative interview with many formal quantitative measures. When we asked mothers about their budgets, we did it in the form of a conversation, not in a survey mode. Many times, architects of multimethod studies are tempted to throw all the scales they can think of at qualitative research subjects. Because most Americans assume an "interview" means a survey, qualitative researchers must spend time convincing their subjects that the conversations they engage in will not be in survey form. Once the respondent becomes free of what I call the "survey mentality," the level of rapport rises dramatically. Adding many closed-ended survey items to an in-depth interview is often harmful to the integrity of the qualitative study.

Multimethod Study Design Issues

In putting together a multimethod research design to assess the effects of a social program, researchers often wonder which should come first, the qualitative or the quantitative. Social scientists have long praised the qualitative tradition for its unique ability to ground more quantitative studies (identify relevant variables) and to generate hypotheses (identify new and surprising relationships) that can be tested more systematically in a survey. On the other hand, qualitative research has sometimes been used to figure out mysteries in the quantitative data after some preliminary analysis has been done. In an ideal world with unlimited budgets, a qualitative/quantitative research design should be iterative. In the Urban Change project, we began the qualitative interviews before fielding the survey. Armed with our initial client interviews, we could critique the survey and suggest alterations, exclusions, and additions. Now that the first round of survey data are in, we are examining the data for new questions that we can ask our subjects. The second round of qualitative research will then feed into the survey to be fielded in two years.

Some Recent Examples

Parents' Fair Share

In 1991, Frank Furstenburg, Kay Sherwood, and Mercer Sullivan conducted focus group interviews with 71 low-income noncustodial fathers as part of an effort to design a demonstration project that could help such fathers gain employment and pay child support. These researchers gathered accounts that offered a fascinating glimpse into how low-income men viewed the official child support system. The results (Furstenburg, Sherwood, and Sullivan 1992) were used to guide the formulation of a program that offered job training and education, assistance with finding employment, and peer support to low-income noncustodial fathers whose child support was in arrears. While they participated, their child support orders were adjusted or lowered so that they could participate in the program.

Once the program, Parents' Fair Share (PFS), had been implemented in seven sites across the country, ethnographer Earl Johnson followed 32 participants of PFS over a two-year period. During this time, he engaged in semistructured in-depth interviews with the men and observed them in their daily lives. Ironically, Johnson's data revealed that despite the fact that fathers in the demonstration program had access to more resources than they had under the old child support regime, PFS fathers viewed the "enhanced" program in much the same way that their focus group counterparts had viewed the "basic" child support system. In both cases, if one's child was on welfare, fathers believed that paying through the formal system offered few rewards. For example, each study found that the child support system's inability to take into account fluctuations in men's economic situations engendered both hostility and fear, that the effect of imposing inflexible payment orders on precariously employed men drove them into severe arrears, and that the child support system's practice of using most of the money to reimburse the state for the welfare benefits it paid to the mother made it unlikely that the fathers would even attempt to obey the law with regard to child support.

However, Johnson's in-depth interviews went further than the focus group interviews, and offered other fascinating clues about other reasons why some fathers in the PFS program failed to comply with one or more requirements. For example, one of Johnson's respondents said he failed to participate in a domestic violence program he had been court-ordered to attend because the program site was located in a rival gang's territory. This respondent felt that encroaching on the territory of these adversaries placed him at risk. When he reported his fears to program staff, they reportedly offered little sympathy for his predicament (Johnson, Levine, and Doolittle 1999, 165).

For other fathers who spoke to Johnson, the costs of attending the PFS program, although seemingly minor to outside observers, were enough to discourage participation. First, the meager bus fare many fathers had to pay to get to the program site in some cases constituted a significant portion of their income. Second, hours spent at PFS in training, education, or peer support meetings meant less time to devote to other income generating activities (many of them informal or illegal). The program carried no stipend for either transportation costs or any compensation for hours of work lost. Some fathers reported to Johnson that their failure to continue in the program was due to a lack of funds to cover their own living expenses, even though they realized that their child support obligations would be held in check only if they continued to participate in PFS.

> The majority were surviving on irregular, unpredictable, odd jobs on, or more often off, the books and both legal or illegal. Often, they had little or no money, and just getting to the program each day was a financial strain. Participation often forced them to give up an opportunity to earn a little income on a given day. This meant that participants had to weigh the usefulness and expectations they had for the program and for themselves against the economic cost of spending part or all of their day in it and having nothing tangible to show at a day's end. The longer a participant stayed in PFS, the tighter his resources became (Johnson et al. 1999, 172).

In addition, Johnson's respondents sometimes had a hard time keeping people who depended on their support—their own mothers or their girlfriends, for example—"off their backs" long enough to complete the program.

Finally, Johnson found that other small glitches foiled fathers' attempts to comply with PFS. Johnson, Levine, and Doolittle write that "participants in this study reported that in many instances PFS seemed unable to help them get the services they wanted or needed, that delays prevented them from pursuing opportunities (for example, tuition funds were released weeks after a training program had begun), and that PFS did not stand behind them in their dealings with other agencies" (Johnson et al. 1999, 170).

Both Johnson's results and those from the focus groups conducted in the early 1990s assisted the program evaluators, who were also concluding an experimental evaluation of the program, to understand the sometimes disappointing results that PFS had on fathers who participated.

New Hope

New Hope was an antipoverty program operating in two inner-city neighborhoods in Milwaukee, Wisconsin, in the mid-1990s. When families volunteered for New Hope, New Hope staff assigned them to either a control or an experimental group. Those in the experimental group had to work at least 30 hours a week to be eligible for program benefits, including wage and child care subsidies and health insurance. If they could not find a job that offered enough hours to fulfill their work requirement, New Hope would provide them with a temporary community service job.

Researchers at the Manpower Demonstration Research Corporation and members of the MacArthur Network on Middle Childhood were given the task of implementing the quantitative analysis, while Tom Wiesner (University of California at Los Angeles) and a team of graduate students at Northwestern University took on the qualitative analysis. The quantitative team drew on a variety of data, including administrative records data and surveys of both families and teachers, which were conducted about two years after families had volunteered for the program. At about the same time (the two-year mark), the ethnographic team began working with a group of 45 families drawn from both the experimental and the control groups. The ethnographic team met periodically with each of these 45 families for the next three years, observing family life and engaging in informal conversations about issues Weisner and his team believed might be salient to their participation in New Hope. Field notes were sorted by topic and shared among members of both the quantitative and ethnographic team. Another notable innovation that improved the fit between the qualitative and quantitative analysis was to involve team members in both the qualitative and quantitative analyses.

Though the sample size of the ethnographic study was too small (22 experimental and 23 control families) to assess overall program effects (see Duncan and Gibson 1999), these researchers used the qualitative data in innovative ways to "tell stories" about the quantitative results; they used vignettes depicting circumstances of individual families to illustrate key quantitative results in vivid and memorable ways. These page-long vignettes helped researchers in the larger research and evaluation team to understand how complex families' situations really were. The vignettes also helped researchers to understand how the New Hope treatment fit within the larger context of families' lives at any time, as well as how the contexts changed over time. The insight they gained from the families allowed the quantitative team to construct quantitative measures that, in later survey waves, will lead to a survey instrument that allows the survey to gather a more complete account of family well-being.

In addition, New Hope's qualitative data proved indispensable for understanding puzzling patterns in the quantitative data. Greg Duncan and Christine Gibson, two of the team members, write

> For example, one of the most important—and initially puzzling—effects of the New Hope experiment was on teacher-reported achievement and behavior of pre-adolescent children. Boys in the experimental group were 0.3 to 0.5 standard deviations better behaved and higher achieving than their control-group counterparts, but there were no such effects for girls.
>
> The survey offered few clues to this gender story. Qualitative interviews suggested that mothers believed that gangs and other neighborhood pressures were much more threatening to their boys than girls, and that mothers in the experimental group channeled more of the program's resources (e.g., child care subsidies for extended-day programs) to their boys. Further quantitative analyses of both New Hope and national-sample survey data supported this interpretation (Duncan and Gibson 1999).

New Hope researchers also found that the ethnographic data were vital for isolating subgroups in the sample that may have used the program in different ways and thus led to different outcomes. An illustration is New Hope's effects on labor supply and earnings.

> The quantitative team knew from the beginning that program effects on work and earnings were heterogeneous. Roughly one-third of the families attracted to New Hope were already working more than 30 hours and viewed the program's benefits as a way of making work and family demands more manageable. If anything, experimental-control differences in the labor supply among these families were negative. In contrast, families not working full-time at baseline viewed New Hope as a way of facilitating a transition to full-time work. On balance, experimental-control effects on labor supply were positive for these families, although stronger in the first than second year of the program. Qualitative interviews pointed to important heterogeneity among this latter set of families. Some, perhaps one-fifth, had multiple problems (e.g., drug dependence, children with severe behavior problems, relatives in ill health) that New Hope's package of benefits could not be expected to overcome. Others had no such apparent problems, and in these cases, both experimental and control families could be expected to do well in Milwaukee's job-rich environment. A third group, however—those who were only one or two barriers away from making it—might well profit the most from the New Hope package of benefits. Extensive quantitative work on barrier-defined subgroups showed this to be the case (Duncan and Gibson 1999).

Duncan and Gibson conclude, "Program effects on the labor supply among families with a small number of barriers were large and, if anything, larger in the second than the first year. This key set of findings would simply not have been discovered were it not for the qualitative work" (Duncan and Gibson 1999).

Conclusion

I have tried to show why client-based qualitative research is useful and to offer some ideas about how it might be done within the context of policy or program evaluations. State welfare reform is both complex and dynamic, and understanding the client's point of view is crucial. Beyond providing memorable and politically powerful anecdotal stories, client-based ethnographic research can offer crucial data that, if woven iteratively into a larger multimethod study, can prove enormously useful in both interpreting survey results and helping researchers design surveys that fit better with the lives and experiences of the research subjects they seek to understand. Client-based qualitative research is particularly useful when combined with program-based implementation research, where the informal structure of a program can be directly observed. Although few studies in the past have combined all three elements, several multisite studies of welfare reform do so. These will provide more insight into the utility and practicality of engaging in multimethod research, and will do so in the context of one of the largest policy changes in the 20th century.

NOTES

1. Our Philadelphia clients also often watch the local or national news, which sometimes reports on a program in one state that is designed differently in another. Again, client confusion may result despite the quality of program implementation.

2. Whereas previously the welfare office could "disregard" (not count) only the first $30 plus one-third of remaining income women earned in the first four months, and could continue to disregard one-third of her earnings after four months (the rest of her earnings were deducted from her welfare check), the new policy meant that the welfare office could disregard 50 percent of her work income, with no reduction at the four-month point.

REFERENCES

Anderson, Elijah. 1978. *A Place on the Corner.* Chicago: University of Chicago Press.
———. 1990. *Streetwise: Race, Class, and Change in an Urban Community.* Chicago: University of Chicago Press.
Becker, Howard S., Everett C. Hughes, Blanche Geer, and Anselm Lo Strauss. 1961. *Boys in White: Student Culture in Medical School.* Chicago: University of Chicago Press.
Bosk, Charles L. 1981. *Forgive and Remember: Managing Medical Failure.* Chicago: University of Chicago Press.

Culhane, Jennifer. 2000. "Low-Income, Noncustodial Fathers in Philadelphia." Unpublished manuscript. Philadelphia: University of Pennsylvania.

Duncan, Greg, and Christina Gibson. 1999. "Qualitative-Quantitative Interactions in the 'New Hope' Experiment." *Poverty Research News* 4(1). Chicago: Joint Center for Poverty Research.

Edin, Kathryn. 1995. "Single Mothers and Child Support: Possibilities and Limits of Child Support Policy." *Child and Youth Services Review* 17(1–2):203–30.

Edin, Kathryn, and Laura Lein. 1997a. *Making Ends Meet: How Single Mothers Survive Welfare and Low-Wage Work*. New York: Russell Sage Foundation.

———. 1997b. "Welfare, Work, and Economic Survival Strategies." *American Sociological Review* 61 (May):253–66.

———. 1998. "The Private Safety Net: Welfare Reform, Social Networks, Community Resources, and Family Well-Being." *Housing Policy Debate* 9(3):541–74.

Furstenburg, Frank F., Jr., Kay E. Sherwood, and Mercer L. Sullivan. 1992. *Caring and Paying: What Fathers and Mothers Say about Child Support*. New York: Manpower Demonstration Research Corporation.

Johnson, Earl, Ann Levine, and Fred Doolittle. 1999. *Fathers' Fair Share: Helping Poor Men Manage Child Support and Fatherhood*. New York: Russell Sage Foundation.

Liebow, Elliot. 1967. *Tally's Corner*. Boston: Little, Brown.

Merton, Robert K., Marjorie Fiske, and Patricia Kendall. 1952. *The Focused Interview: A Manual*. New York: Columbia University, Bureau of Applied Social Research.

Murray, Charles A. 1984. *Losing Ground: American Social Policy, 1950–1980*. New York: Basic Books.

Nelson, Timothy, Kathryn Edin, and Susan Clampet-Lundquist. 1999. "Doing the Best I Can: What Poor Non-Custodial Fathers Say about Their Families." Paper presented at the conference "Absent Fathers," Harvard University, April.

Rainwater, Lee. 1970. *Behind Ghetto Walls: Black Families in a Federal Slum*. Chicago: Aldine.

Stack, Carol B. 1970. *All Our Kin: Strategies for Survival in a Black Community*. New York: Harper and Row.

Strauss, Anselm, and Juliet Corbin. 1990. *Basics of Qualitative Research: Grounded Theory Procedures and Techniques*. Newbury Park, Calif.: Sage Publications.

Suttles, Gerald. 1968. *Social Order of the Slum: Ethnicity and Territory in the Inner City*. Chicago: University of Chicago Press.

Valentine, Bettylou. 1978. *Hustling and Other Hard Work: Lifestyles in the Ghetto*. New York: Free Press.

Whyte, William F. 1955. *Street Corner Society: The Social Structure of an Italian Slum*. Chicago: University of Chicago Press.

Willis, Paul E. 1977. *Learning to Labour: How Working Class Kids Get Working Class Jobs*. Farnborough, England: Saxon House.

9

What Lies behind the Impacts?

Implementation Research in the Context of Net Impact Studies

Kay E. Sherwood and Fred Doolittle

Implementation research conducted in the context of an impact evaluation has as its primary goal explaining the impact findings of such a study. Although the measurement of differences between program and control or comparison group outcomes is the "bottom line" of impact evaluation, without good complementary implementation research it is difficult for the funders of program interventions and for program administrators and future program designers to decide what to do next. Should a program with positive net impacts be replicated? Not necessarily. For example, if a strong net decrease in government expenditures on public assistance were found to be attributable to welfare agency staff ignoring program regulations (for example, by refusing to hand out applications for assistance until a person had visited the welfare office at least twice), the program might not be touted a success or a model to replicate. A program with negligible net impacts should not necessarily be discarded as a meritless idea either. The implementation analysis of such a program might reveal that less than a third of the intended participants actually got the intended "treatment" for reasons that would be avoidable in the future. In that case, interested policymakers and program designers might conclude that the program idea had not been given a fair test; they might conclude that implementation problems could be and should be fixed, rather than that the idea should be discarded.

Implementation research in the context of an impact evaluation has grown more sophisticated over the last two decades, because policymakers and others concerned about investing public funds in social programs have been eager for a better picture of the nature of program administration and the reasons for observed impact findings—and they have been willing to pay for the work needed to develop this information. In the field of welfare research, the growing complexity of reforms—moving beyond job search or workfare requirements—has contributed to policymakers' interest in understanding the sources of impact findings, fostered a willingness to invest greater resources in implementation research, and pushed researchers to develop new research methods. This interest harkens back to the 1970s, when several large and well-funded impact studies of innovative programs were financed by the federal government, after which social policy researchers entered a period of much leaner funding. Many of the welfare reform studies of the early- to mid-1980s were done under authority of federal waivers with funding shared by states and the federal government and boosted by private foundation support. Those studies typically did not support rich implementation research or even the full range of impact analysis.

Advances in implementation research designed to explain impact findings have also occurred because of the way knowledge building about welfare reforms takes place. In the United States, welfare reform evaluations are part of a multidisciplinary public/private policy research enterprise in which information about what works is accumulated program by program, evaluation by evaluation, with the ultimate objective of crafting good public policies. Policymakers want to avoid costly and doomed experiments and invest in policies with potential. To support that goal, researchers try to answer the policymakers' questions about what to scrap, what to modify, and what to replicate. Building the knowledge to do it requires explanations of *why* successful policies and programs have worked and why others have not, and why some have been modestly successful and some have generated significant changes. Absent such explanations, each new policy initiative is a shot in the twilight of partial information about where not to aim.

Implementation research plays an important role in explaining impact evaluation results because, whereas impacts are a simple measured difference between the outcomes of a group targeted by a program intervention and a similar comparison or control group not served or excluded from the intervention,[1] this measured difference is a function of a complicated, and often interacting, set of circumstances. Impacts (positive or negative) of a welfare reform intervention, for example, can be driven by

- the quality and intensity (or amount) of the intervention reaching those people with access to the intervention;
- the baseline level of similar activity among the group not served by the intervention (the control or comparison group);
- the characteristics of those people targeted by the intervention, including their beliefs, expectations, and hopes for fertility, family formation, and investments in education; and
- a host of external conditions, such as the local labor market, the cost of living and the cost of working, the availability and cost of child care, and transportation.

It is the task of implementation research in the context of an impact evaluation, in collaboration with impact analysis, to sort out which of these factors (or possibly others) explain why the intervention being evaluated produced the measured result that it did and, under the best conditions, how much of the result might be attributable to which factor.[2]

Complicating the goals of implementation research within impact evaluation, however, are two important policy problems. First is the time sensitivity of the audience for implementation findings. The people who make up the audience—usually executive branch government officials and legislators—often face difficult administrative and policy choices as program implementation progresses and they often ask for formative evaluation feedback from implementation analysis long before impact results are in. They want to know if they are on the right track, or if they should be changing features of their programs before, rather than after, there is information about program effects. Sometimes they want to know if they should continue to supply resources originally committed and stay the course with an initiative when other budgetary demands arise.

The second complicating policy issue is the role of site variation in impact results. In addition to the factors described that drive program impacts, in a multiple-site evaluation variations in implementation (broadly defined) might account for variations in impacts across sites. Social programs are notoriously variable from place to place, even when their features are closely specified and regulated. Because the challenge to the implementation researcher is to *connect* findings on implementation to impact findings, variation across sites can be an important tool in solving the puzzle of what explains impacts. Thus, site-level analysis often becomes central to implementation analysis in the context of impact evaluations—in part, because it is a means of generating more data points or observations to have something credible and meaningful to say about the connection between implementation experience and impacts. The difficulty here is how an intervention is bounded for study. Along some dimensions, a 58-county program will look like 58 programs and thus merit close study in at least several "representative" locations. Similarly, a county with 10 welfare offices might, for some implementation research purposes, have 10 programs.

This chapter discusses three questions that are usually the focus of implementation research conducted in the context of an impact evaluation. The chapter closes by exploring briefly the implications of these questions for methods used in this type of implementation research and the ways in which the problems of time sensitivity and site variation tend to play out, as well as our views of how implementation researchers should handle these issues.

Throughout the chapter, we use the terms *intervention* and *program* interchangeably, although we recognize that some social policies, including some welfare reforms, do not constitute a program "service" in the traditional sense of that term. For example, time limits on eligibility for cash assistance under the Temporary Assistance for Needy Families (TANF) program are a policy and an intervention, but not a program or service as those are usually understood. We have adopted the economists' use of the term *behavior* for this chapter as well, which usually denotes activities and outcomes of individual people without assuming causes or interactions among causative factors. In the economists' dialect, "work behavior" may be the result of the beliefs, desires, and efforts of individuals, the impersonal action of the labor market, or some combination of personal and environmental characteristics. To economists, it is all "behavior."

Key Questions of Implementation Research in an Impact Study

Good implementation research in the context of impact studies must help the evaluators answer these questions: Do the conditions needed for a strong impact study exist? What explains the pattern of impact estimates? How can successful programs or interventions be replicated? As we hope to make clear in this discussion, the boundary between impact and implementation research can blur. In a successful evaluation, the two work together.

Do the Conditions Needed for a Strong Impact Study Exist?

The first job of implementation research within an impact evaluation is to help determine whether several conditions for carrying out a valid impact study exist at the time the impact study begins (or existed when the program was being implemented). In this role, implementation research supplements and often overlaps with the work that impact analysts do. Although the division of labor is not sharp, impact researchers usually worry about confirming, statistically, that the control or comparison group and the program group are equivalent in their measured characteristics, and creating a sample large enough to detect impacts of the expected magnitude at a high level of significance. Implementation researchers, on the other hand, focus on the features of the program or policy that may affect the interpretation of the impact study—information that can also be used to help explain impact findings (to be discussed in the next section). Our discussion of the role of implementation research in examining the conditions needed for a strong impact study is divided into three subsections, each concerned with an important question about those conditions: Is there a logical or empirical basis for the design of the program or intervention that suggests that it has a reasonable chance of producing impacts? Did the program or intervention get a "fair test?" And did the program or intervention produce a real difference between the experiences of the group included and the control or comparison group?

IS THERE GOOD REASON TO BELIEVE THAT THE INTERVENTION HAS A CHANCE OF MAKING A DIFFERENCE TO THE TARGET GROUP?
This is a threshold criterion that, in a different form, may also be an empirical question for implementation research. To meet this criterion, the intervention under study must be predicated on some evidence, however suggestive, that the lever employed will move the object in question. Social science research on poverty, employment, and family issues encompasses a broad set of theories about how to improve the health, work, income, education, and life chances of poor people. A host of cash assistance formulas, incentives and disincentives, services, opportunities, persuasive techniques, technologies, substitutes for key developmental rela-

tionships, even transformational belief systems, have been the bases for welfare reforms. Whatever the means chosen for reform, evaluation designers must take into account what an intervention can be expected to achieve *on average,* which is the built-in standard for impact evaluation when the outcomes of one group (those who were exposed to the treatment) are compared with the outcomes of another (those who were not). For example, a six-week intervention that is expected to move welfare recipients with less than a high school education into $10-an-hour jobs with benefits in the private sector and keep them working and moving up in wages and benefits over a follow-up year would be aiming for results "outside the box," based on the achievements of past interventions. The six-week intervention would have to be operating in an unusually tight labor market or have unusual features for these expectations to be justified.

The task of implementation researchers in this case would be to look for features of the intervention, or the environment in which it was implemented, to support its implicit theory—that is, that relatively brief job preparation is what welfare recipients need to land good entry-level jobs and advance. Not finding either an unusual labor market or unusual program features, implementation researchers might conclude that the intervention did not have a realistic chance to make a difference. It could have been the wrong intervention for the labor market conditions, the wrong locality for the intervention, the wrong target group for the intervention, or the wrong type or duration of intervention for the selected target group and locality. In these circumstances, implementation researchers might report "no chance," meaning a faulty design, or leave it to the impact analysis to find that the intervention just didn't work. However, it would still be the task of implementation analysis to determine why.

Both this criterion of a reasonable theory and the fair test criterion discussed below point to a set of issues in impact-related implementation research that we will call "evaluator activism." Most researchers would prefer to assure before an evaluation begins that, to the maximum extent possible, the intervention has a realistic chance to make a difference and will receive a fair test. Under the best conditions, collaboration between the program designers and the evaluators enables the evaluation and the intervention to be designed simultaneously to assure these conditions. When this activist role is not possible, evaluators sometimes fall back to the position of making these judgments after the fact.

What makes the reasonable theory criterion more important to impact studies than to other types of evaluation is the extraordinary level of resources required for impact evaluation. It is difficult, if not unethical, for an impact evaluator to go into a multiyear, multimillion-dollar project believing that the intervention in question could not possibly produce positive findings or findings that accurately reflect how the program would normally work (although evaluators have been wrong in such judgments). It is equally difficult for an investor in a multiyear, multimillion-dollar project to learn at the end that the project's central idea was faulty, especially if the program's logic or test conditions could have been improved by a different approach to implementation or by a different evaluation design.[3]

DID THE PROGRAM OR POLICY UNDER STUDY RECEIVE A FAIR TEST?

An important, overarching condition for a valid impact evaluation is that the program or policy under study is implemented well enough to produce effects, if effects could be produced by the intervention. Arguably, this is a more complicated judgment than is undertaken in any other type of implementation research. The key research question across all types of implementation research is "What happened?"—that is, did the program or policy under study materialize and, if so, what form did it take? For some types of implementation research, the question is more pointed: "What happened compared with what was supposed to or expected to happen?" The added burden of implementation research in the context of an impact study is the identification of a threshold level of implementation necessary for a true test of the intervention's power. Thus, a key question of impact-related implementation analysis is this: *Did the program or policy under study get a "fair test"?* The following discussion presents our view of the elements of a "fair test."

The intended target group was reached. Social policy interventions are most often targeted to particular groups who are seen as needing or likely to benefit from the intervention. If, in the course of implementing an evaluation of a targeted intervention, a research sample builds up that does not include the intended target group, or does not include enough target group members to produce statistically significant findings for that group, the impact study is jeopardized. In studies of mandatory programs covering all welfare recipients, this is not likely to be an issue. But in programs with substantial and subjective exemptions, or in voluntary programs, it can be difficult to recruit and serve the intended population in large enough numbers to meet policy goals or to satisfy the requirements of the research design. (In addition to pointing toward poor conditions for valid impact research, this would be a finding about the program under study.)

To document this element of a fair test of the intervention, the implementation analysis must determine (1) the proportion of sample members (in both control or comparison and program groups) with the essential targeting characteristics; (2) the number "reached" by the policy or program under study (see the next section for more on the meaning of this); and (3) whether *enough* target group members met the definition of "reached" to support a conclusion that the intervention under study had the potential to succeed for them. This final, difficult determination is essential to an interpretation of impact results because if the proportion of targeted individuals in the entire research sample was small, any positive intervention results for the entire research sample could not clearly be claimed as relevant for the intended group. Further, if only a small proportion of the program group sample was exposed to a specifically defined form or "dose" of the intervention, any statistically significant program impacts detected could not necessarily be attributed to that form or dose of the intervention; some difference between the experiences of the program group and control or comparison group members outside that description of the intervention could have produced such a result.

Both the representation of the target group in the full sample and the "penetration" of the treatment within the program group sample are important because impact analysis compares the control or comparison group results—an average—with the average results for the program group, including everyone who was inadvertently included in either group and everyone who turned out to be unavailable, uninterested, or otherwise unreachable. In random assignment–style impact evaluations, it is up to the managers of the "test" to ensure that the intervention recruits, assigns, and serves, or not, the intended groups to the maximum extent possible.

The program or policy was adequately in effect or available. Most social interventions have several components, dimensions, or pathways. Thus, a fair test judgment entails defining the *essential* elements of the program or policy under study—that is, those that the program designers and evaluators believe are needed for impacts to be observed. Then, implementation research must examine variations in implementation, focusing on questions such as these:

- Which components or dimensions were in place or operating *over what periods*, particularly in relation to when the impact sample was drawn? Did some of the early participants get less than later ones because of a slow start-up?

- Which components or dimensions of the intervention under study operated *at what capacity*, particularly in relation to the rate at which the impact sample was drawn? Were there too few program slots or opportunities at any point, resulting in down time and nonparticipation?
- Which components or dimensions of the intervention were in place or operating, at what capacity, *in which parts of the geographic area that was supposed to be covered*, particularly if the characteristics of the target group members varied according to geography? Did city dwellers have access to more than rural residents?
- What *variations in the intervention's methods or approaches* occurred, when and where? Were program rules enforced more strictly in some locations or for some sample members?

Finally, taking into consideration all the major variations in implementation, the analysis must determine whether a threshold level of program services provision or policy intervention was achieved for the target group to be potentially "exposed" enough to be affected. A fair test of a social policy or program does not require excellent or even good implementation; it requires "good enough" implementation. Researchers are thus looking for gaps in the exposure of the program group to the intended treatment—that is, the times and places that potential participants could not have gotten what they were supposed to get—to conclude whether there was an opportunity for impacts.

A gap in exposure to the intervention treatment, or variation in the strength or capacity of the intervention, does not necessarily portend a poor showing in impacts. Studies of the Center for Employment Training (CET) program conducted during the mid-1980s illustrate the need to have a realistic view of implementation. At CET, service funding was a continuing difficulty and the program had to suspend intake and service start-up at times. Some research sample members thus faced substantial delays between selection into the sample and the start of program services. Nevertheless, CET produced strong impacts in two separate impact studies (Burghardt et al. 1992; Cave et al. 1993).

Program designers are often overly optimistic about participation. As a result, implementation researchers often face the task of deciding what constitutes an adequate exposure to an intervention under study when participation levels fall below the original projections. Is exposure to the program, for example, "receiving information," "being offered or invited to participate," "being served in any capacity or quantity," or "participating in or receiving a specified set or sequence of services for a specified length of time?" The last measure is sometimes appealing to program operators, because they tend to prefer having the effectiveness of their services or interventions judged on the outcomes of participants who got the intended types and amounts of treatment. Program operators can be frustrated when an impact study research sample is "diluted" by a substantial percentage of people who do not actually receive the intended services. But using a standard of exposure to an intended sequence and length of service is often too stringent a measure of the *availability* of services. When participation levels drop below intended levels, it can be because of a mismatch between service offerings and participant interests, needs, or ability to participate continuously. Rather than necessarily being an indication of the lack of availability of services, lower-than-intended participation levels are more often a central finding about program design or implementation.

The intensity, "dose," or quality of the intervention was adequate. This criterion for a fair test can be based on the assumptions and theories of the program designers or policy authors about what *amount* of the intervention is needed to make a difference. Alternatively, operational benchmarks intended to drive program operations might guide implementation researchers about what constitutes an adequate amount of an intervention. Efforts to develop a theory of change for the intervention during a design stage might produce research guides as well. But, if no amount of service or marker of adequacy was specified at the outset, evaluators can construct a standard drawing from either past interventions or new theories. In some evaluations, however, the adequate amount or quality of the policy or program under study is an empirical question that will yield a research finding, instead of a criterion of a fair test. This might occur in several instances: when there is no relevant experience to draw upon from past interventions; when the program designers and policy authors assume that *any* amount or quality of the service or intervention being evaluated has the potential to improve the outcomes of participants; or when two or more versions of a program are being evaluated side by side to determine which level or type of service or intervention produces the best outcomes.

We find that the necessary intensity, dose, or quality needed for a fair test of an intervention is often greater than would be achieved in the average, nonresearch implementation environment, but less than what the authors of the intervention hoped for or envisioned. Some program designers have envisioned extended service plans for disadvantaged young people, for example, which have proved difficult to attain. In one voluntary program for young mothers receiving welfare, the program design called for a service sequence of up to one year with close to full-time involvement in education, job training, and other services, but the average length of time that participants were active in the program was about $6\frac{1}{2}$ months and their average attendance during the first (education) phase of the program was less than half-time (Quint, Fink, and Rowser 1991).

The key tasks of implementation researchers charged with determining whether a program or policy had a fair test by this criterion are to measure and describe the intensity, dose, and quality of the program or policy under study; calibrate them relative to the intervention designers' dictates, other interventions, or an independent standard to determine whether the program or policy achieved the threshold; and present a broader conclusion about "How much is enough?" of the intervention to expect change or, possibly, "How much is not enough?"

Some implementation researchers prefer not to take the risks associated with this judgment; they simply present the data on "how much" and participant opinions on "how good," leaving for the evaluation audience the judgment about adequacy for a fair test. Others prefer to stick to measures of participation by the targeted group or duration of exposure, avoiding the difficult questions of quality. Creating objective rating schemes for quality of service is the most difficult way to develop judgments of a fair test, and few studies have tried it.

Did the Program Produce a Real Service Difference?

A third implementation research question and another condition for a strong and useful impact analysis is this: *Did the program or policy produce real differences in the experience of the program and control or comparison groups?* Even if an impact study is carefully designed and monitored to assure that only the target group is reached, only the program group (not the control or comparison group) is getting the intervention, and the intervention is sufficiently available and powerful, the experiences of the control or comparison group members can determine whether the intervention produces impacts. This happens because impact analysis measures only the *difference* in outcomes for two groups of people, one exposed to a policy or provided a service and the other not exposed to that same policy or provided that same service. Impact analysis does not assume or assure that control or comparison group members partake of zero services or that they are unaffected by any other relevant policy. In the real world, people who do not get selected for an intervention sometimes search for and participate in other services and activities, and they make choices and changes in their lives, even if the intervention evaluation is designed to minimize assistance to them. The level of control or comparison group activity is the baseline above which an intervention must significantly increase program or policy "inputs" for the program group to expect a difference in measurable outcomes.

To determine whether there is a real difference in the experiences of the program groups and control or comparison groups, implementation researchers must document and measure who got what and who did what, whether initiated by the program under study or by the individuals in the study sample. If the intervention was designed to improve the income of the target group by teaching people in the program group how to look for work, for example, an implementation analysis would determine the proportion and characteristics of the program group members who participated in job search instruction offered under the intervention's auspices, and their hours of participation, as well as the proportion and characteristics of control or comparison group members who participated in any similar instruction offered by another service provider and their hours of participation. The analysis might further compare the experiences of the two groups based on observations of the types of job search instruction available in the locality of the intervention, focusing on any significant differences in the style, intensity, or quality of the instruction. Finally, implementation analysis in this case would determine the proportion and characteristics of both the program group members and control or comparison group members who found jobs on their own without any assistance.

One possible implementation story in this case is that the intervention achieved a high rate of participation in its job search workshops and the workshops were high energy, interesting, and apparently effective because most participants found jobs, but that such workshops had become ubiquitous in the locality and control or comparison group members were participating in workshops given by community colleges and adult schools that were similar to the intervention's workshops and at almost the same rate as the program group. In this event, the implementation analysis would conclude that there was little difference in the experience of the two groups.[4] If there were also no impacts or small impacts, this finding of a small difference in services might be the primary explanation.[5]

An intervention intended to affect the job search activity of a welfare program group by telling the individuals that they will lose their public assistance benefits unless they look for work necessitates a different kind of examination of program group and control or comparison group experiences. Whereas it would be essential to measure and document the job search activities of each group as well as any help they received with job search, the focus of the implementation analysis in this intervention would be the program's message: What were program group members actually told about job search and the consequences of not searching? When were they told? By whom? Under what circumstances? How many times? What did program group members understand about job search, the participation requirement, and the consequences of not searching? What did they hear? When? From whom? What did they think about the message and its meaning for them? Was there any awareness among control or comparison group members about the message? How did they hear the message? What did they understand? How did they think it might affect them in the present or in the future?[6]

The critical difference in the experiences of program and control or comparison group members that an implementation study would seek to identify in this case is their understanding of or belief about required job search and the consequences of not searching for work. If a high proportion of the program group members heard the message intended and believed in the consequences whereas few control or comparison group members either were aware of the requirement and the consequences or believed that it had anything to do with them in the present or the future, then the implementation analysis would conclude that the condition of difference existed for a valid impact evaluation. On the other hand, if few program group members understood the message accurately or few believed in the consequences, and the control or comparison group was similarly unreached, the implementation analysis would conclude that *on this dimension* there was no significant difference in experience.

In the case of an intervention that is dependent on the highly fallible outcome of human communication, implementation researchers might also explore whether the process of trying to send the intervention's message inadvertently created some other difference in experience between program group members and the control or comparison group's members. For example, the number of contacts between program staff and members of the two groups might have been significantly different, or a higher level of assistance with job search might have been available to the program group, regardless of whether they "got the message." If the intervention turned out to have impacts, implementation researchers would look to these other dimensions of difference between the experiences of the two groups to explain the impact findings.

Similar issues have arisen in studies of other types of welfare reforms. In studies of incentives to work and income support tied to full-time employment, a focus on sample members' understanding of new program services and requirements has also proven important. The research on the New Hope project in Milwaukee included a detailed examination of this issue (Brock et al. 1997). In studies of time limits on aid, research has focused on how recipients understand and interpret the message that aid will not continue indefinitely and on how they fashion a response (see, for example, Brown, Bloom, and Butler 1997).

What Explains the Impact Results?

The core task of implementation research conducted in the context of an impact study is to answer the question, Why did the evaluation produce the observed impact findings? Important collateral questions include these: If there were no impacts, what went wrong? If there were impacts, what caused them? If impacts varied by study site or subgroup, why?

This task seems straightforward but is, in fact, difficult for four reasons.

1. Explanations for the pattern of impact findings stand on shakier scientific ground than the basic impact estimates. Typically, such explanations are founded in correlations, not the firmer relationships that yield the basic impact estimates, for which there is a strong case for causality. Typically, also, there are competing explanations for impact findings, and isolating any one or a few explanations is often more art and judgment than science. Even when there are multiple sites, and variation is observed in the way sites implemented the intervention, and differences in site impacts are statistically significant, it remains difficult to isolate the reasons for impact findings, as will be discussed in more detail later in this chapter.[7] In the end, implementation researchers must usually settle for hypotheses—*potential* explanations. Thus, implementation

analysis in the context of an impact evaluation, perhaps more than other types of implementation analysis, must be grounded in relevant cumulative knowledge, which can provide a framework for developing hypotheses about the sources of the impact estimates. A fresh look at "what happened" is often useful, but interpretation of impact results that is innocent of prior attempts to achieve the same or similar ends is not.

2. Implementation analysis and impact analysis tend to merge in the process of explanation. In fact, when an impact study is being designed, when it is being carried out in the field, and when the results are being analyzed, an implementation-impact team is often created to examine all possible sources of the impact results. The broad questions posed above intentionally cover not only the possibility that something about the intervention explains the impact results, but that something about the evaluation conditions or evaluation design may also account for the results. In the role of explicator, the evaluator, or the evaluation team, examines the characteristics and experiences of the target group, the availability, quantity, and quality of the service or policy under study, the environment in which the program or policy was implemented, *and* the features of the evaluation that might have affected either the behavior of sample members or the direction or magnitude of the impact estimates. For example, one unhappy (but not rare) finding of impact/implementation analysis might be that the impact sample was not large enough to detect differences between program group and control or comparison group outcomes of the magnitude consistent with results of similar interventions evaluated in the past. The reason might be that the program or policy under study called for volunteers and the implementing organization could not generate enough targeted volunteers to meet the sample goal.

3. There is a time lag between the intervention events—targeted people participating in services or reached by a policy—and the final measure of their outcomes. Programs and policies change during the multiyear period of data collection and analysis that is typical for an impact evaluation. Often, an intervention is no longer operating when the final impact analysis is completed. This can occur through gradual reforms of public programs; it is common for agencies to respond to weak impact findings by asserting that the program studied has been improved. The scheduled end of

demonstration efforts also creates the time lag. A recent example is the New Hope demonstration. The program was closing up shop at the time the first impact findings were being released. The consequence is that descriptions of the intervention cannot be rechecked when something unexpected turns up in an impact analysis.

4. Finally, yet another source of difficulty is the near impossibility of revising the key elements of the evaluation design. Additional analysis of data collected on the individuals in the sample is possible. For example, if the implementation research suggests that the intervention implemented early in the evaluation period was substantially different from the later intervention, the sample might be divided into early and late cohorts for analysis (assuming that the sample was large enough for this). But the specific individuals who make up the study sample, the data collected about sample members at sample intake and about members' program- or policy-related activities, and data collected about sample members' experiences when they were exposed to the program or policy under study are forever fixed—for methodological as well as time-sensitive reasons.

The process of collecting these data—how they were defined, how they were reported and recorded—and sometimes the methods used to analyze them, become part of the raw material for explaining the results. The reason is that, in an impact study, evaluators usually cannot go back and collect data overlooked in the research design stage, for example, or change the data collection strategies if responses from sample members are inadequate in some way. In the unhappy example above, the conclusion of no detectable impacts might be explained as the *possible* result of a too-small sample, but this problem cannot be corrected after the fact. In the canon of interventions subjected to impact evaluation, the finding for the example program would have to remain that it produced no measurable impacts. Some might hold that the program or policy could be effective at some level or for some people and the inadequacy of the sample size just makes this impossible to specify. Nevertheless, no alternative reality of the program or policy is possible from the evaluator's perspective.

If explaining impacts is an uncertain science at present and methodologically challenging, how do implementation researchers go about it? They are guided by theory, by past evaluations of similar interventions or interventions with similar goals, by research on the populations targeted by the intervention under study, by intimate acquaintance with impact analysis, and by observation and interaction with the targeted people and the program staff who between them generate some of the changes that the impact analysis measures. The contributions to explanation of each of these guides are described below.

A THEORY OF IMPACTS AS A GUIDE TO EXPLANATION

Although impact estimates are based on differences between group averages, the underlying dynamic of social programs and social policy is that, in the face of a changed set of circumstances created by the program or policy, individual people will change their own behavior. Thus, the theory of how impacts might be produced in any social policy or program experiment must be founded specifically in the levers known to or reasonably expected to induce people to live their lives differently. Given what is known about the difficulty of changing certain work and self-sufficiency behaviors even when they are recognized as ineffective, and what is known about the determinants of economic status, inventing policy or programs that can lever significant change is an ambitious undertaking.[8] A theory of impacts that is an effective guide to implementation analysis must both fit the intent of the policy or program under evaluation *and* be grounded in the reality of how individuals change.

A theory of impacts must also specify the path by which anticipated changes are expected to occur. For example, a prominent theory of the 1970s and early 1980s about why some welfare recipients were staying on assistance for years instead of working was that they did not know how to find job openings and land jobs and that their own behavior in the job search process was often counterproductive.[9] Teach them about how the job market works, teach them how to make a good first impression, provide structure and support to boost motivation and persistence in looking for jobs, and welfare recipients could go to work, the theory went. The Job Club model (usually attributed to Nathan H. Azrin [see Mangum 1982, 62]) based on this theory has been a remarkably enduring welfare-to-work approach and the theory has proved predictive for many welfare recipients, although in the late 1980s and in the 1990s it was recognized that poverty and welfare dependence were not reduced as a result of welfare recipients *going to work*. Staying employed and earning enough to support a family modestly are problems that were not addressed by the theory.

Specifying the theoretical path from status quo to desired outcomes matters to the implementation researcher's ability to explain impacts because it provides clues about where to look for the explanations. If an intervention under study provided job search training for welfare recipients and nothing else by design, the implementation research would set out to confirm the underlying theory of impacts by determining

- the rate of participation in training workshops by the program group;
- the rate of participation in similar activities by control or comparison group members;
- what had actually been taught in the workshops;
- a measure of what workshop participants learned;
- what workshop activity looked like (how time was spent in workshops);
- a measure of the amount of time participants spent in workshops;
- a measure of job searching carried out by workshop participants and nonparticipants in the program group and by control or comparison group members;
- what program group members, including both workshop participants and nonparticipants, thought about the program, its goals, and changes made in their lives;
- conditions in the local labor market;
- features of the welfare benefit package that might influence recipients' choices about working; and
- availability of services needed to support working parents.

These types of information are directly related to the theory that job search skills make the difference for the target group. Positive significant impacts might be explained primarily by the theory if implementation research showed that some or all of the following conditions were present:

- There was a high rate of participation in training workshops by participants.
- The control or comparison group did not generally receive similar assistance.
- The workshop teaching and learning was focused on how to get interviews with prospective employers and how to perform in these interviews.
- Workshop participants generally spent their workshop time in the principal intended activities of learning, practicing, and trying to get interviews with prospective employers.

- The average amount of program participation was adequate to carry out the intended program activities.
- The members of the control or comparison group had a significantly lower rate of job search (as measured by employer contacts or interviews, for example) or received lower quality services than program group members.
- Program group members generally believed that they could work and could be helped by the program to find jobs.
- Neither the local labor market nor the welfare benefits package constituted a barrier to the program's success.
- Program participants were generally able to manage the child care, transportation, and other logistics of the change from unemployment to work.

The proposed theory would be ruled out as an explanation for significant positive impacts, however, if there were important gaps in the predicted path of impacts for this hypothetical job search intervention. For example, if workshop participation had been low, if participants spent their workshop time sleeping or socializing, or if participants got few interviews as a result of their workshop activities, positive impacts would have to be explained by something other than the *intended* intervention. Unintentionally, the program group might have experienced something that the control or comparison group did not and the unintended difference in experiences might explain the impacts. In this event, the implementation researcher would broaden the search for explanations by turning to other guides.

Ruling out explanations for impact results is a powerful role for implementation analysis. For example, a program that had no measurable impacts and was implemented as intended, based on the findings of implementation research, would need rethinking—particularly in its theory and delivery system. Good implementation research could shorten the search for explanations by eliminating as a cause shortcomings in the way the program or policy concept was translated into actual services or interventions for the targeted population.

If there were no measurable impacts of the hypothetical job search workshop program and the fair test criteria had been met ("good enough" implementation and a difference in program group and control or comparison group experiences), the implementation researcher would turn to the environment in which the program was implemented. Perhaps the job market had been flooded with unskilled or entry-level workers, or jobs for unskilled applicants were scarce. Perhaps there was no public transportation or there were few openings in after-school child care programs. Perhaps the average starting wages for entry-level work were so low that welfare recipients making the transition to work would not see a net income gain. Perhaps the working conditions in most of the jobs available for unskilled workers were extraordinarily difficult. Perhaps the predominant value of program group members was to be full-time caretakers for their children, regardless of the cost.

To be prepared for the case of no measurable impacts, the evaluation team—implementation researchers and impact analysts—need to have a plan in place that enables them to examine patterns of outcomes in detail. For example, the evaluators should answer questions such as these: Did program group members start jobs at a higher rate but stop working quickly? Behind the averages for the program group and the control or comparison group, was there a pattern of more people working and earning a little compared with a few people working and earning a lot? Were the characteristics of the program group members who worked similar to or different from those of the control or comparison group members who worked?

The Evaluation Record of Similar Interventions and Related Research on the Targeted Population As a Guide to Explanation

In impact evaluations, researchers cannot rely solely on the event path embedded in a particular theory of impacts. Some of the most important clues for an explanation as well as guides for judging the adequacy of implementation for a fair test come from previous interventions. Examples of the accumulated knowledge that can inform the search for explanations for observed impacts, in highly condensed and simplified form, include these:

- Job development and/or a "growth" job market are essential elements of the most successful job search programs.
- Taking people out of the labor market to involve them in a poorly run program offering weak services can produce negative impacts.
- In a good labor market, the welfare recipients likely to be involved in a welfare-to-work program have more barriers to work than those involved when the labor market is oversupplied.

- It is difficult to preselect welfare recipients who will succeed at entering the labor market because personal circumstances are the most important barrier to work for this population and these are difficult to predict.
- Poor people, especially poor mothers, experience a lot of disruptions in the kind of daily routine needed to participate in education or training programs, or to work.
- Control or comparison group use of services can be high.
- The labor market experiences of men and women—at the low end of the market, especially—are different enough to suggest separate analyses.
- It is possible for people to put in the expected "seat time" in an adult education program but not make significant competence gains.
- Participation in the best programs—especially voluntary programs—never approaches 100 percent.
- Welfare recipients supplement their public assistance income in various ways to make ends meet, so officially reported income does not tell the whole story about work incentives.
- There are different outcomes for sequenced versus simultaneous service designs.

Using such lessons from previous studies, implementation researchers can build contingencies into their plans for data collection and analysis as well as construct thresholds of "good enough" program implementation to apply the fair test criteria. For example, consider a welfare reform intervention introduced in the context of time limits that targeted older mothers who had been out of the labor market for many years and whose first language was not English. The intervention is designed to first help the participants improve their English language skills in a classroom setting and then, after they are speaking and writing English at a specified competence level, provide job search assistance. In the absence of guides from past interventions and research, the implementation research conducted for an impact study of this welfare-to-work intervention might focus on the amount of time the women spent in the classroom and the apparent quality of the teaching, the rate at which they moved on to job search in the service sequence and the characteristics of those who did and did not progress in this way, their in-program educational achievements, and the amount and quality of the job search assistance.

This approach to implementation research may miss the story of the intervention. Evaluations of past interventions suggest that movement from English language instruction to job search via a competence test might be infrequent for the targeted group (Pauly 1995). To capture the complete story here, the implementation research might be expanded to include an examination of the previous English language training experiences of the targeted group (using their first languages for any interviewing) as well as their attitudes and beliefs about work and welfare, home situations, future plans, and alternative means of support to try to understand why they would or would not benefit from the intervention.

If there were a finding of positive impacts, it would be important to explain how this intervention differed from similar programs evaluated in the past—an explanation that might depend on a new factor in the intervention, such as time limits on welfare receipt; or on the personal circumstances, attitudes, and beliefs of the mothers; the attitudes, efforts, and messages of the program staff; the quality of the English language instruction; or some of each. If there were no impacts, the implementation researchers would be prepared to look in the areas where past interventions have hypothesized the reasons lie. For example, a large proportion of the women may believe that time limits on public assistance will not affect them or they may not want to face the coming change. Some may report that they plan to return to their birth countries or go live with their adult children; some may have teenagers at home whom they wish to continue to supervise after school; some may attend English classes for the social benefits but learn little; some may believe that learning English is impossible for them. In other words, the explanation of impact findings in this case may be a complicated story of cultural and social change, rather than a simple story about welfare-to-work policies and programs.

Research findings about the targeted population are useful guides, too. In addition to the extensive body of research on the causes and consequences of poverty, much is known about the skills, behaviors, life events, and beliefs of some groups of low-income people. So, for example, because a large proportion of female welfare recipients report having been adult victims of domestic violence or childhood victims of physical, emotional, or sexual abuse, implementation research to explain impact findings of any intervention targeted to welfare recipients might entail connecting victim-related behaviors to outcomes. For victims, fears and feelings of unworthiness may have a stronger effect on work behavior than a welfare-to-work intervention, even one with significant financial incentives.

THE THEORIES, METHODS, AND QUIRKS OF IMPACT ANALYSIS: OTHER SOURCES OF EXPLANATION

As noted above, impact results can be driven either by the performance of the intervention being tested or by the methods used to measure such performance. Implementation researchers must have detailed knowledge of how impacts were estimated to fill out their inquiry of what caused an impact finding. The most important areas of impact analysis for this inquiry are these:

- *How the impact sample was drawn.*
  This might suggest something about who is in the sample that cannot be established by analyzing baseline characteristics, especially sample members' interest, motivation, and awareness about the intervention.
- *The size of the impact sample and its implications for the evaluators' ability to determine significance.*
  This is a central concern of impact evaluators at both the design and the analysis stages of a study. If the impact researchers are not going to be able to detect policy-relevant impacts because the sample size is too small, the scope and importance of implementation research, as well as its focus, may be affected. Some studies with these methodological problems might be revised to emphasize what can be learned through implementation research, particularly whether the targeted group was receiving the intended service or treatment at the intended level.
- *The point of random assignment (in an experimental design).*
  In a sequence of pre-program events or activities, the point at which individuals enter the impact sample has important implications for the readiness of program group members to participate in services, the likelihood that they will participate, and the nature and amount of services received by the control group.
- *Analysis issues raised by testing an intervention in multiple sites.*
  Implementation research can contribute to the decision about whether it is appropriate to pool samples across sites based on the type and degree of sites' common elements, or whether analysis must be done site by site.

THE PERSPECTIVES OF PROGRAM STAFF AND
TARGET GROUP MEMBERS ON PROGRAM IMPACTS

The ideas that policymakers and program designers have about how to affect the behavior of the target group are not always consistent with what target group members and frontline program staff say. To cover all contingencies and be prepared to explain impacts, implementation researchers must know what the people most closely involved think about the prospects for an intervention. It is common to conduct structured interviews, focus groups, and surveys with two groups: staff implementing the intervention under study, and participants and those who have either chosen not to participate or been unable to access program services. This type of systematic data collection can illuminate differences in the intervention across sites or over time. Implementation researchers also often engage in informal discussions with staff and participants to bounce ideas off them about program implementation and effects and to develop hypotheses about why the program is operated as it is.[10]

LEARNING FROM SITE VARIATION IN IMPLEMENTATION AND IMPACTS

In multisite evaluations, program implementation and impacts almost always vary across the sites. This presents an opportunity to investigate the links between particular contextual conditions and implementation practices, and site-level impacts—a useful tactic that has not been without problems and controversies. A first step, often overlooked, is to determine whether the observed site differences in impacts are, in fact, statistically significant. In testing a program in multiple places, purely random variation can produce site differences. Thus, it is important to determine whether the observed site differences are large enough to be unlikely to have emerged by chance. If this threshold test is passed, there are still complexities.

One fundamental problem is that there are often many more ways in which the sites differ (in program implementation, participant characteristics, and context) than there are sites. When researchers try to test hypotheses about the source of site variation in impacts using statistical methods, they usually run up against a problem of limited degrees of freedom in the statistical models. In this case, the degrees of freedom are defined as the number of sites minus one—so, for example, in a six-site study, only five possible explanations for impacts can be tested statistically.

Aggregating findings across studies is one way to increase the degrees of freedom for a multisite analysis. One ongoing effort that has taken this approach seeks to explore how public management approaches and governance practices affect program outcomes and effectiveness. This project aggregates findings across several welfare reform impact studies to create many more sites (observations) than would be available in a single study. Data about context and implementation practice are collected in a similar way across these studies, making it possible to construct statistical models to estimate the influence of management practices and local conditions on site impacts.[11]

A second complication in learning from site variation arises out of the dictates of classical statistical theory. Traditional statistical analysis requires an analyst to specify the hypotheses to be tested before observing the data on which the hypotheses will be tested. In the context of explaining site impacts, this means that the analyst "only gets one shot" at using the data for tests of the source of site differences. If the initial test of hypotheses specified in advance does not identify links between context and implementation practices and site impacts, that is all the hypothesis-testing possible with those data. According to classical statistical theory, if one then goes back into the data and finds some relationship not previously anticipated and tested, this is not a finding proved by the data; instead, it is only a hypothesis to be tested on other data. Implementation researchers vary greatly in their enthusiasm for and fidelity to this classical statistical model.[12]

How Can Successful Interventions Be Replicated?

The final major question addressed by implementation research in the context of an impact study is this: *What* further *information does implementation research have to provide to enable others to replicate a successful intervention?* The audience for this information is practitioners—the program designers, managers, and administrators who turn social policy goals into the infrastructure and organizations needed to change the behavior of individual targeted people. Their concerns are a more concrete version of the explanations for impacts that are of interest to policymakers. Those who would replicate a successful intervention need to know first whether its impacts result from the power of the intervention's treatment, or from a low level of similar services or policies available in the site locations, as measured by those reaching the control or comparison groups, or from conditions of the environment (and which ones). Then, if conditions in the practitioners' environments are propitious, they need to know specifically what the treatment consisted of and the mechanisms and tools used to get the quantity and quality of the treatment to targeted individuals. Thus, among further subjects for inquiry to inform a replication effort are staffing, governance, facilities and equipment, information systems, marketing, and financing.

STAFFING

Staffing patterns are of interest in most social policy interventions because person-to-person interaction is often a primary mechanism to accomplish the steps leading to behavior change in individual targeted people.[13] Key questions about staffing are these: How many staff per targeted person were employed in what positions? What were their qualifications, skills, and training, and their attitudes about the intervention and the targeted group? What were the main sources of staff and what was the process for selecting them to work in the intervention program? What salaries, benefits, and other inducements did they receive? What were their terms of employment in the intervention program—for example, were the jobs permanent or temporary, could the staff choose to return to their previous jobs, did they receive performance bonuses, and, if so, what were the terms of these? What changes in staffing occurred over the course of the intervention's test? (These questions supplement the inquiry necessary to determine whether the intervention had a fair test and to explain the results of the impact analysis; for those purposes, implementation research will already have undertaken the task of documenting what the intervention staff actually did.)

A practitioner seeking to replicate a successful intervention may not be able to match all of these staffing conditions. However, detailed information about the conditions provides a basis to judge what an equivalent or closely approximate staffing configuration might look like in the practitioner's circumstances. In particular, it tells the replicating practitioner whether the staffing of the successful intervention was unusual for the type of program or policy implementation and, therefore, likely to contribute to its success. For example, if a successful welfare reform intervention was staffed in a selective process with master's-level people who were paid $10,000 a year more than staff in similar positions and they had the potential to earn performance bonuses, and the program had a staff-to-recipient ratio of 1:25, the practitioner would conclude that attempting replication with a typical staffing configuration for welfare-to-work programs would risk the success that was the point of the replication effort.

GOVERNANCE

Governance is an area where much implementation research has been focused, in part because the field is dominated by political scientists and sociologists, who tend to see implementation as affected primarily by a set of relationships among institutions, their constituents, and their component parts or levels. In this view, broadly speaking, the idea for an intervention would be mediated through these relationships and take its final form based on formal and informal controls, power, discretion, and technical expertise exercised by the relevant players. In particular, investigators of the process of implementation of public policy have focused on command structures, differing incentives within different parts of the public policy implementation systems, and ambiguity or clarity of the original policy intent.[14]

The degree to which governance affects implementation performance and, in turn, the success or failure of a social intervention, is an open question, but practitioners seeking to replicate good performance need to know about the governance structures, arrangements, understandings, and practices of the model intervention to avoid identifiable governance barriers to implementation. This is an area of implementation research in which the study of site variation has been particularly fruitful because in the same intervention, different site governance structures and practices may be found to vary in a pattern that fits variation in site performance or impacts. In turn, this fact leads researchers to hypothesize a cause-and-effect relationship between governance and performance and give the practitioners examples of governance within the same intervention context both to emulate and to avoid (see Lynn, Heinrich, and Hill 1999; Riccio, Friedlander, and Freedman 1994; and Riccio et al. 1999).

The basic questions for implementation research on governance are these: Which institutions and organizations were involved in the intervention, what were their roles and responsibilities, and what were the formal and informal ways in which they related to each other? How did these structures and relationships facilitate or impede implementation of the intervention? Who were the major decisionmakers, what were their positions in these structures, and how did their beliefs, goals, and actions shape the intervention, from conception through design, negotiation, implementation, and management? Detailed questions about a specific intervention include these:

- Was there a designated lead agency, a collaboration of partners, or some other structure for making the intervention happen?

- How were funds for the intervention distributed, on what basis, and through what mechanisms?
- How and on what basis was it determined which partners or departments or units would be responsible for which intervention functions?
- How did the involved players communicate with one another and what did they communicate about?
- How and by whom were standards for performance set and monitored?
- How and by whom was it determined what the intervention's staffing configuration, compensation, training, and supervision would be?
- How were staff hired and fired and on what basis?
- What were the areas of discretion for staff, supervisors, managers, partner organization heads, department or unit heads, and others involved in implementation?
- What were the "styles" of management in each partner organization, department, or unit and at each level of these, from frontline staff to chief—for example, directive, participatory, rule-based, information-based, exception-based?
- What changes in governance or organizational culture in each of the players' organizations were undertaken to implement the intervention?
- What changes actually occurred in each instance?

Management and organizational behavior theory and empirical research on governance, as they apply to the multipartner, public/private/nonprofit organizational partnerships that are characteristic of social policy interventions, offer only bits and pieces of guidance to the practitioner who would replicate a successful intervention. Thus, the value of answers to the detailed questions above is not always to enable the practitioner to replicate the governance of a successful intervention. Rather, these answers are sometimes the necessary foundation for the implementation researcher to identify problematic governance structures, arrangements, and practices that practitioners should avoid. (They may also aid theory building in implementation research.) An example of implementation research that serves both purposes is an examination of performance-based contracting as a governance practice of a successful intervention in which varying methods of setting the performance goals are documented. The research might reveal that in one site, the methods seemed to lead to acrimonious or resentful relationships between the parties and seemed to slow down implementation whereas methods adopted in another site appeared to cement cooperation and speed up implementation.

FACILITIES AND EQUIPMENT

With the exception of management information systems discussed below, social programs are notoriously low tech, and implementation research has rarely described facilities and equipment in ways that are useful to program operators or looked in this area for aids to performance. Attractive facilities or high-tech equipment are noted because they are unusual. Practitioners often elevate the importance of these, however, in the belief that better-than-the-norm surroundings for staff and clients in a social program convey a message that these people are important, which might improve job satisfaction for the staff and participation and/or compliance among clients. At a minimum, practitioners seeking to replicate a successful intervention would need to know whether there were any facilities and equipment essential to getting the treatment or service to the targeted group—for example, transportation or communications media in rural areas, networked computers in a multisite intervention, or video machines for job search clients to practice interviewing in job search workshops.

INFORMATION SYSTEMS

Computer-based information systems are essential to managing social programs and policies and the subject of much discussion among practitioners outside the sphere of implementation research. We believe that practitioners seeking to replicate a successful intervention need to know whether the information systems used in the intervention had features particularly suited to the specific governance structure, services, staffing configuration or staff makeup, or scale of the intervention. But we do not believe that implementation research conducted in the context of an impact study is the best vehicle for transferring knowledge about how to design and install these systems from one practitioner to another—mainly because the transfer is best accomplished by hands-on work in which a potential replicator can see an MIS (management information system) in operation and see samples of output as well as read about how it works, but also because the detail required to describe such systems can overwhelm and discourage the general reader of implementation literature who is looking for lessons to apply to his or her program and practice.

MARKETING

Marketing techniques and messages are an underappreciated aspect of the performance of social interventions. Social programs or policies are "marketed" not just to potential participants, but to staff, partner organizations, elected officials, the public at large, potential funders, and a host of individuals and institutions whose cooperation, support, or both is needed to pull off a new intervention. Who constitutes the audience and who is the marketer depends on where the idea originates. To be helpful to practitioners seeking to replicate a successful intervention, implementation research must document the messages, the media, and the inducements used to persuade all the stakeholders to participate in the desired ways. Of particular interest to practitioners are the messages, media, and inducements that seemed to work in situations of expected conflict or resistance—for example, across organizational boundaries, when the benefits of participation were not obvious, or when significant changes in personal behavior or beliefs were entailed.

FINANCING

In an impact study, the question of financing is often considered only in the context of a benefit-cost study—a type of analysis that sometimes, but not always, follows estimation of impacts. In the benefit-cost framework, "net costs" per targeted participant—that is, the difference between those incurred on behalf of the program group in an impact sample and those incurred on behalf of a control or comparison group—are the standard measure. Sometimes these are computed per component or program function as well. Net costs, however, are not useful to practitioners interested in building and budgeting an intervention from a starting point of zero. Practitioners usually need to know the total costs of implementing each separate component (or function) of an intervention in standard line-item budgeting categories and the potential sources of variation in costs. In an oversimplified example, a successful welfare reform intervention that included job search assistance for 75 percent of the target group annually, community service jobs for 30 percent annually, child care assistance for 80 percent annually, and a major saturation strategy that called for 80 percent to be involved in work activities at a specified level every month would suggest the need for the following set of cost figures for practitioners to replicate it:

- The cost per actual participant in the job search assistance component to run the component, including all "in-workshop" expenses for personnel, facilities, equipment, consumable supplies, and expense payments to participants, and including the costs of tracking in-workshop attendance and activities, but excluding all costs of getting participants to the workshop and following up on dropouts or those who were supposed to attend but did not.
- The cost per actual participant in the community service jobs component to run the component, including all personnel and other than personnel costs to recruit employers, place participants at worksites, monitor participants and worksites, help participants find regular jobs, and track and report on all in-component attendance and activities, but excluding the costs of following up on dropouts or those who were supposed to attend but did not.
- The cost per targeted person (personnel and other than personnel costs) to implement the saturation strategy—that is, to do all the program's marketing, participant recruitment, enrollment, assessment, assignment, communication with no-shows and dropouts, enforcement of sanctions, and tracking and reporting on program-wide participation and status.
- The cost per user of child care assistance to assess eligibility, need, or both; make the payments, arrangements, or both; monitor the connection between program participation and eligibility for child care assistance; license, register, or monitor the providers; and track and report on the use of child care assistance.

With these cost figures, practitioners can estimate their own financial needs for a replication based on the program scale they plan to achieve and their known personnel and other costs (taking into account the qualifications of the intervention staff and any unusual features of facilities, equipment, etc.). Important sources of variation for an implementation analysis to include might be whether existing facilities were used in the intervention or new facilities had to be built, leased, or rented; the availability and labor market for the staff hired for the intervention; and the market for child care in the intervention location. Practitioners are also typically interested in funding sources, particularly the way different sources with different purposes, requirements, and restrictions can be put together to create an affordable and manageable program. Thus, implementation analysis that facilitates replication should detail the sources and features of funding in an impact study intervention.[15]

Implications of Answers to the Key Questions
for Implementation Research Methodology

This chapter began by arguing that the primary goal of implementation research in the context of an impact study is to explain the impact findings. Although there are many complexities to that task and additional questions are often addressed, this explanatory goal heavily influences the research methods and data collection strategies used. It also places a premium on planning: Data must be specified and collected *in anticipation* of a host of impact results, both positive and negative.

One of the most important effects of the explanatory goal on implementation research methodology is the focus on the relationship between the intervention and the individual. Because impacts are derived from changes in individuals' behavior, there is often an effort to find ways to attach measures of an intervention's context, its characteristics, and service implementation to individuals in the research sample. The program measures, together with the numerous measures of individual background characteristics and program participation typically collected in impact studies, enable analysts to define many different subgroups of the research sample in an effort to identify people for whom the intervention worked more and less well. Variation in an intervention's effects—whether this occurs on the basis of characteristics of individuals in the sample or characteristics of the intervention—is the richest mine of explanations for impact results. For multisite studies, individual sample members are also linked to specific sites to enable researchers to examine variation in impacts across sites. If contextual conditions or program offerings change over time, analysts move beyond site designations (presumed to represent differences in context and services) and also designate the time period during which each individual sample member was served.

The goal of explaining impact results also drives this type of implementation research toward quantitative measures that are continuous, rather than categorical, variables. The use of staff and participant surveys to develop indices of implementation practice at the site level, instead of treating sites as undifferentiated bundles of attributes, is an example of this research strategy. In the welfare-to-work field, researchers have developed rankings of staff's emphasis on various program goals or of participants' perceptions of their obligations while receiving public assistance, which are then used to group similar sites and to distribute sites along key implementation dimensions. These are the initial steps in connecting site variations in implementation to site variations in impacts.

Program participation—usually considered a subject of implementation research—is often a key variable in impact analysis and, therefore, is quantified, often using continuous measures, and identified with individual research sample members. For example, impact analysts may want to determine the relationship between the "dosage" of program services and impacts, which requires person-specific measures of participation, such as hours of attendance in program components.

The goal of describing and characterizing the service difference produced by the program or intervention—necessary to determining whether the program or intervention got a fair test—also has implications for data collection. The current "best practice" standard, based on hard lessons learned in several major evaluations, is to use identical measures and data collection methods for the program group and control or comparison group. The lessons come from some studies in the poverty field in which researchers used program tracking data from a local management information system (MIS) to measure participation in the program under study (by far the best measure of program activity) and then used surveys for measuring participation in all other programs by both the program and the comparison group. This mixing of data collection methods has not worked well because it has proven virtually impossible to design survey questions that prompt program group members to accurately distinguish between services received from the program under study and services received from other sources.[16] As a result, it has been difficult to get an accurate measure of the total difference in services between the two groups using mixed-mode data collection strategies. Now, surveys are typically used to collect all program participation data for impact analysis, but there is also the option of tracking down MIS records from all, or almost all, possible local programs of a similar nature and using this source exclusively for both the program and control or comparison groups.

Although individualized (person-identified) quantitative measures of program implementation dominate implementation research in the context of an impact study, there is clearly a role for qualitative data. Field research (observation of services, interviews with staff, etc.) plays an important role in assessing the reasonableness of the underlying program theory, deciding whether program services were of sufficient quality to produce a fair test, and developing lessons for replication. Ethnographic research can play a unique role in impact studies if it is done early in the project and used to develop hypotheses that are investigated further through subsequent quantitative work. In addition, ethnographic research is useful in understanding how program services are understood and experienced by participants and those who chose not to participate (see, for example, Furstenberg, Sherwood, and Sullivan 1992; Johnson, Levine, and Doolittle 1999; and Quint et al. 1999).

Finally, as many of the new welfare reforms lead to a move away from random assignment studies (which provide a relatively clear-cut answer to certain types of questions) to a variety of nonexperimental methods for estimating program impacts, implementation research will become a more important source of answers about program effects. Because non-experimental methods have a greater potential for selection bias than experimental methods, it will be important to surround key research questions by using multiple analytic methods. For example, a careful look through the implementation research lens at whether the underlying theory of change embedded in a program actually played out can contribute much to the assessment of program impacts.[17]

Managing Time Sensitivity and Multiple-Site Problems

In this section, we return to two themes introduced early in the chapter: the desire or even demand of administrators and policymakers for early feedback on program operations, and the complexity of using site differences to understand the influences on program impacts. With the previous material as background, we offer our reflections on how to balance the competing demands in these two areas.

The evaluation literature encompasses theories and models that offer widely varying solutions to the problems and needs of people "on the ground." Summative, formative, action, and empowerment evaluation proponents, the classical experimenters, the nonexperimental statisticians, the practitioners of quantitative and qualitative methodologies and their disciplinary variations are more or less attached to objectivity, independence, confidence in the findings, steady-state program environments, confidentiality, trust, the customer, the knowledge base, and other concepts that bear on whether to provide early feedback on evaluation research to the people making decisions about the program or intervention being evaluated (see Patton 1990; Shadish, Cook, and Leviton 1991). The framework this chapter proposes implies a clear answer to the issue of early feedback, whether it is considered formative or something else. In our view, the goal of impact research is to provide a fair test of the effects of a program or policy. Thus, if researchers learn through implementation research about ways in which the test could be made fairer, that information should be conveyed to people who can improve the test early in the evaluation, the sooner the better. We discussed three broad dimensions of a fair test—the target group was reached, the treatment was adequately available, and the treatment was of adequate intensity, dose, or quality. These imply that the evaluator could provide early feedback on a variety of program operation topics.

On multiple sites, our sense is that in any single study with relatively few sites, conflict between the classical statistical model and careful reflection on possible causes of variation in site impacts may not be important because neither method is likely to produce conclusive evidence for a strong link between context, practice, and impacts. We expect real learning about these relationships to emerge through the process of building up a series of consistent findings. The effort to aggregate across studies, develop consistent measures of program and context, and perform statistical analyses to test relationships holds promise for insights. However, this approach depends vitally on the nature of the site descriptive variables available for the analysis, so continued work to refine them and include more measures of the quantity and quality of services is necessary.

Conclusion

Implementation research in the context of an impact study demands an extraordinary amount of forethought. Once the members of the impact study research sample receive services, the opportunity to capture good information on their experiences has usually passed. It often proves difficult to adjust an impact study as interesting findings emerge. The movement from the specific to the general (inductive research), which might be laudable in other types of implementation research, does not work well in the tightly coupled design of an impact study with implementation research. The sources for an implementation research design in this context are often existing research findings about similar programs and the theory of change articulated about the program under study. Rarely is there time to develop the research design as you go.

Impact-related implementation research appears to be moving in opposite directions simultaneously. On one hand, there is a move to quantify, tighten the linkages with the impact analysis (through similar data collection techniques and analytic methods), and develop larger samples through aggregation across studies. On the other hand, ethnographic work is becoming more accepted and is now used more frequently to generate hypotheses testable in an intervention and to explain impact research results. Both directions seem useful given the current paucity of findings connecting implementation practices to impacts, and given the need for multiple research methods to strengthen evaluations employing nonexperimental impact estimation techniques.

We conclude with an appeal to researchers doing impact-related implementation research to stay grounded in what is known about how people change their behavior, the kinds of services or policies likely to produce such change, and the task of looking at the extent, nature, and quality of opportunities that interventions under study provide for potentially transformative interactions between staff and participants and between participants and their larger environment. Because this is where we believe impacts are born, mastering these interactions (being present at their creation) would be a major contribution to future research.

NOTES

1. We use the term *control group* to refer to the research group created through random assignment in an experimental study that represents the "world without the program"; *comparison group* refers to the group serving a similar function in a non-experimental study whose members are not randomly selected.

2. Authors of other chapters in this volume identify description as a key task of implementation research as well. We treat description as necessary for this special type of implementation research to succeed at explanation.

3. Policies that are highly visible or controversial might merit an impact evaluation even if the evaluators do not believe their underlying theories to be plausible.

4. As discussed further below, it is critical for an accurate measure of service differences that the same data sources are used to measure the program group's use of services and the control or comparison group's use of services.

5. One of the problems the New Chance Demonstration encountered was an unexpectedly high level of services for the control group and lower than desired participation in program services for the program group. This no doubt contributed to the finding of no impacts on many key outcomes. (See Quint et al. 1994.)

6. In the Abt Associates study of the Indiana welfare reform program, researchers sought to understand what the program and control group members heard about the various new requirements and offered recommendations to clarify the treatment difference between the two groups. (See Fein et al. 1997.)

7. For a discussion of the difficulty of explaining site variation in impacts, see Orr (1999).

8. Mainstream social science, especially poverty research, has emphasized the importance of parents' income and education on the well-being and eventual economic success of children. See, for example, Haveman and Wolfe (1994) and Duncan and Brooks-Gunn (1997). Some poverty research challenges the importance of parental income while still finding the major determinants of the eventual economic success of children in parental characteristics and behaviors. See, for example, Mayer (1997). Michael Lewis (1999) seeks to overturn the influence of developmental theory—that is, present behavior is best explained by the past—on social policy, and replace it with a theory of "behavior in context," which calls for better care, not cures, as the objective of social interventions. His is not the mainstream view, however. A recent psychoanalytic investigation of work problems reinforces the developmental view as it relates to adult work behavior. See Axelrod (1999).

9. For a comprehensive review of the theoretical roots of job search programs, see Mangum (1982).

10. In the Parents' Fair Share Demonstration, for example, a field researcher remained in contact with over 30 parents for several years, engaging in wide-ranging conversations about program services, the local context, and the parents' lives outside of the program (Johnson, Levine, and Doolittle 1999).

11. See two papers prepared for a Workshop on Models and Methods for the Empirical Study of Governance and Public Management, the University of Arizona, April 29–May 1, 1999: (1) Riccio et al. (1999) and (2) Lynn, Heinrich, and Hill (1999).

12. The variety is illustrated by contrasting the analysis done in the National JTPA Study with that done in the evaluation of California's GAIN program. See Orr et al. (1995) and Riccio, Friedlander, and Freedman (1994).

13. Personalized attention and trusting relationships between staff and clients are two of the management practices being tested in the work by the MDRC team of Riccio, Bloom, Orenstein, and Small (1999) and the University of Chicago team of Lynn, Heinrich, and Hill (1999). Fostering caring relationships between adults and young people is also one of the principles of much youth development theory. See, for example, Public/Private Ventures (1993), and Gambone and Arbreton (1997).

14. For reviews of the theoretical policy implementation literature, see Brock (1992); Matland (1995); and Mazmanian and Sabatier (1989, chapters 1 and 2).

15. For a detailed description of cost analysis that can be helpful to practitioners of welfare reform, see Greenberg and Appenzeller (1998).

16. This problem was most extreme in the National JTPA Study because, in many respects, JTPA was a funding source rather than a source of a particular kind of service.

17. For elaboration of evaluation strategies based on theories of change, see the series of reports from the Aspen Institute Roundtable on Comprehensive Community Initiatives for Children and Families, including Connell et al. (1995) and Fulbright-Anderson, Kubisch, and Connell (1997, 1998).

REFERENCES

Axelrod, Steven D. 1999. *Work and the Evolving Self: Theoretical and Clinical Considerations.* Hillsdale, N.J.: Analytic Press.

Brock, Thomas Wayne. 1992. "The Implementation of Welfare Reform: Policy and Organizational Effects on Service Delivery in Los Angeles County." Ph.D. diss., University of California at Los Angeles.

Brock, Thomas, Fred Doolittle, Veronica Fellerath, and Michael Wiseman. 1997. *Creating New Hope: Implementation of a Program to Reduce Poverty and Reform Welfare.* New York: Manpower Demonstration Research Corporation.

Brown, Amy, Dan Bloom, and David Butler. 1997. *The View from the Field: As Time Limits Approach, Welfare Recipients and Staff Talk about Their Attitudes and Expectations.* New York: Manpower Demonstration Research Corporation.

Burghardt, John, Anu Rangarajan, Anne Gordon, and Ellen Kisker. 1992. *Evaluation of the Minority Female Single Parent Demonstration: Volume I: Summary Report.* Princeton, N.J.: Mathematica Policy Research.

Cave, George, Hans Bos, Fred Doolittle, and Cyril Toussaint. 1993. *JOBSTART: Final Report on a Program for School Dropouts.* New York: Manpower Demonstration Research Corporation.

Connell, James P., Anne C. Kubisch, Lisbeth B. Schorr, and Carol H. Weiss, eds. 1995. *New Approaches to Evaluating Community Initiatives. Volume I: Concepts, Methods, and Contexts.* Queenstown, Md.: Aspen Institute.

Duncan, Greg J., and Jeanne Brooks-Gunn, eds. 1997. *Consequences of Growing Up Poor.* New York: Russell Sage Foundation.

Fein, David, Erik Beecroft, Jennifer Karweit, Pamela Holcomb, Sandra Clark, Carolyn O'Brian, and Caroline Ratcliffe. 1997. *The Indiana Welfare Reform Evaluation: Assessing Program Implementation and Early Impacts on Cash Assistance.* Cambridge, Mass.: Abt Associates.

Fulbright-Anderson, Karen, Anne C. Kubisch, and James P. Connell, eds. 1997. *Voices from the Field: Learning from the Early Work of Comprehensive Community Initiatives.* Queenstown, Md.: Aspen Institute.

———.1998. *New Approaches to Evaluating Community Initiatives. Volume II: Theory, Measurement, and Analysis.* Queenstown, Md.: Aspen Institute.

Furstenberg, Frank F., Jr., Kay E. Sherwood, and Mercer L. Sullivan. 1992. *Caring and Paying: What Fathers and Mothers Say about Child Support.* New York: Manpower Demonstration Research Corporation.

Gambone, Michelle Alberti, and Amy J. A. Arbreton.1997. *Safe Havens: The Contributions of Youth Organizations to Healthy Adolescent Development.* Philadelphia, Pa.: Public/Private Ventures.

Greenberg, David H., and Ute Appenzeller. 1998. *Cost Analysis Step by Step: A How-to Guide for Planners and Providers of Welfare-to-Work and Other Employment and Training Programs.* New York: Manpower Demonstration Research Corporation.

Haveman, Robert, and Barbara Wolfe. 1994. *Succeeding Generations: On the Effects of Investments in Children.* New York: Russell Sage Foundation.

Johnson, Earl S., Ann Levine, and Fred C. Doolittle. 1999. *Fathers' Fair Share.* New York: Russell Sage Foundation.

Lewis, Michael. 1999. *Altering Fate: Why the Past Does Not Predict the Future.* New York: Guilford Press.

Lynn, Laurence E., Jr., Carolyn J. Heinrich, and Carolyn J. Hill. 1999. "The Empirical Study of Governance: Theories, Models, and Methods." Paper presented at a Workshop on Models and Methods for the Empirical Study of Governance and Public Management, University of Arizona, April 29–May 1.

Mangum, Stephen L. 1982. *Job Search: A Review of the Literature*. Salt Lake City, Utah: Olympus Research Centers (for the U.S. Department of Labor), Feb. 1.

Matland, Richard E. 1995. "Synthesizing the Implementation Literature: The Ambiguity-Conflict Model of Policy Implementation." *Journal of Public Administration Research and Theory* 5(2):145–74.

Mayer, Susan E. 1997. *What Money Can't Buy: Family Income and Children's Life Chances*. Cambridge, Mass.: Harvard University Press.

Mazmanian, Daniel A., and Paul A. Sabatier. 1989. *Implementation and Public Policy*. Lanham, Md.: University Press of America, chapters 1 and 2 (Originally published by Scott, Foresman and Company, 1983).

Orr, Larry. 1999. *Social Experiments: Evaluating Public Programs with Experimental Methods*. Thousand Oaks, Calif.: Sage Publications.

Orr, Larry L., Howard S. Bloom, Stephen H. Bell, Fred Doolittle, Winston Lin, and George Cave. 1995. *Does Training for the Disadvantaged Work? Evidence from the National JTPA Study*. Washington, D.C.: Urban Institute Press.

Patton, Michael Quinn. 1990. *Qualitative Evaluation and Research Methods*. Newbury Park, Calif.: Sage Publications.

Pauly, Edward, with Cristina DiMeo. 1995. *The JOBS Evaluation. Adult Education for People on AFDC: A Synthesis of Research*. Washington, D.C.: U.S. Department of Health and Human Services.

Public/Private Ventures. 1993. "Community Change for Youth Development: Establishing Long-Term Supports in Communities for the Growth and Development of Young People. A Concept Paper." Philadelphia, Pa.: Public/Private Ventures.

Quint, Janet, Barbara Fink, and Sharon Rowser. 1991. *New Chance: Implementing a Comprehensive Program for Disadvantaged Young Mothers and Their Children*. New York: Manpower Demonstration Research Corporation.

Quint, Janet, Denise F. Polit, Hans Bos, and George Cave. 1994. *New Chance: Interim Findings on a Comprehensive Program for Disadvantaged Young Mothers and Their Children*. New York: Manpower Demonstration Research Corporation.

Quint, Janet, Kathryn Edin, Maria L. Buck, Barbara Fink, Yolanda C. Padilla, Olis Simmons-Hewitt, and Mary Eustace Valmont. 1999. *Big Cities and Welfare Reform: Early Implementation and Ethnographic Findings from the Project on Devolution and Urban Change*. New York: Manpower Demonstration Research Corporation.

Riccio, James, Daniel Friedlander, and Stephen Freedman. 1994. *GAIN: Benefits, Costs, and Three-Year Impacts of a Welfare-to-Work Program*. New York: Manpower Demonstration Research Corporation.

Riccio, James, Howard Bloom, Alan Orenstein, and Electra Small. 1999. "Overview: Public Management and the Effectiveness of Welfare-to-Work Programs." Paper presented at a Workshop on Models and Methods for the Empirical Study of Governance and Public Management, University of Arizona, April 29–May 1.

Shadish, William R., Thomas D. Cook, and Laura Leviton. 1991. *Foundations of Program Evaluation: Theories of Practice*. Newbury Park, Calif.: Sage Publications.

PART THREE
Using Data to Understand Implementation

The third part focuses on data collection methods. Like the choice of analytic strategies, data collection methods are dictated by the underlying research questions and target populations of interest. There exists no one method appropriate for all studies. Chapter 10 covers most of the conventional techniques; chapter 11 deals with a data source of increasing importance—administrative data.

Approaches to Data Collection for Implementation Analysis (chapter 10). Given the diversity and complexity of implementation studies, Charlesworth and Born warn against the temptation to prescribe particular data collection approaches for particular types of studies. In addition to the general admonition repeated throughout the volume that several types of data collection are important for validity and reliability, these authors make the more specific point that feasibility often plays a critical role in shaping the nature of the data collection strategies chosen. "Timelines and budgets are only two of the many real-world constraints imposed on researchers and the ideal method of data collection may not be the method that, ultimately, is used."

Charlesworth and Born describe the advantages and disadvantages of the major primary data collection strategies used by implementation analysts, along with examples of their use in the welfare reform evaluation context.

They begin with a discussion of *in-person interviews,* pointing out that these can be in the qualitative tradition (with unstructured or semi-structured interviews) or can draw on the quantitative tradition (with highly structured and primarily closed-ended items). The advantage the authors cite for in-person interviews is their ability to collect relatively complete information about personal characteristics and the respondent's surrounding environment. This method maximizes the chances that non-respondents and noncontacts can be traced (and the sample characteristics maintained). Disadvantages include the difficulty of ensuring respondent confidentiality, the problem of interviewer effects, and the relatively large amount of time and resources needed to use the approach successfully (including the need for highly skilled interviewers and the time needed to locate and schedule the interviews). The authors also caution that in-person interviews using the qualitative approach can appear deceptively simple. It is easy to start asking unstructured questions, so the need for considerable methodological planning before entering the field may not be apparent until poor data quality teaches this lesson when it is too late.

Telephone surveys have become a popular method of data collection in the past 30 years, now that more than 9 of 10 U.S. households have telephones and computer-assisted telephone interviewing systems have greatly improved quality control. Advantages of the method include data collection speed, the ease of encompassing a geographically dispersed sample, and relatively low cost. Disadvantages include inability to use visual aids, limited information about refusals and noncontacts, and the danger of bias: households that lack phones are heavily concentrated among the poor and otherwise disadvantaged groups in the population.

Self-administered questionnaires ask respondents to provide data with no researcher intervention or facilitation. Mail surveys typically cost less even than research involving administrative data (see next section). Their lack of interviewer influence also reduces social desirability bias (the tendency of respondents to say what they think people want to hear), and some analysts believe self-administration is more likely to solicit truthful information on sensitive issues. Their disadvantages include low response rates, bias resulting from higher response rates for better educated respondents, and freedom of the respondent to answer questions in any order (which necessitates designing questionnaires so that interpretation is not dependent on question sequence).

Direct observation has a long and rich history in the social sciences. Its use is almost always advantageous because of its great potential to identify unanticipated issues. Here again, the approach can be quantitative or qualitative. The quantitative tradition calls for simple observation with precise operationalization and measurement, the goal being standardization and control. The qualitative tradition emphasizes participant observation, which does not establish predetermined categories of measurement, but rather involves a focusing process that progresses from general description to more refined content as additional issues of interest emerge. Simple observation is regarded as one of the least obtrusive of all research techniques. A necessary implication, of course, is that the respondents' roles are passive. For both simple and participant observation, reliance on the subjective perception of the researcher runs the risk of personal bias. This and related validity concerns can be guarded against by using multiple observers, systematizing observation as much as possible, and varying its time and place.

The *focus group* approach involves group discussion among perhaps 7 to 12 individuals, lasting typically from one to two hours. Participants are selected because they have certain characteristics in common that relate to the topic of interest. A facilitator (often the researcher) creates a comfortable environment that allows expression of different perceptions and points of view. This approach is almost always used to collect qualitative data, although quantitative data can be collected in the focus group context. Its strengths include quick data production at lower cost than individual interviewing. Disadvantages include inability (1) to know whether group behavior mirrors individual behavior and (2) to generalize with confidence to larger populations due to the small number of participants and the convenience nature of most samples. The focus group approach also suffers in comparison with observation, because the setting is unnatural and generally limited to spoken behavior.

Use of Administrative Data for Implementation Research (chapter 11). Administrative data are data regularly and consistently collected in support of a program's functioning and stored within its information system. Although administrative databases are not typically collected for research purposes, they are often thought of as having great potential research value and have been used effectively in a variety of program evaluation contexts.

The fact that administrative data now exist for nearly every federal or state social program, and for many general populations, gives some idea of the promise of this type of data. Its promise is some way from being fully realized, however, as discussed by Robert Goerge. For a particular program, the data are typically longitudinal, population-based, and accurate for the most important features of the program. But administrative databases, in most cases, are not currently linked at the individual or provider level across programs. In addition, it is often difficult to gain access to the data and, if access is obtained, it can be technically extremely challenging and time-consuming to create longitudinal research files. Further, since quality varies widely, each program dataset and field or variable must be assessed individually for accuracy and general utility. Generally, the data used directly for determining eligibility, client tracking, or accounting and reimbursement functions are more reliable than data not required for day-to-day program functioning.

The good news is that it is increasingly likely that state and county governments will create data warehouses, which will require the formulation of uniform standards for storing, formatting, and documenting administrative data for research purposes. But it will take a number of years before such warehouses are in general use. In the meantime, the difficulties of using such data may outweigh their promise for many analysts, particularly in projects with limited data development budgets.

10

Approaches to Data Collection for Implementation Analysis

Leanne Charlesworth and Catherine Born

Implementation in the policy context generally refers to the process of carrying out a basic policy decision or to the interaction between the setting of policy goals and actions geared to achieving them (Lipsky 1980; Mazmanian and Sabatier 1983; Pressman and Wildavsky 1973). Implementation analyses focus on the nature of this process and factors that may affect the achievement of policy objectives. Because a tremendous number of factors may influence the achievement of such objectives, the nature and foci of implementation analyses vary widely. Factors contributing to policy success or failure are also at times beyond the scope of such analyses. For example, welfare policy implementation failures may stem from inadequate definition of the problem or issue of concern or from generally inadequate structural supports in the welfare infrastructure (Goodwin and Moen 1983). As Pressman and Wildavsky (1973) point out, perfectly ordinary circumstances can also present serious obstacles to implementation. Implementation studies thus examine tangible aspects of the implementation process while remaining aware of these realities.

When studying welfare policy implementation, the researcher may draw upon a number of data collection approaches. For example, qualitative and quantitative data may be obtained from or recorded by study participants, an independent observer or team of observers, or existing data sources or repositories. Data collection approaches frequently drawn upon in the social sciences and examined here include in-person interviews, telephone surveys, self-administered questionnaires, observation, focus groups, and secondary analysis of existing data. Although each is presented separately, the reality is that combining two or more approaches frequently yields the most valuable information and insight. As no approach is perfect, multiple approaches are usually preferred.

Although tempting, it is overly simplistic if not dangerous to universally prescribe particular data collection approaches for particular types of studies. As Holcomb and Nightingale suggest in chapter 3 of this volume, implementation analyses are diverse and complex. Whereas each individual analysis must be guided by a carefully developed conceptual framework, implementation studies as a group (and even similar study types) do not share a particular research design or theoretical model. The data collection approach, or approaches, most appropriate for a particular study will depend upon a variety of factors including, for example, the research purpose, questions, or hypotheses and the resources and data sources available to the study. The researcher must weigh the advantages and disadvantages of each approach as well as the ability of the approach to answer the research questions of interest. In sum, data collection must be approached with flexibility.

Using this premise, this chapter offers general guidelines and issues to consider when comparing various data collection approaches. Specifically, we provide an overview of the major primary data collection approaches, plus a brief discussion of content analysis of existing documents—their advantages and disadvantages from a traditional social science research perspective, and the use of each approach in welfare policy implementation research. Ultimately, the value of each approach to any particular implementation analysis depends upon issues inherent to the approach as well as the match between the approach and the specific analysis.

In-Person Interviews

Various interview types fall under the in-person (or face-to-face) interview heading. The qualitative-quantitative continuum provides a useful framework for understanding some of the basic distinctions among in-person interviews. In-person interviews drawing upon the qualitative tradition are generally either unstructured or semistructured. Interviews drawing upon the quantitative tradition are typically highly structured and contain primarily closed-ended items.

During unstructured in-person interviews, the researcher typically introduces the topic of interest but the interview does not follow a particular order or consist of predetermined items (Rubin and Rubin 1995). In semistructured interviews there is room for exploration of unanticipated issues, but typically the interviewer introduces the topic and follows a somewhat consistent order with some use of predetermined items. Structured interviews, in contrast, are based on a positivist or quantitative tradition. That is, the topic of the interview, items, and item order are typically predetermined and standardized across interviews (Neuman 1994).

Advantages and Disadvantages

The advantages of in-person interviews are identified in figure 10.1. In-person interviews allow collection of information about personal characteristics and the respondent's surrounding environment, supplementary information that may be valuable in interpreting study results. They may yield more complete responses in general, but specifically to sensitive questions because the interviewer is present to probe for additional information or to encourage the respondent to answer the question. When compared with all other methods, in-person interviews place the fewest limits on the type and length of questioning possible (Frey and Oishi 1995).

The in-person interview, however, also has several important disadvantages. For example, ensuring respondent confidentiality is difficult, because respondents are aware that the interviewer knows many of the respondent's identifying characteristics. In addition, interviewer effects are typically greatest in in-person interviewing. Although respondents may be more likely to answer sensitive questions, the possibility of obtaining socially desirable answers is high because of the effect of the interviewer's presence. The more personalized the interview, the more likely it is that this will happen (Frey and Oishi 1995).

A relatively large amount of time and resources must be available to employ this approach successfully (Czaja and Blair 1996). Interviewers must be highly skilled, and often much time is required to locate respondents and arrange as well as conduct interviews. In-person interviews,

Figure 10.1. Advantages of In-Person Interviews

- High response rates
- Possibility for lengthy and complex items and interview
- High researcher control of question order, response situation
- Success with open-ended questions
- Use of visual materials, observation-based data possible
- Researcher-respondent rapport building possible
- High-quality response recording
- Low sampling frame and response bias
- Rich, voluminous data possible

however, vary in their degree of difficulty. As might be expected, high-quality unstructured interviews are typically the most challenging to conduct. They require an interviewer who is familiar with the topic and with the methodological options available, as well as the conceptual issues involved with research and knowledge building through this approach (Kvale 1996). Although the difficulty of the interviewing task can be diminished by careful design of questions and adequate interviewer training, extensive reliance upon open-ended questions always necessitates an experienced and skilled interviewer and leads to data that are challenging and time-consuming to code and analyze (Miller 1991). Thus in general, but particularly during in-person interviews, open-ended questions should be used with a specific purpose in mind.

We also caution that in-person interviews appear deceptively simple. It is easy to begin unstructured or semistructured interviewing without a great deal of planning or foresight regarding methodological issues. Contributing to this deceptive simplicity is the fact that the qualitative research community has developed relatively few standardized rules and methodological conventions. As a result, methodological decisions may at times be made on the spot, based on the researcher's experience and rationale (Kvale 1996). This often decreases the quality of data obtained through this approach.

Common criticisms leveled at qualitative interviewing include the argument that the approach is not scientific or objective and should be used only in exploratory research. The approach can be too person-dependent (different interviewers may come up with different questions and probes), analysis may be excessively subjective (different analysts may find entirely different meaning) and, for a variety of reasons, findings frequently lack generalizability. However, these "flaws" can also be viewed as strengths and the deliberate use of the subjective method for in-depth understanding of the perspectives of participants can produce invaluable results. This is particularly true if understanding participants' views or opinions is an explicit goal of the research. In fact, from the perspective of qualitative researchers, traditional quantitative interviewing lacks depth and produces findings that are somewhat lacking in context (Kvale 1996; Rubin and Rubin 1995).

Full consideration of these competing points of view requires examination of paradigmatic issues beyond the scope of the present discussion.[1] It is, however, essential to recognize that all approaches to in-person interviewing specifically and data collection in general have certain advantages and disadvantages; in-person interviewing and other forms of qualitative data collection are simply easier to criticize because the quantitative approach dominates most perspectives and evaluative criteria.

Use in Welfare Policy Implementation Research

In-person interviewing has been used extensively in welfare implementation studies and is a major data collection tool used in field research to gather narrative descriptions of program development and functioning and to understand the practices, experiences, attitudes, or perceptions of administrators, workers, or clients. In particular, this approach can be used to gather descriptions of the program model, client flow, and other program processes. As would be expected, the degree of structure within such interviews varies widely. It is most important that the interview approach chosen is consistent with the goal of the study. For example, highly structured in-person interviews are useful for identifying quantifiable similarities or differences across sites or individuals. Semi- or unstructured interviews are more common and are useful for gathering narrative descriptions of program processes and professional practices as well as exploring individual perceptions. Sample items consistent with interviews of varying degrees of structure are provided in figure 10.2. It is important to recognize that the primary difference among unstructured, semistructured, and structured interviews is the nature of the entire interview rather than individual items.

The welfare policy implementation literature is rich in examples of ways in-person interviews can be used to yield important descriptive data

Figure 10.2. Sample Questions by Type of In-Person Interview

Unstructured	Semistructured	Structured
• Could you describe the typical intake process in your office? • Could you elaborate on what happens during the second component that you just described?	• Would you describe the intake process in your office as very flexible, flexible, or not at all flexible? • What is it about your process that causes you to characterize it that way?	• Would you describe the intake process in your office as very flexible, flexible, or not at all flexible? • Are you very satisfied, moderately satisfied, or unsatisfied with the intake process within your office?

and progress information about the translation of policy into practice. For example, Riccio et al. (1989) relied upon face-to-face interviews with department managerial, supervisory, and line staff, as well as interviews with external service providers, to inform the field research component of their Greater Avenues for Independence (GAIN) study. Holcomb et al. (1998) relied upon informal in-person interviews (with state and local administrators as well as frontline staff and employers) in their comparison of five states implementing work-oriented strategies.

Fein et al. (1998) describe semistructured, in-person interviews (with administrators and staff from state and local welfare offices as well as staff from other relevant local agencies) as a primary data collection method used in the process study component of their evaluation of welfare reform in Indiana. In those interviews, consistent topics were organization and service delivery structure, client flow, perceptions of reform goals, training, cultural changes, policy requirements and provisions, and program changes.[2]

In-person interviews are often used in combination with observation. In their examination of post-reform changes in worker-client transactions, Meyers, Glaser, and MacDonald (1998) used semistructured worker interviews to supplement data obtained through observation of worker-client transactions. In those interviews, the researchers probed the general topics of work responsibilities, understanding of program priorities, and the information viewed as most important to communicate to clients.[3] Sandfort (1997) drew upon ethnographic methods and employed semistructured interviewing with frontline staff and managers in five distinct organizations within two Michigan counties. During interviews, she focused on the nature of staff and organizational experiences, responsibilities, opinions of welfare reform, views of clients, and daily activities. She then drew upon those data to reach conclusions about barriers to the implementation of comprehensive reforms.

Scrivener et al. (1998), in Manpower Demonstration Research Corporation's (MDRC's) implementation study component of its Portland (Oregon) welfare-to-work program evaluation, also conducted in-person interviews with clients, administrators, case managers, and other service providers. Interviews focused on management philosophies and structure, enforcement of the participation mandate, service availability, the nature of interactions between staff and clients, and interagency relations. The approach was used as one of a number of data collection strategies and helped provide the basis for conclusions reached about program implementation and functioning.

Fletcher, Winter, and Gaddis (1998) used in-person interviews with welfare administrators and staff in their study of the implementation of welfare reform in Iowa. To inform the community case study component of this project, the researchers conducted in-person interviews with key community informants and recipient families. Those interview data were in turn supplemented by focus group discussions with line workers.

Bloom, Andes, and Nicholson (1998), in MDRC's study of welfare reform implementation in Connecticut, conducted in-person interviews with line staff, supervisors, and managers. In addition, field researchers reviewed 25 specific cases with the workers assigned to those cases to investigate the processes and reasoning behind extensions granted to cases that had reached welfare time limits. The interview and case review data enhanced the researchers' understanding of some of the not-so-obvious qualitative factors affecting initial implementation of policy initiatives and program functioning.[4]

As suggested by the widespread reliance on this data collection approach among implementation researchers, the in-person interview is particularly useful for gathering perceptual and descriptive data on program functioning and for generating and informing "next steps" or areas of importance in a research project. This approach is most frequently used to gather information on the perceptions and activities of persons on the front lines, such as managers and workers. The semistructured in-person interview's flexibility is particularly well suited for use in implementation studies because such studies are typically exploratory in nature, frequently requiring the ability to investigate and probe unanticipated topics.

When used as one component of field research, in-person interviews are an excellent tool. They help generate general impressions and increase the depth of researchers' understanding in case studies. But several methodological challenges or areas for improvement and caution exist (see figure 10.3). It is important to ensure that interview content and placement on the structure continuum are consistent with the general study design and objectives. For example, in case studies in which the researcher's knowledge is integral to study findings, unstructured interviewing is preferable. For cross-site or cross-interviewer analyses, however, semistructured or structured interviewing is virtually always essential to sound data analysis and interpretation of results.

Also, a weakness among implementation researchers in general is that the specific interviewing approach used is often described vaguely in published reports, which makes it difficult to replicate the approach, discern the quality and quantity of the data collected, and assess the consistency of the specific approach with the research objectives. Particularly in view of the criticisms often leveled at qualitative, interview-based welfare research studies, it is imperative to convey to the research audience how many and which individuals were interviewed, the approach to interviewing, and the topics covered. If multiple interviewers were used, training and cross-interviewer consistency should also be addressed. Methods of recording interviewees' responses (for example, whether interviews were audiotaped) and of data analysis should also be described. This information is necessary to demonstrate that the methods used and data obtained, at least theoretically, provide a sound basis for reaching conclusions about program functioning or emphases.

Figure 10.3. In-Person Interviews: Issues to Consider

- Degree of structure desired
- Logistics (arranging and conducting)
- Data recording approach
- Sample representativeness
- Interviewer skill and training; cross-interviewer consistency
- Analysis approach (time and resources available)
- Respondent confidentiality concerns
- Social desirability bias

Related to this is the caution noted earlier that in-person interviews appear deceptively simple and semistructured or unstructured interviews can be commenced by novice researchers without great attention to planning or methodological issues. The ease with which such studies can be mounted leaves this method of data collection open to abuse. A number of studies examining the implementation of recent welfare reforms have relied solely on client or staff interviews and have suffered from weaknesses such as underdeveloped methods and theoretical bases or study designs inconsistent with research objectives. Because many of today's implementation studies are funded by government entities in great need of research evidence to aid in the ongoing development of policies and programs, it is critical to hold such research to high standards.

Thus implementation researchers must become methodical and explicit about in-person interview practices and procedures. Full articulation of the theoretical reasoning behind selection of this approach and detailed explanation of the steps involved are needed to guide the efforts of less experienced implementation researchers. Also, work remains to be done in linking data obtained through this approach to more quantitative outcome data. A final challenge in this area is to report explicitly on information gained through interviews. In reporting study findings, it is implicitly understood that researchers gain a great deal of knowledge about policy and program implementation through in-person interviewing; unfortunately, this knowledge at times is underemphasized relative to data more easily quantified. This relative neglect may be due to a lack of methodological rigor or simply to inadequate methodological description in published reports. Both deserve attention.

Telephone Surveys

The telephone survey became a popular method of data collection beginning in the 1970s, when the proportion of U.S. households with telephones began to exceed 90 percent (Lavrakas 1987). Because the majority of the population now owns a telephone and random digit dialing techniques make it easy to access unlisted and new numbers, the telephone survey is now heavily relied upon for data collection (Frey and Oishi 1995).

Integration of the computer and automated systems into telephone interviewing has brought great improvements in telephone surveys. Computer-assisted telephone interviewing (CATI) systems generally enhance quality control, particularly if a supervisor is able to monitor interviews. Telephone interviewing that incorporates such computer-based systems has the potential to be highly efficient, cost-effective, and accurate.

Advantages and Disadvantages

The telephone survey offers several potential advantages (see figure 10.4). Its most significant strengths include the speed of data collection, the fact that the sample may be geographically dispersed, and the relatively inexpensive nature of the approach. Also, although individual items must be relatively short and straightforward, the general questionnaire, or interview, may be complex (Czaja and Blair 1996; Frey and Oishi 1995).

However, telephone surveys also present several significant disadvantages, including the inability to use visual aids and the limited information usually available to the researcher about refusals and noncontacts. Certain populations, particularly low-income individuals, are likely to lack telephones or to change telephone numbers frequently (Miller 1991). The telephone survey has traditionally been thought less useful for examination of sensitive topics but, because in-person and telephone methods each present distinct advantages in this area, it is difficult to generalize about the relative ability of each approach to obtain embarrassing or sensitive data. In general, though, the rapport between the respondent and interviewer is of a fairly low quality in telephone interviews.

Newer telephone interviewing techniques such as CATI have dramatically increased the sophistication of interviews possible by phone (Frey and Oishi 1995). Despite these improvements, telephone surveys remain

Figure 10.4. Advantages of Telephone Surveys

- Rapid data collection
- Wide geographic distribution of sample
- Large sample size possible
- Complex instrument (interview) possible
- High researcher control of question order
- High-quality response recording possible
- High response rate
- Low cost
- Potential rapid analysis and feedback of data

limited in the type and length of items and interviews that can be effectively employed (Czaja and Blair 1996). For example, it is possible to use open-ended questions in telephone interviews, but the advantages of such questions are often lost due to the difficulty of recording responses in their entirety (whether on paper or within a CATI system) given the necessarily fast-paced nature of telephone interviewing.

Use in Welfare Policy Implementation Research

Telephone surveys, like in-person interviews, have been used with a variety of implementation study participants including clients, program staff, and the general public. Most frequently, such surveys are used to obtain data from clients on their perceptions of, and experiences with, a new program or policy; the approach is also occasionally used with program staff. For example, Seefeldt, Sandfort, and Danziger (1998) used structured telephone interviews (consisting of open-ended items) with local work program managers in their study of initial welfare reform implementation in Michigan. The interviews focused on organizational conditions, management practices, service technology, interagency collaboration, and perceptions of clients, economic conditions, and reform initiatives. The data produced were subsequently used to examine the relationship between implementation choices (particularly delivery system structure) and outcomes (proportion of recipients combining welfare and work and proportion of recipients leaving welfare due to employment earnings) (see Sandfort, Seefeldt, and Danziger 1998).

In more traditional use of the telephone survey, Meyers (1993) conducted telephone interviews with GAIN participants to examine the perceived adequacy of child care and the relationship between adequacy and participant success. Participants were recruited in person (at GAIN program sites) and interviewed by phone at three different points, with each interview taking place at a selected stage in program participation. Fraker (1998), in Mathematica's study of the implementation of the Iowa Limited Benefit Plan, conducted telephone interviews with a small sample of plan participants. The interviews were supplemented by more in-depth personal interviews with a small subsample of respondents. Using the reverse approach, Hagen and Davis (1994) followed their in-person interviews of clients with brief telephone interviews (several months later) that focused on assessing participants' progress in the Job Opportunities and Basic Skills (JOBS) program. The in-person interview and telephone survey data were then used in combination to reach conclusions about clients' perceptions of the new program and to identify implementation problems and successes. MDRC also included telephone interviews with clients (along with staff self-administered surveys) to investigate the reasons behind clients' responses to new initiatives in Vermont, Florida, and Minnesota. Telephone interview data were then compared with worker survey data to examine the accuracy of staff perceptions of the reasons for clients' actions (Knox 1998).

Similarly, Bloom, Kemple, and Rogers-Dillon (1997) and Bloom et al. (1998) used telephone surveys of clients to examine Connecticut and Florida's implementation of welfare reform; in both cases, the surveys focused on client experiences during initial program implementation. The University of Maryland is using telephone surveys of random samples of welfare leavers to supplement its longitudinal welfare reform outcomes study, and South Carolina has used the telephone survey method to uncover clients' perceptions of how they have been faring since the implementation of PRWORA-based welfare reform.[5]

In sum, in implementation research to date, telephone surveys have most frequently been used with program participants and use of this method increased during the first few years of welfare reform. In addition to the advantages already noted, telephone surveys permit use of large samples, making it easier to ensure that the sample is representative of the population of interest and improving the ability to perform subgroup analyses. This is particularly useful to implementation studies interested in specific subpopulations; for example, sanctioned cases, successful cases, or recidivists. And, due to the compatibility of telephone interviewing with a highly structured interview containing primarily closed-ended items, quantitative data are easily obtained through this approach. Figure 10.5 contains examples of items compatible with telephone interviews. Such quantitative data are relatively easy to analyze and can be used to quickly identify frequently reported client issues and trends of relevance to program implementation. Thus data obtained through telephone interviews with clients may guide or improve policy and program implementation.

As noted in figure 10.6, several issues should be considered in employing the telephone interview as a data collection approach. In particular, although telephone surveys generally yield high response rates, research with welfare program participants is likely to do so primarily when targeting current participants; surveys targeting former program participants

Figure 10.5. Sample Telephone Survey Items

- In the past two years, has your (cash assistance) been cut off because you didn't do something your case worker wanted you to do?
  ☐ Yes ☐ No ☐ Don't recall ☐ Refused

- Other than odd jobs, how many months has it been since you last worked full-time for pay?
  ☐ Fewer than 6 months   ☐ More than 2 years
  ☐ Between 6 months and 9 months   ☐ Don't know
  ☐ Between 10 months and 12 months   ☐ Refused
  ☐ Between 13 months and 2 years

---

may experience quite low response rates. And in general, because of the traditional challenges experienced when conducting research with low-income populations, the well-known advantages of telephone surveys are often not readily available to researchers seeking the input of welfare program participants.

Self-Administered Questionnaires

Self-administered questionnaires, whether distributed in person or by mail, ask respondents to complete a task unique to this data collection approach; in both cases, the respondent directly provides data with no researcher intervention or facilitation (Fowler 1995). Although mail surveys in particular have a fairly long history in social science research, their disadvantages are well known. However, they are still widely used

Figure 10.6. Telephone Surveys: Issues to Consider

- Limited information regarding refusals and noncontacts
- Potentially low coverage among certain populations (low-income, highly mobile, less educated, non-English-speaking)
- Limited item complexity, not conducive to use of open-ended questions
- Use of visual material not possible
- Cross-interviewer consistency
- Approach to response recording
- Social desirability bias

and may be useful in situations in which the research sample is widely distributed but is relatively invested in the study, resources are limited, or respondents need privacy and time to think about their answers or to consult personal records (Mangione 1995). If the number of research questions or items is limited and most are closed-ended or work better when presented visually rather than orally, the mail survey may be a wise choice.

Advantages and Disadvantages

Figure 10.7 lists the major advantages of the mail survey. Mail surveys are typically less expensive than in-person or telephone interviews. Bourque and Fielder (1995) estimate that a questionnaire completed by mail costs approximately 50 percent less than one administered by telephone and 75 percent less than one administered in person. It is also likely that mail surveys are less expensive than research involving administrative data.[6] Although response rates are generally lowest with this approach, some respondents prefer completing a self-administered questionnaire at their convenience to committing to a particular day and time for a telephone or in-person interview. In addition, minimal research resources—including equipment and personnel—are needed.

Often, sensitive questions are more likely to be answered due to the heightened sense of anonymity felt by respondents. Many researchers believe respondents are more likely to give complete and truthful information (particularly on sensitive topics) in a mail survey or other self-administered questionnaire than in an interview, though evidence suggests that telephone and in-person interviews may be as effective and even more accurate (Bourque and Fielder 1995). As with all data collection approaches, these conflicting findings may be primarily due to study

*Figure 10.7. Advantages of Mail Surveys
and Other Self-Administered Questionnaires*

• Low cost   • Respondent access to office/household records
• Wide geographic distribution of sample   • Conduciveness to sensitive questions
• Possibility of large sample size
• Unlimited respondent response time and privacy   • Low social desirability bias

differences, interviewer skill and ability to establish rapport, the extent to which respondents believe data are confidential or anonymous, or the manner in which the individual items and general questionnaire are structured. However, mail surveys and other self-administered questionnaires do avoid some of the difficulties of securing personal information; such approaches produce the least interviewer influence and, consequently, social desirability bias (Bourque and Fielder 1995; Czaja and Blair 1996; Mangione 1995).

In considering the disadvantages of this approach, the researcher must be aware that the respondent may view the entire questionnaire before beginning and may respond to items in any order. In addition, in answering each item, the respondent is able to view all response options before selecting one. Although it is possible to keep sampling frame bias somewhat low, the disadvantages include a relatively high response bias (in particular, highly educated individuals are more likely to respond) and generally low response rates. Respondents are less likely to respond to open-ended questions and, as noted, the researcher's control of the response situation is poor. Interviews may therefore be preferred to mail surveys and other self-administered questionnaires because the interviewer can play a role in enhancing respondent participation, guiding the questioning, and clarifying the meaning of questions or responses (Frey and Oishi 1995).

An important area to consider when using the self-administered approach is questionnaire construction (which should be carefully attended to regardless of the particular approach selected). For example, traditional instrumentation issues must be considered; scales or indices should be reliable and valid. With self-administered questionnaires, the purpose should be as clear and straightforward as possible and the questionnaire itself should be short, clear, and composed of primarily closed-ended items. Question order should not be critical; it must be acceptable and expected that respondents may complete the questionnaire "out of order," skip certain sections, or otherwise violate ideal respondent behavior. It is also important to note that the individual targeted by the questionnaire may not be the person who actually completes it. In addition, time issues should be considered; for example, one cannot be certain of the exact date on which the questionnaire was completed. And although mail surveys are generally viewed as relatively quick, individual turnaround time may not be as fast as expected or needed (Czaja and Blair 1996).

Many of the major disadvantages of mail and other self-administered questionnaires have to do with sampling issues (Bourque and Fielder 1995). The representativeness of the sample is affected by the availability of a complete and accurate list of the population. And, as noted, response rates (even in high-quality, intensive efforts) are consistently lower than those secured through telephone and in-person interviews. A variety of methods such as additional response incentives and follow-up using alternative data collection approaches may be used to obtain information about or from nonresponders. Although such methods are often time consuming and expensive, a high level of nonresponse necessitates such efforts to ensure that the sample is representative.

Low response rates continue to plague mail surveys for many reasons. Reading difficulties may affect response, particularly among certain populations. Among the general population, the illiteracy rate is estimated at approximately 20 percent (Bourque and Fielder 1995); among low-income and other disadvantaged populations, we can assume the rate is higher. Individuals unable to speak English are highly unlikely to complete a questionnaire printed only in English. Thus data from multiple-language populations generally are not accurately collected using the self-administered questionnaire approach. And as noted, for various reasons including residential instability, less educated individuals are less likely to respond to mail surveys (Mangione 1995). Response bias is a disadvantage of particular relevance to data collection efforts targeting the welfare recipient population.

Use in Welfare Policy Implementation Research

In the context of implementation study, a major strength of mail and other self-administered surveys is that respondents can pick the time that is best for them to complete such surveys. This is a particular asset when respondents are managers or frontline workers with busy or fluctuating schedules. This is also one reason that mail surveys and other self-administered questionnaires are frequently used with program staff. The respondent is able to review documents or access other information that may be necessary for accurate item completion. In implementation studies, the method is thus often used to obtain data that respondents can provide only by accessing their office records. Mail or other self-administered surveys also often ask respondents to rate issues or items on quantitative scales; such ratings may be more accurate when the respondent has adequate time to think about the accuracy of the rating and is able to see the scale continuum. Examples of items consistent with this approach are provided in figure 10.8.

In their examination of welfare reform implementation in Maryland, Born, Charlesworth, and Hyde (1998) carried out a mail survey of frontline workers in local welfare agencies across the state. The survey focused on dimensions such as reform perceptions, staff responsibilities, time allocation, and client assessment emphases and was used to compare agency procedures and worker practices across jurisdictions. Bloom, Kemple, and Rogers-Dillon (1997) and Bloom, Andes, and Nicholson (1998) used self-administered staff surveys in Connecticut and Florida to investigate program functioning and implementation issues. Fein et al. (1998) drew upon a statewide mail survey of local welfare office directors (focusing on perceptions of objectives and effectiveness of reform as well as the ways in which reform had affected staff, operations, and clients) as one component of their examination of reform implementation in Indiana.

As part of their GAIN study, Riccio et al. (1989) administered a survey to work program and eligibility staff (as well as supervisors) focused on staff perspectives on job responsibilities, interactions with welfare recipients, relative emphasis on GAIN goals, job satisfaction and morale, and perceptions of welfare recipients' motivations to become self-supporting (see also Riccio and Friedlander 1992). Survey data were then used to characterize the manner in which counties implemented the GAIN model, for example, categorizing a county's ideology toward sanctions and emphasis on personalized attention. Eventually, these data were linked to outcomes; specifically, the relationship between agency emphases and client outcomes (welfare receipt and earnings) was explored (see Riccio and Orenstein 1996). A self-administered survey of program participants was also used to measure client attitudes toward the GAIN program in general (Riccio and Hasenfeld 1996).

Figure 10.8. Sample Mail and Self-Administered Questionnaire Items

- Overall, how would you describe the availability of support services for your clients?
  ☐ Not available   ☐ Sometimes available   ☐ Usually available   ☐ Always available

- During an average week, what percentage of your time is spent in face-to-face contact with clients? _____%

Somewhat similarly, Hasenfeld and Weaver (1996) relied upon a survey of frontline workers to create a series of independent and dependent variables; these data were then analyzed to determine the relationship between organizational arrangements (primarily worker practices) and client compliance with program requirements. Weaver and Hasenfeld (1997) also used self-administered client questionnaires to gather participant data (particularly, perceptions of workers and case management practices). These data were subsequently used to reexamine relationships between case management practices and client compliance with program requirements, with participants' assessments of the program included as additional variables of interest.

As described by Lurie (chapter 5 of this volume), field network research depends upon a structured, self-administered instrument (containing open-ended items) used in a unique manner. The instrument is completed by field researchers (or senior policy analysts); the analysts themselves, however, may gather data through any number of strategies including observation, in-person interviews, and analysis of existing documents (Hagen 1994). Thus Nathan and Gais (1999) drew upon the instrument responses of senior policy analysts in forming their conclusions regarding the initial implementation of recent welfare reform efforts within 20 states.

Hagen and Lurie (1994), in their examination of the implementation of the JOBS program across 10 states, supplemented field network research with a self-administered questionnaire given to frontline workers. This questionnaire collected data on workers' perceptions of reform and clients, job roles and responsibilities, time allocation, and personal emphases, among other issues. These data were combined with data gathered through field work, including interviews with clients, to form impressions of JOBS implementation progress across states.

Surveys administered on site, as would be expected, obtain much higher response rates than those conducted by mail. In general, both types of self-administered questionnaires are highly useful in implementation research. The data obtained (for example, worker responses to a series of closed-ended items) can be used to quantify agency tendencies or practices. However, before selecting this approach (see figure 10.9), one must be aware that the data that can be collected are limited; it is impossible to collect rich descriptive or narrative information because questions must be fairly simple and straightforward. Also, in implementation research to date, the number of workers (or other respondents) used to characterize

Figure 10.9. Mail Surveys/Self-Administered Questionnaires: Issues to Consider

- Low response rate
- Cross-study (instrument) comparability
- Questionnaire construction
- Respondent literacy level
- Limited item and questionnaire complexity and length
- Low researcher control of response situation
- Response bias
- Limited use of open-ended questions

agencies in this manner is, at times, small. In agencies with a limited number of frontline staff, this may be acceptable; however, response rate issues must always be examined before placing confidence in study assertions or conclusions.

Across implementation analyses, the number of distinct questionnaires used limits the ability to compare findings. At this stage in welfare policy implementation research, many questionnaires used with frontline staff have targeted similar attitudinal and behavioral issues. Rather than constantly creating new questionnaires or scales to measure worker attitudes or practices, it is wise (when possible and appropriate) to draw upon established, high-quality instruments or scales for replication and comparison purposes.

Observation

In the social sciences, direct observation has a long and rich history. In 1958, Gold described a now well-known observation continuum that identified four potential observer roles. At one end is the complete observer, detached from the interaction or phenomenon under observation. At the other extreme is the complete participant, whose research observations and participation in the observed situation take place simultaneously. The two roles that fall in the middle and blend features of each extreme are observer-participant and participant-observer.

Observation is one of the most basic forms of research and, in welfare reform implementation studies, is likely to be used in conjunction with other data collection approaches. Traditionally regarded as one of the least intrusive forms of data collection, simple observation (or in Gold's classic typology, the complete "observer" role) involves simply following the flow of events. However, the researcher's observations are distinct from those of the layperson in that they should be systematic and purposive (Adler and Adler 1998).

As with in-person interviewing, the quantitative–qualitative distinction is relevant to understanding types of observation. The quantitative research tradition calls for observation involving precise operationalization and measurement of the variables of interest, the goal being standardization and control. In the qualitative research tradition, however, participant observation has dominated (Adler and Adler 1998). Such observation does not typically establish predetermined categories of measurement. Rather, following a grounded theory-building approach, data collection occurs first and categories, or concepts, are then generated from the data (Glaser and Strauss 1967). Field research within organizational or community settings typically relies upon participant observation.

Qualitative researchers have identified different observer roles as well as different stages of the observational process. Essentially, these stages entail a focusing process in which observation progresses from general description to more specific content of interest. As observation progresses, the research question becomes more refined, but additional issues of interest usually emerge. Often, early observation informs and narrows future observation, if this is a logical part of the research process taking place (Adler and Adler 1998).

Observation, paradigmatic issues aside, generally is improved by a systematic approach involving the use of observation guides or other tools to aid in data collection. Observation guides should determine primary topics of interest but allow for open-ended responses, focusing the observation task but being generally flexible enough to allow data to be collected on unexpected dimensions. Observation schedules are similar but attempt to bring a more narrow focus to the observation effort. Both types of tools often draw upon the processes and rules of content analysis (Bogdan and Biklen 1992).

Observation guides or schedules are typically used in multisubject or multisite research involving teams because they are particularly useful for gathering comparable data across sites or subjects and aid in attempts to establish trends or cross-site findings. They should also be used by solitary researchers who observe a single site or event and wish to make data collection as systematic as possible. However, the use of observation guides or schedules can undermine the strength of the qualitative approach. In general, such tools should be used only when consistent with the research goals. Such tools may inappropriately focus the research effort on the production of numerical counts rather than new concepts and understanding (Bogdan and Biklen 1992). However, if the production of numerical counts is the research goal, then use of such guides is essential.

Advantages and Disadvantages

The use of observation is almost always advantageous (see figure 10.10). One strength of observation, particularly in the qualitative tradition, is the great potential for the discovery of new and unanticipated issues and findings, as well as concept or theory generation (Glaser and Strauss 1967). Observation based on the quantitative tradition (located toward the "complete observer" end of the Gold continuum) is traditionally regarded as the least intrusive of all research techniques. Observation can enhance the overall rigor of any research effort; when it is used in combination with other methods, data triangulation can inform and enrich findings. Like all data collection approaches, then, observation perhaps has most to offer when used as an integrated rather than solitary method.

A fairly obvious limitation of observation is directly related to one of its strengths. That is, observation's unobtrusive nature necessarily implies that respondents' roles are passive. Also, observation relies upon the subjective perceptions of the researcher and thus is subject to personal biases (Adler and Adler 1998). One step that may be taken to address this issue is to employ multiple observers so that findings can be cross-checked, but this introduces issues of intercoder, or inter-rater, reliability. Findings generated through observation(s) based on the qualitative tradition often cannot be subjected to statistical analysis, and one's level of confidence in (and the generalizability of) findings so obtained may be compromised.

To address such concerns, the quantity and nature of observations should be carefully considered in advance. Observation should be as sys-

Figure 10.10. Advantages of Observation

- Potential for discovery of new ideas, issues, and hypothesis generation
- Minimal researcher effects
- Triangulation of additional data, findings
- Discovery of data, information discrepancies

tematic as possible given the research purposes, and time and place of observation should be varied to enhance data validity. Systematic observation should be repeated across varying conditions. In such situations, if findings are replicated, a higher degree of confidence and credibility may be obtained.

Use in Welfare Policy Implementation Research

Welfare policy implementation research has long relied upon observation as a major component of fieldwork, primarily to form general impressions of program structure, functioning, and emphases. It is often through observation that new issues and areas for further inquiry are identified. For the most part, implementation researchers are still fine-tuning their use of more quantitative, systematic observation, a difficult method given the dynamic nature of the policy implementation process and policy implementation settings (welfare agencies and their partner organizations). Thus more qualitative approaches to observation have been most common and particularly valuable—perhaps invaluable—at initial study stages as a means to understand actual program functioning (as opposed to stated policy) and to inform research questions and study planning.

Examples of the use of observation in implementation research are plentiful. Riccio et al. (1989) used observation of orientations, customer appraisals, job search workshops, and basic education classes to inform field research in their evaluation of the GAIN program. Born, Charlesworth, and Hyde (1998) supplemented management and staff in-person interviews with observation of eligibility interviews, customer assessments, orientations, and other on-site activities to examine customer pathways and assessment practices in Maryland. Similarly, Fein et al. (1998) observed program activities such as intake and assessment, orientation sessions, and "self-sufficiency planning" interviews in their study of reform implementation in Indiana.

Brodkin (1997) relied upon observation of worker-client interactions and processes such as orientation, assessment, and job search and job readiness sessions as a major data collection approach in her case study of reform implementation; observational data were used primarily to enhance the researcher's depth of understanding. In particular, Brodkin employed observation and the case study method to identify general factors that affected bureaucratic discretion in welfare policy implementation. Sandfort (1997) drew upon participant observation (in local welfare offices) in her field research. Specifically, she shadowed individual workers, observed staff and management team meetings, social events, orientation sessions, classroom activities, and paperwork completion.

Meyers, Glaser, and MacDonald (1998) used observation of worker-client transactions (intake and redetermination interviews) as the primary data collection approach in their study of welfare reform implementation in California. Using a structured observation form, researchers focused on the frequency with which certain topics were discussed, the content of other discussion that may have taken place, and case characteristics. These observational data were later coded on two dimensions (content and use of positive discretion) to assess workers' behavior following reform implementation.

Weaver and Hasenfeld (1997) used systematic observation of GAIN activities (case management, orientation, and conciliation sessions as well as other routine interactions) to develop a detailed qualitative description of agency case management activities. Subsequently, when combined with supplemental data (participants' perceptions obtained through self-administered questionnaires) on case management practices under the new welfare-to-work program, the relationships between such practices, participants' assessments of the program, and compliance with program requirements were able to be examined.

Unquestionably, observation is of fundamental importance in implementation studies, especially in generating new research questions and hypotheses, informing study planning, and allowing the researcher, usually an outsider, to gain understanding of program functioning and agency practices. Sample observation guide items are provided in figure 10.11. To date, observation has primarily been used as a data triangulation tool to supplement data gained through other methods. Although extremely valuable as an adjunct approach, observation also has potential

Figure 10.11. Sample Observation Guide Items

- Space for on-site customer activities appears to be
  0   1   2   3   4   5   6   7   8
  Extremely limited   More than adequate
- Are there welfare-to-work informational materials in the waiting area?
  ☐ No ☐ Yes ☐ Not applicable   Other: _____

as the major data collection method. For example, characterization of the "typical" worker-client interaction may be best served by extensive, systematic observation producing descriptive quantitative and qualitative data about such interactions.

Figure 10.12 lists several methodological issues to which attention should be devoted before observation is chosen as a data collection approach. For example, consistency across observers is critical. The rigor of observation-based data collection strategies can be improved, specifically, by developing systematic approaches that stress reliability and validity. Client characteristics (e.g., demographics, but also case history or status), worker characteristics (e.g., worker position or type and level of experience), and agency characteristics (e.g., program structure and distinct types of worker-client interactions) all affect the interaction observed and the ability to compare observational data across sites. If generalizability is desired, researchers must observe a sufficient volume of interactions and use a consistent approach to observation.

Implementation studies have much to gain by confronting such methodological challenges. For example, if observational data were viewed as highly reliable, characterizations of typical worker-client interactions would be based primarily on such data, which arguably more directly reflect program functioning than the indirect, potentially biased descriptions of such functioning provided by those who participate in worker-client interactions. Although the obstacles associated with the use of observation as a major data collection approach are formidable, overcoming the obstacles may be well worth the effort involved.

Focus Groups

The focus group, described by Morgan as "a research technique that collects data through group interaction on a topic determined by the researcher" (1996, 130), generally involves from 7 to 12 individuals, and

Figure 10.12. Observation: Issues to Consider

• Systematization, rigor	• Limited generalizability
• Cross-observer, situation, and site consistency	• Subjectivity (researcher-dependent)
	• Respondent passivity

group discussion typically lasts from one to two hours. In the group for-mat, participants discuss a particular topic under the direction of a facili-tator who promotes interaction and ensures that discussion remains on the topic of interest to the research. The amount of direction can vary widely and will influence the type and quality of data obtained from participants. Among other issues, the amount of structure provided by the facilitator should be determined by the broader research focus and questions. Facil-itator skill is crucial because the facilitator is key to ensuring that group discussion goes smoothly; training in group dynamics and interview skills is essential (Morgan 1996; Stewart and Shamdasani 1990).

Focus group participants are typically unfamiliar with one another and are selected because they have certain characteristics in common that relate to the topic of the focus group. The role of the facilitator, or researcher, is to create a comfortable environment that allows expression of different perceptions and points of view. Krueger thus defines the focus group as a "carefully planned discussion designed to obtain perceptions on a defined area of interest in a permissive, nonthreatening environ-ment" during which "group members influence each other by respond-ing to ideas and comments in the discussion" (Krueger 1988; 18). Focus groups differ from other group interactions in that the goal is not to reach consensus or make recommendations; instead, focus groups are designed to determine the perceptions, feelings, and manner of thinking of partic-ipants about phenomena of interest. From the qualitative perspective, the researcher derives understanding from discussion rather than confirma-tion of a predetermined hypothesis.

Depending upon the research goal, it may be helpful to carefully pre-determine and sequence discussion topics. In virtually all cases, ques-tions should be asked in a natural, logical sequence and attention given to the thought processes used by participants as they consider the issues under discussion. Through systematic analysis of the data produced, the researcher gains insight into participants' perceptions.

Although quantitative data can be collected in the focus group context, this approach is virtually always used to collect qualitative data. Tradi-tionally, focus groups were thought of as most useful for designing survey questionnaires, primarily because they provide a means of exploring the way potential respondents talk about objects and events. And indeed, such exploration is useful for developing appropriate question wording and response alternatives for closed-ended survey items. Focus groups are also very useful for exploratory research, when little is known about the phenomenon of interest. They are often used early in a research project, followed by other approaches that provide more quantifiable findings. In this tradition, focus groups have been useful when undertaken after analysis of large-scale surveys or other research projects to inform the interpretation of quantitative findings.

However, focus groups are versatile, useful for obtaining general information about a topic of interest or for refining questions or hypotheses for further research using quantitative or more intensive qualitative methods (Stewart and Shamdasani 1990). For example, such groups can be combined with follow-up, in-person interviews with individual participants to explore specific opinions and experiences in more depth. In general, focus groups often stimulate new ideas, diagnose potential problems with a new program or service, and generate impressions of services, institutions, or other objects of interest.

Advantages and Disadvantages

Focus groups have several strengths (see figure 10.13), including the ability to provide data quickly and at less cost than if each individual were interviewed separately, while still allowing the researcher to interact directly with respondents. Respondents can qualify their answers and the researcher can observe nonverbal responses. Respondents can also react to and build upon their own or others' previous responses, which may lead to the individual or group production of ideas that may not have emerged in individual interviews (Krueger 1988; Stewart and Shamdasani 1990).

Focus groups have high face validity; that is, the technique is easily understood and the results can be expressed in lay terminology, easily digested by those to whom the information is presented (Krueger 1988). The researcher is able to observe the extent and nature of participant

Figure 10.13. Advantages of Focus Groups

- Respondent use of own words, associations, categorizations
- Rapid identification of distinct experiences, perspectives, and suggestions
- Quick data collection period
- Response explanation, probing possible
- Group synergy, production of ideas
- Rich, voluminous data

agreement (or disagreement) and can ask for comparisons of experiences and views rather than simply "aggregating individual data to speculate about whether or why the individual interviewees differ" (Morgan 1996, 139). However, although the focus group provides an opportunity to collect data on and through group interaction, the researcher does not know if this group behavior mirrors individual behavior. And although the researcher may define the discussion topics (so, relatively speaking, focus groups are more controlled than observation), because of the participant-defined nature of group interaction, the focus group setting is typically less controlled than individual interviewing.

Several other disadvantages are encountered when focus groups are selected as the primary data collection approach. Focus groups typically produce "soft" data, difficult to analyze and challenging to summarize. Because of the typically small number of participants and the convenience nature of most samples, the ability to generalize to larger populations is often compromised. The interaction of participants with one another and with the facilitator may bring undesirable effects; in particular, responses are not independent of one another and a dominant or opinionated group participant may bias the results. Contrary to popular belief, moreover, Fern (1982) found that individual interviews may produce more ideas from each individual. The evidence in this area is unclear and conflicting; because of the different settings and the processes that occur therein, individual interviews and focus groups clearly produce differences in what and how much is said. And, the nature of interaction within focus groups may lead researchers or the research audience to place greater faith in findings than is actually warranted because of the credibility that is sometimes attached to anecdote or "live" respondents (Stewart and Shamdasani 1990). This is dangerous because findings may lack validity for a number of reasons; for example, facilitators may bias results by (unknowingly) providing cues about what type of responses or answers are desirable.

Krueger (1988) adds to these disadvantages the fact that group members may "take over" the course of the discussion, potentially leading to detours and valuable time spent on irrelevant topics. Also, groups can vary considerably—even with the same facilitator in place across groups. Under the same conditions, one group may be more energetic and talkative than others; thus enough groups must be included to balance such idiosyncrasies. Focus groups are also somewhat difficult to assemble, and must be conducted in an environment conducive to conversation.

In reality, focus groups often present more logistical problems than individual interviews. They may require less in the way of a prepared interview, but in this sense they suffer from deceptive simplicity. Lack of preparation on the part of the researcher or facilitator easily leads to "relatively chaotic data collection, with little comparability from group to group" (Morgan 1988, 18). The generally higher level of researcher control over interaction that exists in an individual interview translates into comparative advantage in managing what data are actually collected. Moreover, the relative financial cost of focus groups and individual interviews is somewhat unclear and depends in part on the amount of time and resources spent on planning and implementing either method.

Use of focus groups must be consistent with the purpose of the research. Focus groups are, for example, inappropriate for determining the prevalence of a given attitude or experience among a population (Ward, Bertrand, and Brown 1991). Telephone surveys are better able to elicit simple "yes" or "no" responses about specific behaviors and experiences and are able to cover more topics in a shorter amount of time (Morgan 1996). As always, there is a trade-off between the depth of data collection approaches such as focus groups and in-person interviews and the breadth of methods such as telephone surveys.

Compared with participant observation, the main advantage of focus groups is the ability to observe a large amount of verbal interaction on a topic in a limited period of time. The facilitator may direct or facilitate the functioning of the group, but this may also be viewed as the most significant disadvantage compared with participant observation. Focus groups are unnatural settings, generally limited to verbal behavior, consisting only of interaction in a somewhat artificial discussion group, created and directed by the researcher. If the goal is examination of natural individual or group behavior, observation is the preferred approach. Indeed, organizations are frequently studied by participant observation because they are structurally well suited to the method (Morgan 1988). Investigation of psychological topics such as attitudes and cognition, however, is more compatible with an interview-based, one-on-one approach.

Use in Welfare Policy Implementation Research

Focus groups have not been widely used in implementation research perhaps because their unique advantages, such as the ability to observe group interaction and exchange of ideas, are not essential to investigations of policy implementation. However, because they are an excellent tool for gathering general perceptual data quickly and for gathering input from individuals who are not literate, focus groups are a useful tool when seeking the general perceptions and experiences of program participants. If quick feedback on program functioning is needed, focus groups are very useful. In addition, this somewhat participant-driven approach is appropriate in "many applied settings where there is a difference in perspective between the researchers and those with whom they need to work" (Morgan 1996, 133). Because welfare reform circa 1996 fundamentally shifts policy implementation and interpretation to the state and, often, substate level, the use of focus groups as a data collection tool may increase in the coming years.

Although historically less popular among implementation researchers, focus groups have been used in several welfare policy implementation studies. As an additional data collection tool in her Michigan study, Sandfort (1997) conducted 13 focus groups, each of which was held with staff in similar positions (frontline or management); discussion focused on organizational change and staff responses to such change. Fraker (1998) employed focus groups as one component of Mathematica's examination of Iowa's Limited Benefit Plan. Specifically, public health nurses and social workers were to visit families assigned to the Plan; focus groups and observation were used as data collection tools and revealed that this aspect of the program (home visiting) was not being carried out as intended.

MDRC used focus groups with clients in its Vermont, Florida, and Minnesota implementation studies to investigate the reasons behind client actions (Knox 1998). Kraft and Bush (1998) conducted a series of focus groups with welfare recipients in New Jersey to examine participants' knowledge of welfare reform and their perspectives on service adequacy and system improvement. Similarly, Bloom et al. (1998) used focus group discussions with clients to examine perceptions of Jobs First in Connecticut.

Thus focus groups may be used to identify salient issues among a particular category of staff or to examine perceptions or thought processes among program participants. Sample focus group guide items are provided in figure 10.14. The most appropriate use of focus groups in the welfare reform implementation context is identification of broad themes or issues that can then be examined in more depth through additional data collection strategies. Like in-person interviews, however, the focus

Figure 10.14. Sample Focus Group Guide Items

• What do you think about the new workshops that are available to program participants? • What suggestions do you have for improving the program?

group appears to be a deceptively simple method, and several issues (see figure 10.15) must be addressed before this approach is adopted. High-quality focus groups call for the careful development of discussion guides and group procedures; analysis is time-consuming and challenging; the moderator or facilitator must be highly skilled and solidly grounded in the research and the specific contribution to the project that the focus group is intended to yield. The appropriateness of this method for the study at hand should always be carefully considered, and adequate time and effort must be invested to yield high-quality data.

Content Analysis of Existing Documents

Analysis of data created or collected by others and archived in some form[7] (such as forms, other program documents, or case records) is typically undertaken using content analysis techniques. Content analysis procedures "create quantitative indicators that assess the degree of attention or concern devoted to units such as themes, categories or issues" (Weber 1990, 70). Content analysis is particularly useful for three types of research problems: (1) those involving a large volume of text, (2) those in which the research topic must be studied at a distance (such as historical documents), and (3) those in which the message(s) in the text are difficult to discern through casual observation (Neuman 1994). Content analysis is, essentially, a data reduction technique.

Figure 10.15. Focus Groups: Issues to Consider

• Degree of facilitator control, direction	• Social desirability bias
• Facilitator skill	• Analysis approach
• Discussion guide development, structure	• Artificial setting
• Logistics (group assembly, environment)	• Limited generalizability
• Sample representativeness	

There are a variety of content analysis techniques, including but not limited to key-word-in-context (KWIC) lists, word frequency lists, retrievals from coded texts, and category counts (Weber 1990). Careful measurement is essential to high-quality written document analysis and observation. The unit of analysis must be determined in advance and the researcher must develop a coding system that includes rules or instructions on how to systematically record the content of interest. Thus both structured observation and contextual analysis, if done well, are systematic, careful, and based on written rules for categorizing or classifying observations or written materials. This type of carefully structured approach enhances the reliability of the data obtained and allows replication to take place.

Coding approaches used in secondary analysis of existing documents vary widely depending on the research focus and questions. Common characteristics of interest include frequency (e.g., of a particular behavior, word, or phrase), direction (e.g., along some continuum such as positive versus negative, slow versus quick), and intensity (e.g., minor versus major or strength versus weakness). Coding may also focus on manifest or latent content, or a combination of the two. Generally, manifest content coding, which focuses on the visible, surface content, tends to be more reliable. Latent content coding, which focuses on the underlying, implicit meaning, is generally less reliable because it is based on the individual coder's knowledge and interpretation of meaning (Neuman 1994).

Advantages and Disadvantages

Secondary analysis of existing documents offers unique advantages (figure 10.16). The approach entails examination of existing data from which the researcher derives intentions or actions, rather than reliance solely upon individuals' perceptions of such intentions or actions. It also offers a strategy for examination of data when no other means of investigation may be viable, such as historical information. Like observation, it is an

Figure 10.16. Advantages of Secondary Analysis, Existing Documents

• Direct access to data otherwise inaccessible	• Triangulation of additional data/findings
• No social desirability bias	
• Low cost	• Identification of discrepancies

extremely useful supplementary data collection approach because it may offer information that respondents are unable to provide verbally.

However, there are clear limits to this type of secondary analysis, and in general its utility depends on the purpose of the research. Often, the data contained within the documents were created for particular purposes and are not in a format, or do not contain key information, necessary for meeting the research objectives. In addition, without information provided by human interpretation and explanation of archival documents, the knowledge that may be gained through document analysis may be limited or interpretation may be flawed. Thus data acquired through this approach often must be supplemented with data collected from individuals who were involved in the events recorded in the documents.

Less immediately apparent limitations are reliability and validity. Like observation, examination of existing documents involving more than one reviewer or coder necessitates examination of intercoder reliability. In the typical quality control process, coders are asked to code the same text independently; consistency across coders is then checked, usually by another member of the research team. Types of reliability of interest (when multiple coders are used) include stability, reproducibility, and accuracy (Weber 1990).[8]

Findings generated through content analysis possess face validity to the extent that the variables identified actually measure the concepts they were intended to measure. That is, there must be correspondence between the coding category and the abstract concept it represents. Reliability and validity problems typically arise in content analysis because of the ambiguity of word meanings, category definitions, and other coding rules (Weber 1990). Although computer-aided analysis introduces new problems and may at times increase validity issues, such analysis enhances reliability when valid coding rules are consistently applied. Computer-aided approaches are typically used only in research projects entailing a substantial amount of content analysis, such as copious interview transcripts or field notes.

Use in Welfare Policy Implementation Research

Program documents are frequently drawn upon in implementation research to understand the intended nature of a program (for example, policy manuals) or to investigate the manner in which messages are conveyed to clients (program forms). Minutes of task force or commission meetings, transcripts of legislative hearings, and other program design documents are a rich source of information in implementation studies. Case records and the data contained therein are used to track client flow or pathways and to identify the decisions workers make under different circumstances. Items consistent with secondary analysis are provided in figure 10.17.

Most frequently, data in client case records are used to examine clients' experiences. Riccio et al. (1989) used GAIN case managers' narrative descriptions from client case records to identify workers' actions, clients' attendance at activities, and status changes. These data were then combined with data recorded on state-required case record forms; together these sources provided the data necessary to create a database of participant flow information. Case record data were also used to code county emphasis on the penalty process, specifically, the proportions of recipients placed in conciliation or sanctioned. Eventually, such data were linked to outcomes by examining the relationship between the emphasis on penalties and the effectiveness of programs, defined by average earnings and cash assistance payments (see Riccio and Hasenfeld 1996). Bloom et al. (1997) examined the implementation of new policy mandates through similar client data, investigating services received by clients and thus, indirectly, implementation of new policy mandates.

Many implementation studies also use analysis of program materials or other written documents to inform their understanding of policies, procedures, or program components. Sandfort (1997), employing a grounded approach to theory building, used program documents to inform her analysis process. Maloy et al. (1998) used review of state documents (supplemented by informal interviewing of state officials) as the primary data source in their examination of diversion practices across states.

Like observational data, existing data are invaluable for data triangulation and may provide a more objective indication of program functioning than data obtained via staff self-report. Case record data are invaluable for understanding program processes across time. In addition, data contained within policy statements and program descriptions are essential to deter-

Figure 10.17. Sample Secondary Analysis Items

- [Informational program document] Is information on support services provided?
- [Case record] Dates and nature of worker contacts with client during past year

mining discrepancies between what was intended and what occurred. Indeed, most implementation studies are not complete without analysis of program and policy documents.

The issues to be considered before relying upon this method are set out in figure 10.18. Implementation researchers must be certain that the documents reviewed are capable of answering the research questions or, at a minimum, of enhancing researchers' understanding of the implementation process. And, as with all data sources, researchers must be aware of nuances. For example, program forms or other documents may be replaced regularly. Thus it is critical to probe such issues when attempting to use such documents to understand program development or differences between past and current functioning. In case record data, information of a certain type (e.g., appointment scheduling) or pertaining to unusual situations (e.g., sanctioning documentation) may be stored in an unexpected place or manner. Again, collection and analysis procedures must be carefully designed and developed.

Conclusion

In well-done welfare policy implementation research, as in all good research, the choice of data collection method should be determined by the research purpose or question. In some situations, identification of an appropriate method is fairly straightforward (see table 10.1). Clients' views of reform or experiences with a new program, for example, simply cannot be ascertained from administrative data and should instead be obtained through an interview-based approach. This type of approach is particularly insightful when multiple, intensive interviews take place over time

Figure 10.18. Secondary Analysis, Existing Documents: Issues to Consider

- Systematic recording of content of interest
- Unit of analysis
- Ambiguous word meanings, category definitions, coding rules
- Ability of data to answer research questions of interest
- Understanding of data nuances
- Cross-coder reliability

Table 10.1. Data Collection Approach and Sample Consistent Research Questions

Approach	Consistent research questions
In-person interviews	• How do staff view the new policy or program? • How do staff describe day-to-day functioning of the program?
Telephone surveys	• Why did the majority of participants leave the program? • Were most program participants satisfied with the services they received?
Mail and self-administered questionnaires	• Among frontline workers, how much time is allocated to distinct job tasks? • To what extent do program staff feel the new policy has changed job functions?
Observation	• How does the program function on a daily basis? • What takes place during worker-client interactions?
Focus groups	• What are possible reasons for low attendance at certain program activities? • Among clients, what program components have been most helpful?
Secondary analysis	• Since the enactment of the new policy, have there been changes in client flow or activity participation rates? • What types of changes have occurred in the information conveyed to program participants via written documents?

(see Edin's discussion in chapter 8 of this volume). If the research question or objective requires direct observation of interactions, activities, or other such phenomena, interviewing alone is not sufficient. Institutional analyses thus typically draw upon a variety of data sources. For example, organizational ethnographies—or "street-level" analyses (see Brodkin's discussion in chapter 7 of this volume)—likely draw upon both interviewing and observation. Accurate data describing program participation patterns before and after implementation of a new policy or program cannot be reliably obtained from client or staff interviews, but should be retrieved from administrative data systems. Program management studies, including performance analyses (see Mead's discussion in chapter 6 of this volume), are therefore likely to draw upon secondary analysis of administrative data as well as observational data.

High-quality implementation studies, of necessity, usually require use of multiple data collection approaches. The challenge is to ascertain correctly the approach best suited to specific questions of interest. However, in virtually all situations, two or more distinct methods together are best able to produce the desired information. For example, conclusions regarding worker practices have greatest validity when based on data ascertained through interviews, self-administered questionnaires, and observation. For some straightforward questions, a single method may be sufficient and two methods may be equally appropriate. For example, descriptive demographic data on clients can probably be obtained equally well from surveys or administrative data. Here the decision about which method to use is typically based on project timelines and the financial and human resources available to support the data collection effort.

Logistical considerations often prohibit use of a particular approach. Timelines and budgets are only two of the many real-world constraints imposed on researchers. The ideal method of data collection may not be the method that, ultimately, is used. If the researcher prefers administrative data but the agency is unwilling to release it, another method must be employed. In contrast, the researcher may have little choice but to use administrative data if the agency is unwilling to release client contact information or to otherwise permit personal contact with clients. Sometimes there is simply no way around data access obstacles. Other times there are ways to reach a negotiated solution that permits the research to go forward without compromising the quality of the data used for analysis.

Such feasibility considerations often play a critical role in shaping the nature of a study. Indeed, feasibility may be of foremost concern and the ideal combination of data collection approaches may not be possible. In such cases, the trade-offs must be thoroughly considered and the most methodologically appropriate and doable approach should be selected. Logistical issues must always be weighed against other concerns such as the quality of the data generated by different approaches and the ability to meet the research objectives without using a particular approach. In welfare policy implementation research, in particular, if feasibility issues affect the choice of approach, the resulting limitations of the data should be clearly stated so that informed interpretation of findings can take place. When multiple methods of data collection are used in a single investigation, the presentation of findings should indicate which types of data are used, and in what manner, to answer each research question.

The bottom line is that the choice of method is almost never as simple or straightforward as our didactic presentation of the available menu of data collection approaches may make it appear. The primary strengths and limitations of each approach should be evaluated (see table 10.2). But in reality, many issues must be considered in making a truly informed choice and numerous obstacles may prevent the optimal strategy from becoming reality. Nonetheless, this is one of the most important decisions that implementation researchers face. Given policymakers' great hunger for empirical data about welfare reform, the high stakes for families and for states, and the plethora of new programs and policies across the nation, it is incumbent upon those who study welfare implementation to gather data that are as reliable and valid as possible.

Policy implementation researchers face a collective necessity to make implementation research as systematic a type of inquiry as possible, to fully report methodological strategies and challenges encountered, and to increase our ability to replicate methods or models. The type of research that has dominated implementation studies—that is, research "in the field"—presents tremendous opportunities for hypothesis generation and knowledge development; however, those directing such research efforts must ensure that methods employed are rigorous and systematic. Moreover, researchers concentrating their efforts on unique areas of data collection and analysis must communicate for triangulation and the exchange of ideas possible through use of multiple methods to occur. If a comprehensive understanding of policy implementation and program functioning is sought, those working with administrative data must com-

Table 10.2. Strengths and Limitations of Approaches to Data Collection

Method	Primary strength	Primary limitation
In-person interviews	Complexity, depth	High cost, time
Telephone surveys	Speed, low cost	Lack of depth, low response rate (TANF populations)
Mail/self-administered questionnaires	Low cost, low social desirability bias	Lack of control, low response rate (mail)
Observation(s)	Complexity, new discoveries	Social desirability bias, time
Focus groups	Complexity, speed	Social desirability bias, lack of control
Secondary analysis of existing data	Low cost, speed	Lack of complexity, lack of depth

Note: TANF = Temporary Assistance to Needy Families.

municate with those conducting field-based research such as observation and in-person interviewing. Similarly, implementation researchers must remain in constant communication with nonresearchers involved in the development and implementation of new policies and programs so that the foci of study and data collection efforts remain relevant. Social science researchers, in general, confront many of the same challenges. However, the degree of difficulty is heightened for implementation researchers because policy implementation is not static. Thus the research and data collection approaches used to study the implementation process must also be adaptive and dynamic.

NOTES

1. See Guba (1990) for discussion of such paradigmatic issues.
2. Bloom, Kemple, and Rogers-Dillon (1997) also used in-person interviews with managers and line staff to inform their field research on implementation of Florida's welfare reform program.
3. Similarly, Brodkin (1997), in her case study of JOBS implementation and program functioning in Illinois, used qualitative in-person interviewing with frontline staff members as one component of her field research.
4. Mead (1996), when conducting field research, also employs in-person interviews but in a more restricted fashion to identify general agency tendencies and emphases. Such interviews are then used to generate hypotheses that are examined through analysis of administrative data, the primary tool used in Mead's examinations of program operations and outcomes.
5. In fact, as elected officials' interest in the early outcomes of PRWORA-driven state reform programs has grown, a number of states have carried out or commissioned client tracking studies, the majority of which (to date) have relied in whole or in part on the use of telephone surveys (see Tweedie, Jarchow, and Wilkins 2001). Attention to implementation issues, however, varies widely.
6. For a discussion of the use of administrative data, see Robert Goerge (chapter 11, this volume).
7. The issues involved in using another form of existing data—administrative records—are discussed in chapter 11 of this volume.
8. A variety of techniques may be used to examine the degree of consistency between coders; for a thorough discussion of such techniques, see Krippendorff (1980).

REFERENCES

Adler, Patricia A., and Peter Adler. 1998. "Observational Techniques." In *Collecting and Interpreting Qualitative Materials,* edited by Norman K. Denzin and Yvonne S. Lincoln (79–109). Thousand Oaks, Calif.: Sage Publications.

Bloom, Dan, Mary Andes, and Claudia Nicholson. 1998. *Jobs First: Early Implementation of Connecticut's Welfare Reform Initiative.* New York: Manpower Demonstration Research Corporation.

Bloom, Dan, James J. Kemple, and Robin Rogers-Dillon. 1997. *The Family Transition Program: Early Impacts of Florida's Initial Time-Limited Welfare Program.* New York: Manpower Demonstration Research Corporation.

Bogdan, Robert C., and Shari K. Biklen. 1992. *Qualitative Research for Education: An Introduction to Theory and Methods.* Boston: Allyn and Bacon.

Born, Catherine E., Leanne Charlesworth, and Mary Hyde. 1998. *Year One Report Volume One: Examining Customer Pathways and Assessment Practices.* Baltimore: University of Maryland School of Social Work.

Bourque, Linda B., and Eve Fielder. 1995. *How to Conduct Self-Administered and Mail Surveys.* Thousand Oaks, Calif.: Sage Publications.

Brodkin, Evelyn Z. 1997. "Inside the Welfare Contract: Discretion and Accountability in State Welfare Administration." *Social Service Review* 71(1):1–29.

Czaja, Ronald, and Johnny Blair. 1996. *Designing Surveys: A Guide to Decisions and Procedures.* Thousand Oaks, Calif.: Pine Forge Press.

Fein, David J., Erik Beecroft, William Hamilton, Wang S. Lee, Pamela A. Holcomb, Terri S. Thompson, and Caroline E. Ratcliffe. 1998. *The Indiana Welfare Reform Evaluation: Program Implementation and Economic Impacts after Two Years.* Indianapolis, Ind.: Family and Social Services Administration.

Fern, Edward F. 1982. "The Use of Focus Groups for Idea Generation: The Effects of Group Size, Acquaintanceship, and Moderator on Response Quantity and Quality." *Journal of Marketing Research* 19(1):1–13.

Fletcher, Cynthia N., Mary Winter, and Barbara J. Gaddis. 1998. "Studying Welfare Reform: Challenges and Opportunities." *Consumer Interests Annual* 44:72–78.

Fowler, Floyd J. 1995. *Improving Survey Questions: Design and Evaluation.* Thousand Oaks, Calif.: Sage Publications.

Fraker, Thomas M. 1998. *Process Evaluation: Implementation and Operations Studies.* Panel presentation at Department of Health and Human Services Conference on Evaluating Welfare Reform, Arlington, Va., May 21.

Frey, James H., and Sabine Mertens Oishi. 1995. *How to Conduct Interviews by Telephone and In Person.* Thousand Oaks, Calif.: Sage Publications.

Glaser, Barney G., and Anselm L. Strauss. 1967. *The Discovery of Grounded Theory: Strategies for Qualitative Research.* Chicago: Aldine.

Gold, Raymond L. 1958. "Roles in Sociological Field Observations." *Social Forces* 36(3):217–33.

Goodwin, Leonard, and Phyllis Moen. 1983. "The Evolution and Implementation of Family Welfare Policy." In *Implementation and Public Policy,* edited by Daniel A. Mazmanian and Paul A. Sabatier (147–68). Glenview, Ill.: Scott, Foresman.

Guba, Egon G. 1990. "The Alternative Paradigm Dialog." In *The Paradigm Dialog,* edited by Egon G. Guba (17–30). Newbury Park, Calif.: Sage Publications.

Hagen, Jan L. 1994. "JOBS and Case Management: Developments in 10 States." *Social Work* 39(2):197–205.

Hagen, Jan L., and Liane Vida Davis. 1994. *Implementing JOBS: The Participants' Perspective.* Albany: Rockefeller Institute of Government, State University of New York.

Hagen, Jan L., and Irene Lurie. 1994. *Implementing JOBS: Case Management Services*. Albany: Rockefeller Institute of Government, State University of New York.

Hasenfeld, Yeheskel, and Dale Weaver. 1996. "Enforcement, Compliance, and Disputes in Welfare-to-Work Programs." *Social Service Review* 70(2):235–56.

Holcomb, Pamela, LaDonna Pavetti, Caroline Ratcliffe, and Susan Riedinger. 1998. "Building an Employment Focused Welfare System: Work First and Other Work-Oriented Strategies in Five States." Washington, D.C.: The Urban Institute. http://aspe.hhs.gov/search/hsp/isp/wfirst/wfsum.htm.

Knox, Vera. 1998. "Process Evaluation: Implementation and Operations Studies." Panel presentation at Department of Health and Human Services Conference on Evaluating Welfare Reform, Arlington, Va., May 21.

Kraft, M. Katherine, and Irene R. Bush. 1998. "Accountable Welfare Reform: What Consumers Think." *Public Administration Review* 58(5):406–17.

Krippendorff, Klaus. 1980. *Content Analysis: An Introduction to Its Methodology*. Beverly Hills, Calif.: Sage Publications.

Krueger, Richard A. 1988. *Focus Groups: A Practical Guide for Applied Research*. Newbury Park, Calif.: Sage Publications.

Kvale, Steinar. 1996. *Interviews: An Introduction to Qualitative Research Interviewing*. Thousand Oaks, Calif.: Sage Publications.

Lavrakas, Paul J. 1987. *Telephone Survey Methods: Sampling, Selection, and Supervision*. Newbury Park, Calif.: Sage Publications.

Lipsky, Michael. 1980. *Street-Level Bureaucracy: Dilemmas of the Individual in Public Services*. New York: Russell Sage Foundation.

Maloy, Kathleen A., LaDonna A. Pavetti, Peter Shin, Julie Darnell, and Lea Scarpulla-Nolan. 1998. *Description and Assessment of State Approaches to Diversion Programs and Activities under Welfare Reform*. Washington, D.C.: U.S. Department of Health and Human Services.

Mangione, Thomas W. 1995. *Mail Surveys: Improving the Quality*. Thousand Oaks, Calif.: Sage Publications.

Mazmanian, Daniel, and Paul A. Sabatier. 1983. *Implementation and Public Policy*. Glenview, Ill.: Scott, Foresman.

Mead, Lawrence M. 1996. "Welfare Policy: The Administrative Frontier." *Journal of Policy Analysis and Management* 15(4):587–600.

Meyers, Marcia K. 1993. "Child Care in JOBS Employment and Training Program: What Difference Does Quality Make?" *Journal of Marriage and the Family* 55(3):767–83.

Meyers, Marcia K., Barney Glaser, and Karin MacDonald. 1998. "On the Front Lines of Welfare Delivery: Are Workers Implementing Policy Reforms?" *Journal of Policy Analysis and Management* 17(1):1–22.

Miller, Delbert C. 1991. *Handbook of Research Design and Measurement*. Newbury Park, Calif.: Sage Publications.

Morgan, David L. 1988. *Focus Groups as Qualitative Research*. Newbury Park, Calif.: Sage Publications.

———. 1996. "Focus Groups." *Annual Review of Sociology* 22:129–52.

Nathan, Richard P., and Thomas L. Gais. 1999. *Overview Report: Implementing the Personal Responsibility Act of 1996*. Albany: Rockefeller Institute of Government, State University of New York.

Neuman, W. Lawrence. 1994. *Social Research Methods: Qualitative and Quantitative Approaches*, 2d ed. Needham Heights, Mass.: Allyn and Bacon.

Pressman, Jeffrey L., and Aaron B. Wildavsky. 1973. *Implementation: How Great Expectations in Washington Are Dashed in Oakland*. Berkeley: University of California Press.

Riccio, James, and Daniel Friedlander. 1992. *GAIN: Program Strategies, Participation Patterns, and First-Year Impacts in Six Counties*. New York: Manpower Demonstration Research Corporation.

Riccio, James, and Yeheskel Hasenfeld. 1996. "Enforcing a Participation Mandate in a Welfare-to-Work Program." *Social Service Review* 70(4):516–42.

Riccio, James, and Alan Orenstein. 1996. "Understanding Best Practices for Operating Welfare-to-Work Programs." *Evaluation Review* 20(1):3–28.

Riccio, James, Barbara Goldman, Gayle Hamilton, Karin Martinson, and Alan Orenstein. 1989. *GAIN: Early Implementation Experiences and Lessons*. New York: Manpower Demonstration Research Corporation.

Rubin, Herbert J., and Irene S. Rubin. 1995. *Qualitative Interviewing: The Art of Hearing Data*. Thousand Oaks, Calif.: Sage Publications.

Sandfort, Jodi, R. 1997. "The Structuring of Front-Line Work: Conditions within Local Welfare and Welfare-to-Work Organizations in Michigan." Paper presented at Annual Conference of the Association for Public Policy Analysis and Management, Washington, D.C., Nov.

Sandfort, Jodi, Kristin K. Seefeldt, and Sandra Danziger. 1998. "Exploring the Effect of Welfare Reform Implementation on the Attainment of Policy Goals: An Examination of Michigan's Counties." Paper presented at Annual Conference of the Association for Public Policy Analysis and Management, New York, Oct. 29–31.

Scrivener, Susan, Gayle Hamilton, Mary Farrell, Stephen Freedman, Daniel Friedlander, Marisa Mitchell, Jodi Nudelman, and Christine Schwartz. 1998. *National Evaluation of Welfare-to-Work Strategies: Implementation, Participation Patterns, Costs, and Two-Year Impacts of the Portland (Oregon) Welfare-to-Work Program*. Washington, D.C.: U.S. Department of Health and Human Services and U.S. Department of Education.

Seefeldt, Kristin S., Jodi Sandfort, and Sandra K. Danziger. 1998. *Moving Toward a Vision of Family Independence: Local Managers' Views of Michigan's Welfare Reforms*. Ann Arbor: University of Michigan School of Social Work, Law, and Public Policy.

Stewart, David W., and Prem N. Shamdasani. 1990. *Focus Groups: Theory and Practice*. Thousand Oaks, Calif.: Sage Publications.

Tweedie, Jack, Courtney Jarchow, and Andrew Wilkins. 2001. *Tracking Recipients after They Leave Welfare*. Denver: National Conference of State Legislatures.

Ward, Victoria M., Jane T. Bertrand, and Lisanne F. Brown. 1991. "The Comparability of Focus Group and Survey Results." *Evaluation Review* 15:266–83.

Weaver, Dale, and Yeheskel Hasenfeld. 1997. "Case Management Practices, Participants' Responses, and Compliance in Welfare-to-Work Programs." *Social Work Research* 21(2):92–100.

Weber, Robert P. 1990. *Basic Content Analysis*. Newbury Park, Calif.: Sage Publications.

11

Use of Administrative Data for Implementation Research

Robert M. Goerge

I t is clear that multiple sources of data and a range of methods are needed for a comprehensive, rigorous implementation study of welfare reform. Surveys of administrators, caseworkers, program applicants and participants, and even the eligible who do not apply should be done to understand the experiences and activities of those involved over time. Ethnographic and other qualitative methods should be used to understand the cultural changes and the meanings that are ascribed to events and decisions. Policy and program documents need to be reviewed to understand the intended actions. Administrative data from both computerized records and paper files that track the events that households and individuals experienced, the decisions caseworkers made, and the characteristics of both individuals and caseworkers can also be an important source of data.

Administrative data are data that are regularly and consistently collected in support of an organization's function and stored within that organization's information system. Administrative databases are created primarily to monitor use, to determine the consumption of resources, and to ascertain the capacity to supply services. Although administrative data are not collected primarily for research purposes, they can become a resource for research and statistics.

Administrative data are culled from systems that have two basic functions. A particular system may stress one function over the other. The first function is reporting for the purpose of accountability or reimbursement from an external or oversight agency (usually a federal one). The second is internal tracking of individuals or the services that they receive to support decisionmaking and other activities of the organization. The tracking function is what we think about when we refer to management information systems. Typically, the tracking system provides richer data, as external reporting in human services is generally limited to eligibility of the individual for services; tracking data assumes, in contrast, that one is interested in information that identifies and characterizes the individual served, the individuals providing the service, and the services themselves.

In this chapter, I describe the use of administrative data in the context of welfare reform for the purposes of researchers examining the implementation and process of reform. After defining administrative data in greater detail, I discuss both the promise that administrative data offer for research and how far one may go with such data. Illustrative examples are provided. These sections are followed by two on the quality of administrative data and the obstacles a researcher may experience in using such data. I end the chapter with a discussion of some of the technical issues that a researcher may encounter once the data have been acquired and the work begins.

Administrative Data and Welfare Reform Research

In an era of results-based management systems and devolution of authority to more local levels, administrative data take on added importance. A recent report by Northwestern University and the University of Chicago's Joint Center for Poverty Research concludes that, in this era of devolution and results-based management, "policymakers and program administrators will require more and better data sources than they now have if they are to adequately monitor program operations and evaluate program outcomes" (Hotz et al. 1998, ix). Currently, national survey data are a prominent source for academic poverty research. However, these surveys are unable to provide sufficient sample sizes at the state and local levels—the level of government at which more responsibility today lies—and in the time that is necessary to undertake policy and programmatic change. Many states and researchers, therefore, are beginning to look to administrative data to fill their new research needs. Further, administrative databases can play a critical role in cross-state comparisons once issues of comparability are resolved. Technology allows easier linking across multiple data sets today, allowing researchers to overcome many past limitations.

Not only does linking data sets together allow evaluators to follow participants longer and through a variety of programs, it also provides data from more than one program, therefore offering the ability to monitor the success of multiple policy goals. For example, states may have the multiple goals of lowering teenage, out-of-wedlock pregnancy and raising school tests scores and graduation rates. Administrative data can be linked in such a way as to monitor those goals. As the Poverty Center report concludes, "[We] are convinced that administrative data can and ought to be one of the important tools in this research effort" (Hotz et al. 1998, 79).

Cancian et al. (1999) compared administrative data, national longitudinal surveys, and target surveys for assessing work, earnings, and well-being after welfare. The strengths of administrative data include their accuracy and timeliness, their coverage of the service population, their longitudinal nature, and the ability to study small subsets of the population. Weaknesses they list are that the data on other family members, other income, and other issues are not comprehensive and that no information is available for the period after they leave welfare. In fact, these weaknesses can be addressed; the way to address them is discussed later in this chapter. Cancian et al. conclude that "a successful strategy for assessing the well-being of those who leave state TANF [Temporary Assistance for Needy Families] programs will combine analyses of state administrative data with improved, targeted state surveys to provide supplementary information" (Cancian et al. 1999, 25). Certainly, if at all possible, linking data from multiple sources to take advantage of their unique strengths is the preferable strategy for answering most research questions.

Administrative data track the major events of the service provision process and, essentially, what is actually implemented at the recipient/ worker level for a particular program. Administrative data are potentially a key source for process studies for two reasons (Hotz et al. 1998). First, using such data seems to be a logical first step inasmuch as they are supposed to track what is implemented. Most tracking systems do not include information on all the steps of a case's participation, but looking at the activities that are tracked is a good first step in an implementation analysis. Second, it is often thought that this is a readily available data source that can be "mined" early and often. As the implementation occurs, analyses can be updated to develop a longitudinal picture of the implementation—

for example, looking at a monthly recording or case closing reasons (employment or sanction). Moreover, administrative data can provide clues to the quality of implementation. The actual operation of the information system from which the administrative data come is part of the implementation of a policy. An inadequate information system likely means that a policy is not being implemented well or that the process of benefit provision is not going as planned. Good implementation often relies on having a well-designed and responsive information system.

However, it is clear that administrative data will not address all issues of process and implementation. For one, issues of program diversion and eligible nonapplicants cannot be addressed with data from information systems used in TANF because such families and individuals are likely not to be tracked in those systems. Although we may be able to track some family members in other administrative systems, such as food stamps, Medicaid, Unemployment Insurance (UI), Supplemental Security Income (SSI), wage reporting, new hire records, child care, and child support, such a record linkage project would be complex and is unlikely to capture the entire range of substantive interest and the population of interest. Some families will be diverted and simply not captured anywhere.

Because administrative data are here to stay, research using such data will not only constitute a report on the functioning of the system at the time of research but also provide a reporting process capable of updating the findings regularly. Rabb and Winstead (see chapter 2 in this volume) talk about the importance of timely data in the program implementation and policymaking processes and the increasing availability and utility of administrative data. Therefore, an investigation of how administrative data are used in implementation research may provide great long-term benefits if the research activities can be institutionalized in the operation of public agencies. The current efforts to develop better indicators rely a great deal on administrative data because of their availability and cost-effectiveness and because of the lack of regular primary data collection at the state or local level. In recent years, there has been tremendous growth in the use of administrative data at state and county public agencies (Brady and Snow 1996; Hotz et al. 1998). The relationship between state agencies and researchers can become a symbiotic one centering on the use of administrative data for improving monitoring, implementation, and evaluation. States providing researchers with a broad range of administrative data could enrich welfare program implementation research. This chapter hopes to provide some of the ways in which that could happen. In turn, researchers have the resources to make administrative data a much more useful source for states and could assist states in improving their knowledge of how welfare reform is being implemented. Except for intermittent targeted surveys, such as those of TANF leavers now being done in many states, state agencies depend on administrative data for their information and could expand their use of the data.

The recent developments in linking administrative data across programs and storing and accessing those linked data sets in database systems called data warehouses add a new potential utility to administrative data. Just as the categorical nature of programs is being questioned and attacked, the utility of categorical (single-program) data is waning. Looking at the process of service provision or the implementation of policy across multiple programs offers the possibility of looking at service provision in a comprehensive way across time and geography and at a richer set of outcomes.

The Definition of Administrative Data

Administrative data in the social program domain are the data collected in the course of service and benefit provision. In this chapter, we limit our definition of administrative data to data on individual transactions or events, and individuals or families involved in those transactions—such as the provision of benefits, sanctions, ending of benefits, and the receipt of human services. This contrasts with information that is the result of aggregation or analysis of recipient or provider events, such as that used in performance analysis (see Mead's discussion in chapter 6 of this volume).

An administrative information system is typically created for one or a group of related services or benefits. In most cases, it is explicitly not collected for research purposes.[1] Administrative data are collected to (1) determine eligibility of individuals and families for a particular benefit; (2) make payments to both recipients and service providers; (3) track service provision and administrative outcomes of those services; (4) track worker and program activity; and (5) produce regular or ad hoc management reports. In the late 1990s, the greater part of this information is collected through computerized information systems. It can therefore be manipulated significantly more easily than when the information was collected and stored in hard copy.

Administrative data are collected through a variety of mechanisms. Typically, the most reliable is the direct entry of information into the information system by the staff member who is interviewing an individual for eligibility or service purposes. Because this direct data entry is not always possible for technical, professional, or legal reasons, in the majority of social programs, paper forms are completed and then either scanned or entered manually by clerks. Technical obstacles include information systems that are not configured to allow all operators to enter information. The current "legacy" information systems, created in the 1970s and 1980s, do not make use of the distributed computing capacities of networking or the Internet where more individuals can take direct advantage of computer access. Entering data on their clients into an information system is not usually an acceptable part of a job description for professional social workers. Also, there may be legal or security restrictions that prevent workers from having direct access to a system, such as in the case of child abuse, substance abuse, HIV/AIDS or mental health services, or information from remote offices or nonpublic providers may be provided through paper or electronic formats.

Administrative data from the latest developed information systems allow accessing data on specific cases instantaneously.[2] This is important because workers are more likely to provide good data if they receive a direct benefit such as immediate access to the data provided. If workers have to wait for paper reports that may come weeks after filling out the forms, they are unlikely to see the benefit of providing accurate data, unless, of course, work performance is evaluated with such data. In these newer systems, transactions can be entered or recalled while the system is running. Workers can retrieve data that they themselves provided or that someone else provided when they sit at a terminal. This is in contrast to systems where all of the transactions are entered at one time through "batch" data entry and information is recalled through "batch" programs that access the data in the off-hours or at a central information systems department, which is typically not accessible to workers. Most systems, even the previous generations of information systems called "legacy" systems, are online systems, but batch systems may still exist in some public agencies.

A similar set of issues surrounds the use of analyses from administrative data by agency managers. If the analyses that they receive are not responsive to their information needs, their support for the information system and for its analysis will decrease. If the data are not being used to plan, assess, or monitor service provision, workers are unlikely to pay attention to collecting data even on the most important items. It is definitely the case that most resources devoted to information systems development are for the collection and storage of data and retrieval of information on specific cases and not on reports or tools aimed to inform managers or agency leadership.

The Promise of Administrative Data

This section presents the types of issues and questions for which administrative data may be an excellent source for research. It is difficult to say with certainty that any data set built from an administrative information system will allow the pursuit of the issues described below because of the tremendous variation in particular program data from jurisdiction to jurisdiction. I generalize here to describe the mode capacities from my experience.

Because of their availability, administrative data have often been thought of as having great potential for research. For a particular program, the data are typically longitudinal, population-based, and accurate for the most important features of the program. Particularly now, because welfare programs and policies vary across states as a result of devolution, the use of administrative data in the context of implementation research is necessary simply to understand what the actual experiences of families in the program are and, in turn, what the "implemented" procedures are, over and above the stated policy. Given that states and in some cases counties can develop and implement their own policies, and that administrative data, by definition, track those families and individuals that participate, a particular study cannot describe who is participating in welfare programs without an analysis of the administrative data. Although interviews of participating families are important to add information that is not contained in the administrative data, one must typically begin with the administrative data to select a representative sample of the recipient populations.

Because administrative data can be the most up-to-date information of their kind available and because studies that use them can be replicated or updated, the data offer the capacity to provide indicators of the most important issues of welfare reform. If the indicators are developed in a multimethod study where the validity and reliability of the administrative data can be assessed, state governments and others monitoring welfare reform can have accurate and timely information for responding to low performance on either effects or implementation of reform.

Because individual reporting or tracking systems focus on a limited set of outcomes and often neglect data fields that are not central to the business at hand, one strategy for improving data is to combine or link administrative databases. The federal government, through the Department of Health and Human Services, has supported states linking administrative data systems for the purpose of studying the effects of welfare reform and other state and federal public assistance programs since 1995 (DHHS 1999). Data warehouses—central, integrated databases of information designed to support decisionmaking and analysis—in the social program domain are becoming more common. They promise to make administrative data more accessible to managers and researchers in all kinds of organizations. Aside from the great benefit of having a comprehensive set of program data in one place, another opportunity for addressing issues of data quality arises as the data warehouses are being built. Inasmuch as "clean" data are necessary to integrate the data, they must be cleaned before they enter the data warehouse.

One inclusion in these data warehouses that is now likely to exist as a result of welfare reform is UI information. Lane and Stevens (1997) use UI records to analyze the transition patterns between participation in income maintenance programs and employment. Kornfeld and Bloom (1997) found that UI records are a valid source of information for studying quarterly earnings of adult women receiving Aid to Families with Dependent Children (AFDC), albeit not so accurate for some other low-income populations. Hotz and Scholz (2001) have recently summarized much of the work on this topic.

Databases such as those described above will be able to provide data that no other source at the state or local level can.[3] When embarking on a longitudinal, prospective study, the researcher will often find that earnings, welfare, and other service receipt data before the start of the study are required. Welfare recipient recall of welfare program participation is inaccurate going back more than three or four years (Kalil et al. 1998), so a researcher should use income maintenance administrative data to access historical information (Gordon, Jacobson, and Fraker 1996).

Administrative data on welfare programs were used to collect information on program participation and effects well before welfare reform,
particularly with the AFDC waiver evaluations (e.g., Bloom, Kemple, and
Rogers-Dillon 1997). Data warehouses offer the potential for going far
beyond those data to include data on other services and programs, such
as welfare-to-work programs, education and training, child support,
child care, child welfare, substance abuse, and mental health services. If
the data warehouses are not yet available, more effort is likely to be
involved in developing other databases. The benefits of developing them,
however, may include long-lasting, positive effects on the research capacity of states. There are often less readily available sources of administrative data (such as birth records, school records data, or Medicaid records)
that may be more cost-effective or may provide data of better quality or
different meaning than survey data. These alternative data sources have
limitations as well but should be considered carefully. The plan for a survey to be done by the evaluator several years after implementation may
take the pressure off state agency staff to obtain other administrative data
and thus have a counterproductive effect. If alternative sources of administrative data are not planned for early on, important opportunities may
be lost, inasmuch as some of the sources (such as school records) require
signed consent forms, and such signatures are most effectively obtained
at program intake (Gordon, Jacobson, and Fraker 1996).

The value of administrative data in studying local variation cannot be
overestimated, and not simply because states are devolving much of the
policymaking to the local level. The neighborhood context is perhaps
even more critical in the implementation of the Personal Responsibility
and Work Opportunity Reconciliation Act (PRWORA) than it was for
the Family Support Act version of welfare. The work requirements of
PRWORA, made more stringent by some states, make recipients more
dependent on the local labor market, child care and transportation resources, substance abuse and domestic violence prevention and treatment programs, and community safety programs. All of these issues are
recognized keys to whether a parent obtains and maintains employment,
and therefore keys to the implementation of welfare reform. In many
cases, administrative data will be able to provide individual data on the
TANF cases, so that the effect of these issues can be assessed at the individual level. More than that, administrative data can characterize the
immediate neighborhoods (and those around them), so that the effect of
the neighborhood context on job seeking, for example, can be assessed.

Administrative data are also central to the development of research that includes survey or other methods. If one intends to sample individuals, welfare offices, counties, or states in a representative manner, administrative data at the individual or aggregate level provide the raw data for such sampling. Particularly when stratified sampling is employed to insure satisfactory subsamples with certain characteristics, administrative data often provide the characteristics, such as caseload size, demographic composition, or "urbanicity." A recent Manpower Demonstration Research Corporation (MDRC) design paper (Michalopoulos, Lalonde, and Verma 1998) provides a good example of how administrative data can be used to select a survey sample. The authors address the problem of families that are eligible for but not receiving TANF by using food stamp data to track a larger population that may include eligible but not receiving families. (Of course, this approach would be problematic if families eligible for food stamps are not applying for this benefit either.)

Information systems have rarely been developed for purposes other than implementing policy or a set of policies. Since the 1970s, whenever social policy changed, there was usually an accompanying change in what was required of information systems or in how they were financed. As the federal government required more accountability from the states during the 1970s and 1980s, the information system development reflected those demands. A majority of state and county information systems before PRWORA were funded by the federal government.

Although the TANF block grant now includes any funds that would in the past have been earmarked for information systems, the principle that the development and use of information systems reflect social policy still holds, but the venue for that analysis now shifts to the state level. We have yet to see how state legislatures will support information systems now that they must pay for the entire system through funds that are in their control. Although many observers think that the disappearance of earmarked federal funding may mean the end of expanded information systems, the fact remains that information systems are a primary means of organizational control; if the information systems lag behind, so will the implementation of new policies and programs and accountability procedures.

The Scope of Administrative Data

Given the categorical nature of social programs, where each program typically has its own set of eligibility criteria, its own set of federal and state funding streams, and its own particular definitions of the unit of benefit receipt (an individual, a family, or a household), information systems have been developed to meet the specific needs of a program, group of programs, or, in rare instances, an entire state or county public agency. Until recently, there has been little effort toward creating online or other databases that link the spectrum of social programs that constitute any human service system or the array of services that a family in need may require or that link records over time. Almost by definition, administrative databases are not linked at the individual or provider level across programs. Even if there is an identifier that is carried across program information systems, the data are not likely to be linked in a way that allows easy analysis across those programs. Linkage also refers to compiling records on an individual over time as well as across programs; it is often necessary to link data from a program over time as well.

Administrative data typically contain information important to the process of determining eligibility and the accounting and reimbursement issues around providing benefits or services. A rule of thumb is that if the data are not directly necessary for either of these two activities, they are unlikely to be accurate enough for research purposes. (This is discussed in greater detail below.) Depending on the database, the following pieces of information are generally contained in most welfare or human service program databases:

- household composition;
- names, birth dates, race/ethnicity, gender, and relationship to head of household of all household members;
- household address;
- eligibility status of each household member;
- reason for and dates of case opening or closing;
- types and dates of service or benefit receipt;
- types and dates of other administrative actions (e.g., sanctions);
- worker or provider identification; and
- other legal status or assessment information, as needed.

Many of the program events of greatest interest will more than likely be tracked well in information systems. Most TANF information systems will be able to report cases that are sanctioned and cases about to reach time limits. What happens after these events in the TANF program or in Food Stamps; Medicaid; Women, Infants, and Children (WIC); or other programs will be tracked in information systems and will provide important data for understanding the continuity of program participation.

The fact that administrative data now exist for nearly every federal or state social program and for many general populations allows examination of how far researchers could go in creating databases that contain comprehensive sets of service receipt and program participation information about individuals across many domains and throughout the life course. Many school systems now computerize demographic, attendance, and achievement data on their entire pupil population; much of this is critical for the adolescents in the TANF populations. Birth and death certificates are now available for an entire generation. Birth data are an important part of many of the goals of welfare reform. Nearly all formal employment is tracked in wage reporting and unemployment insurance data.[4] All hospital discharges are tracked in many states.

Some of the data described above are typically thought of as representing outcomes in an impact study (i.e., employment, births, deaths, hospitalizations, achievement). However, each outcome is also an input into other processes of service provision or an event in an individual's or a family's life. For example, knowing the fertility rate of welfare recipients is a critical piece of information for both past and future operation of welfare programs. Given family caps, how a family reacts when a child is born is an important process that must be understood. Another example is that inasmuch as knowing the employment of the parent is key to understanding child care demand, job status is a key variable for determining whether child care policy is being effectively implemented.

The Quality of Administrative Data

The quality of administrative data varies as widely as that of data collected for research purposes (Goerge and Lee 1999). Just as a response rate for a social survey can vary from 40 to 90 percent depending on the efforts made to locate respondents and complete interviews, a particular administrative data set may be reliable because of administrative mechanisms used to ensure the accuracy of the information collected. Analogous issues exist with surveys related to the maintenance of longitudinal records and the accuracy of each data item collected.

Just as there are good and bad survey data sets, there are also good and bad administrative data sets. Each administrative data set and each field or variable must be assessed individually for accuracy and general utility. A particular data set may be ideal to answer one group of questions in the evaluation of a program and inappropriate for another. The combination of the research questions and the available administrative data will thus determine the quality of a particular data set. Just as it becomes relatively well known among researchers using a particular survey data set which variables are valid or reliable, there are more and less accurate fields within an administrative data set.

There is no substitute for in-depth knowledge of the administration of the program or service system from which the administrative data originates (see Born, Drake, and Needell in Spano and Eckenrode 1998; and Mead's discussion in chapter 6 of this volume). If this knowledge, including detailed information about how the programs are managed and administrative data are collected and used in the daily conduct of the program, is not readily available to the potential user of the data, then that information must be collected directly from administrators, frontline workers, and information system managers. It is important in many cases to work in partnership with the state agency on data development tasks. This effort may be independent of partnering with the state in the evaluation or research. Data development tasks must be separated from the often narrowly focused research itself.

Implementation research assumes a study over some time—often a period of years. Perhaps the biggest issue concerning the relevance of administrative data to implementation research is the creation of longitudinal files from the data contained in information systems (Goerge, Voorhis, and Lee 1994). Most administrative data are stored in cross-sectional formats that contain all the activities of active recipients during a particular span of time. This is done because of the size of the population of recipients and the number of transactions, the cost of online storage space, and the lack of a reason, up until welfare reform, to track cases over time. Because AFDC was an entitlement, there was no need to know the historical receipt of benefits for a particular family except for addressing issues of sanctioning month to month. The best-case scenario for longitudinal data that "pull" from information systems covers a two-year period. State data systems typically lacked a longitudinal focus; for example, few states, if any, were prepared to track a five-year cumulative history of cash assistance receipt when welfare reform was enacted in 1996 (Brady and Snow 1996).

The solution to this problem goes beyond simply combining cross-sections to create a longitudinal record. The challenge is to link cases, households, and individuals in those units over time. Because there was no need for an agency to make sure that a family that came in for a second episode of AFDC had the same case identification number as it had in the first episode, identification numbers of cases or for individuals in those cases may have been duplicated over time. To unduplicate records over time, it is often necessary to implement complex record-linkage (computer matching) algorithms (Goerge, Voorhis, and Lee 1994; Newcombe 1988). It may be that using Social Security numbers is an inadequate method for linking records (Goerge and Lee 1999).

The second aspect of quality—that of each data item collected—depends much more on the prevention or identification of errors. Again, a rule of thumb is that if the data are not directly necessary for determining eligibility or the accounting and reimbursement issues around providing benefits or services, they are unlikely to be of satisfactory accuracy for research purposes. If individual pieces of data are audited for accuracy by the agency, or in some cases a federal agency, a higher level can be expected. An additional benefit of data directly entered by a caseworker is that the quality of the data is checked every time the worker views the data. If someone incorrectly entered a piece of information, it may then be corrected.

Many systems employ edit checks, which prevent the entering of information that is out of range or invalid. However, this does not ensure accuracy, because it is possible that an entry can be in-range or valid and still not be correct. For example, inversion of a day and month of a date can be easily corrected when the month is above 12, but when it is not, there is no way in which a simple edit check can ensure accuracy.

Administrative data are seldom checked in a comprehensive, systematic, manual, or clerical (active) way. In most cases, such work is undertaken by researchers to ensure that the data (either administrative or survey) they are using are accurate. Even then, if a third data source is not available, it is often difficult to choose the most accurate source of data. One area in which there has been significant work is the recall of income and welfare program receipt. This is clearly a case where administrative data constitute a superior record of what a client received, and when.

Obstacles in the Identification of and Access to Administrative Data

Aside from quality, a host of additional issues often prevent researchers from using administrative data. A researcher may know that a program information system exists, but learning about what is available for analytic purposes is often a research project in itself. Good documentation is rare, and the processes by which researchers can access that documentation are not straightforward even if its existence is known.

Once a particular administrative data set is known to exist, there is usually no formal process for actually obtaining access to it. The first obstacle is usually that program managers seldom want external individuals or organizations to have a data set that can be used to evaluate the managers' work. Often, however, there is no formal reason a researcher cannot get the data set. If granted, requests for administrative data can take many months, depending on the workload of the agency and the importance of the request for the agency. Obviously, if a researcher has a contract with an agency, that relationship should facilitate access, but it does not always, inasmuch as the control of the data may be in a different part of the organization from the one that has jurisdiction over the contract.

There are certainly some good reasons that an agency will not share data with a researcher. Often, federal or state law prevents the sharing of administrative data outside the agency unless stringent criteria are met. For example, the law states that Medicaid data (data from other programs) should be shared only when the analysis of that data is intended for the management or improvement of the program. Inasmuch as this is rather ambiguous, the statute can be interpreted loosely. It is often up to researchers to make the argument that their particular case meets the criteria set forth in statute. The restrictions are particularly salient when researchers request data that contain identifying information for individuals—often necessary for linking individuals across programs.

The Structure of Administrative Data for Research Purposes

The techniques of using administrative data for research purposes are not universally known or easily learned. Unlike survey research, where programs of academic instruction are available and where public-use data sets are typically well documented, there are no standards for storing, formatting, or documenting administrative data for research purposes. The individuals or groups who have used administrative data in the past have done so in relative isolation, often because public-use data sets were an unlikely product of this work, given confidentiality and political concerns and the lack of support for reporting on the methods used.

The increasing likelihood that state and county governments will create data warehouses makes it more likely that researchers will have only minimal data management tasks (similar to survey analysis) when they obtain administrative data. However, it is likely to be a number of years before data warehouses are in universal use. In the meantime, researchers who want to use administrative data will still have to either get the government agency to put it into a structure that they can use, which usually requires an unsatisfactory waiting period, or do it themselves. In the next few paragraphs, we shall discuss specifically what that means.

Whereas researchers using surveys must at times contend with complex skip patterns, the researcher who uses administrative data must contend with data structures that are relational, hierarchical, or a combination of the two. Reformatting these data into a flat file or event-history format is usually not a trivial task. This step most often comes before the record-linkage step described earlier, inasmuch as a researcher would want to cull all identifying information into one file for the use of record-linkage programs.

One strategy that researchers at Chapin Hall have employed is to separate information on "entities" into separate files or "tables" (Brookshire 1993). A basic separation of individuals and events allows for a data model that provides sufficient flexibility to undertake a wide range of analyses. Linked to the table of individuals (the "people" table) is a table that links individuals and events, so that we know who experienced what events. We expand this structure, adding to the "people" table another table that defines relationships between individuals so we are able to create families or households or sibling groups or whatever groupings are possible or necessary for the research.

In some instances, the event table may be separated into many event tables that correspond to all of the service events provided by an agency or into tables that contain only one kind of event. To a certain degree, this choice is predicated on technical issues and the size of the population being analyzed. However, the data model should also reflect the priorities of the research or, if the database is going to support multiple research projects, the most flexible structure.

Conclusion

In this chapter, some issues around the use of administrative data for implementation research have been introduced so that those who want to use or extend the use of administrative data have guidance in doing so. Although it is probably true that the use of administrative data is not a first option for most implementation research, there have been successes in addressing all of the issues discussed above. The advantages of using administrative data for certain kinds of information are clear. The challenge is to reduce the evident disadvantages of using it.

NOTES

1. The primary exceptions to this are birth and death certificates and other health tracking systems.

2. This is technically known as "on-line transactional processing" (OLTP).

3. The effort by the U.S. Census Bureau, the Survey of Program Dynamics, will provide longitudinal data from before welfare reform at a national level (1996–2001).

4. Self-employment, independent contracting, and federal and railroad employment are notable exceptions.

REFERENCES

Bloom, Dan, James J. Kemple, and R. Rogers-Dillon. 1997. *The Family Transition Program: Implementation and Early Impacts of Florida's Time-Limited Welfare Program.* New York: Manpower Demonstration Research Corporation.

Brady, Henry E., and Barbara W. Snow. 1996. *Data Systems and Statistical Requirements for the Personal Responsibility and Work Opportunity Act of 1996.* Berkeley: University of California Data Archive and Technical Assistance.

Brookshire, Robert G. 1993. "A Relational Database Primer." *Social Science Computer Review* 11(2):197–213.

Cancian, Maria, Robert Haveman, Thomas Kaplan, Daniel Meyer, and Barbara Wolfe. 1999. "Work, Earnings, and Well-Being after Welfare: What Do We Know?" *Focus* 20(2):22–25. http://www.ssc.wisc.edu/irp/focus/foc202.pdf. (Accessed July 9, 2002.)

DHHS. See U.S. Department of Health and Human Services.

Goerge, Robert M., and Bong Joo Lee. 1999. "Matching and Cleaning Administrative Data." Paper presented at Panel on Data and Methods for Measuring the Effect of Changes in Social Welfare Programs, Committee on National Statistics, National Research Council, Washington, D.C., Dec. 16–17.

Goerge, Robert M., John Van Voorhis, and Bong Joo Lee. 1994. "Illinois's Longitudinal and Relational Child and Family Research Database." *Social Science Computer Review* 12(3):351–65.

Gordon, Anne, Jonathan Jacobson, and Thomas Fraker. 1996. *Approaches to Evaluating Welfare Reform: Lessons from Five State Demonstrations.* Princeton, N.J.: Mathematica Policy Research.

Hotz, V. Joseph, and John Karl Scholz. 2001. "Measuring Employment and Income for Low-Income Populations with Administrative and Survey Data." Madison: Institute for Research on Poverty, University of Wisconsin. IPR Discussion Paper 1224-01. http://www.ssc.wisc.edu/irp/pubs/dp122401.pdf. (Accessed July 9, 2002.)

Hotz, V. Joseph, Robert M. Goerge, Julie Balzekas, and Francis Margolin, eds. 1998. "Administrative Data for Policy-Relevant Research: Assessment of Current Utility and Recommendations for Development. A Report of the Advisory Panel on Research Uses of Administrative Data of the Northwestern University/University of Chicago Joint Center for Poverty Research." Chicago: Northwestern University/University of Chicago Joint Center for Poverty Research. http://www.jcpr.org/report.html. (Accessed July 9, 2002.)

Kalil, Ariel, P. Lindsay Chase-Lansdale, Rebekah Coley, Robert Goerge, and Bong Joo Lee. 1998. "Correspondence between Individual and Administrative Reports of Welfare Receipt." Paper presented at Annual Workshop, National Association for Welfare Research and Statistics, Chicago, Aug. 2–5.

Kornfeld, Robert, and Howard Bloom. 1997. "Measuring Program Impacts in Earnings and Employment: Do UI Wage Reports from Employers Agree With Surveys of Individuals?" JCPR Working Paper 1. Chicago: Northwestern University/University of Chicago Joint Center for Poverty Research.

Lane, Julia, and David Stevens. 1997. "Welfare-to-Work Policy: Employer Hiring and Retention of Former Welfare Recipients." JCPR Working Paper 3. Chicago: Northwestern University/University of Chicago Joint Center for Poverty Research.

Michalopoulos, Charles, Johannes M. Bos, Robert Lalonde, and Nandita Verma. 1998. "Assessing the Impact of Welfare Reform on Urban Communities: The Urban Change Project and Methodological Considerations." MDRC Working Paper. New York: Manpower Demonstration Research Corporation.

Newcombe, Howard B. 1988. *Handbook of Record Linkage: Methods for Health and Statistical Studies, Administration, and Business.* Oxford, England: Oxford University Press.

Spano, Sedra, and John Eckenrode. 1998. "Administrative Data in Child Welfare: Research Strategies and Prospects for the Future." Paper presented at Meeting on National Data Archive on Child Abuse and Neglect, Cornell University, Ithaca, N.Y., June 26–27.

U.S. Department of Health and Human Services. 1999. "Administrative Data Linking Grants." http://aspe.hhs.gov/hsp/adminlink. (Accessed July 9, 2002.)

PART FOUR
Pursuing Excellence

The final part draws some conclusions and looks to the future. *Where We Go from Here* (chapter 12). Rebecca Maynard and Tom Corbett conclude that the changing policy environment is placing greater emphasis on accountability, which, in turn, will place greater emphasis on knowledge-based decisionmaking at the policy and program level. One implication, in her judgment, is that there will be less support for and interest in research designed primarily to serve academic needs and interests—and more demand for projects designed specifically to obtain the information policymakers want and need. This new evaluation environment will put more stress on joint projects that are explicitly designed to break down disciplinary and methodological walls. It will address policy-driven questions rather than questions posed by analysts to serve their own academic interests. And it will, in consequence, be forced increasingly to use question-driven research methods and data collection strategies. Maynard and Corbett end their discussion with examples of ways the various implementation evaluation methods described in Part Two of the book might be combined with one another, and with impact evaluation strategies, to meet the spectrum of needs posed by the new demands of the policy and program world.

12

Where We Go from Here

Rebecca A. Maynard and Thomas Corbett

The social welfare policy environment has changed dramatically in the past decade. In part, changes have been prompted by the emergence of a stronger, more policy-focused body of evidence regarding social problems and the efficacy of various strategies for improving conditions. Importantly for the research community, the new policy landscape places a much stronger emphasis on accountability. That emphasis, in turn, increases the importance of knowledge-based decisionmaking at both the program and the policy level in ways that have triggered an expansion in the demand for and support of research. Just as critically, shifts in the policy landscape require the use of a broader set of analytic tools to respond to the range of questions being asked.

Policymakers have increased their demands for research to sharpen their understanding of social problems and goals, identify the menu of policy and program options to address particular needs, assess the relative strengths and limitations of options, and shape the development of detailed policy implementation guidelines. Program directors have developed an appreciation for and are increasingly relying on research to guide them in the translation of policy and program support into client intervention and service strategies. Correspondingly, there has been a decline in interest in and support for basic research to expand our general understanding of social phenomena through the development and testing of social, psychological, economic, and political theories. On the other hand, new policy and institutional forms are driving the research agenda in new and exciting directions. Not surprisingly, research agendas eventually reflect, and are shaped by, shifts in policy direction.

Forty Years of Interplay between Policy Content and Analytic Methods

Rigorous study of the processes through which policies are formulated and implemented is experiencing a renaissance—reemerging as salient strategies for understanding the challenges associated with social welfare reform. This rebirth of interest in implementation analysis should not be surprising. Analytic approaches, like the substance of policy, evidence a cyclical character where certain perspectives experience periods of relative dominance and decline (O'Connell 2001). Over the past several decades, we have witnessed an observable, albeit tenuous, connection between trends in social policy and preferences among analytic methods.

The 1960s and early 1970s witnessed a dramatic growth in social policy innovation. Policymakers seized upon a window of opportunity to address a host of societal ills through a spate of legislation bundled up in the broad themes of the Great Society and the War on Poverty. These initiatives, both diverse and ambitious, attempted to transform the way individuals, families, and communities functioned. Although parts of the War on Poverty were national initiatives designed to ensure access to a minimal level of resources, many others operated through state and local authorities, for example, community action agencies. Thus, the War on Poverty can be characterized by its complexity, requiring a sophisticated application of policy initiatives and advanced management techniques. Not surprisingly, dominant research questions of the era were these: "How can policymakers who establish a new program ensure that it is carried out as intended?" and "How can policymakers and program operators judge whether programs have achieved their intended goals?"

The thwarted optimism of the War on Poverty era led to the first generation of implementation studies. For the most part, the central issue involved exploring the processes through which good intentions failed to achieve desired outcomes. Because faith in the federal government's public purposes was high during this period, the appearance of program failure often was attributed to the processes through which national intent was pursued at the local level. It proved challenging for the national government to design programs and oversight strategies adequate to ensure successful implementation by local jurisdictions and the agencies that actually carried out the programs. The implementation analyses of this period sought to better understand the failure of national program and policy initiatives and to secure lessons that would enhance the success of federal programs administered through other levels of government (Derthick 1972; Pressman and Wildavsky 1973).

Arguably, the complex, multi-initiative ambitions encompassed in the Great Society settled into a more discrete set of entitlement programs, perhaps partly as a response to the management and implementation failures found in the first generation of reform initiatives. Cash assistance to low-income families became more of an entitlement, with assistance that was largely divorced from behavioral expectations. New in-kind support programs were started or expanded (especially Medicaid and Food Stamps). These income and in-kind support programs often stressed uniformity of treatment and due process concerns. Local variation and innovation often was discouraged.

Research was dominated by econometric studies or large experiments designed to answer fundamental concerns about the behavioral response to program design features. For example, would changes in welfare guarantees or benefit reduction rates affect labor supply? Several large experiments in the 1970s were designed to influence particular areas of national policy such as income support, housing, and health care. The most significant of these included the negative income tax, housing, and health insurance experiments. Other large-scale experiments in the 1970s tested innovative strategies to address needs of particular target populations in anticipation of new areas of national program development. For example, the National Supported Work Demonstration tested transitional employment support for ex-addicts, ex-offenders, young school dropouts, and long-term welfare recipients (Hollister, Kemper, and Maynard 1984).

This period corresponded to a more authoritative view of management in which a commonly held view was that programs could achieve their formal goals if they were better designed and based on better understanding of the problems. Top-level decisionmakers must expend sufficient political will and resources; those at the operational level must be competent and motivated. Ultimately, the new view of program and policy implementation evolved to one in which the various actors could work together if certain conditions were met, particularly around goal consensus. But where goals were unclear, control might well percolate downward. The work of Daniel Mazmanian and Paul Sabatier (1983) reflected this middle period.

Since the mid-1980s, social welfare policy has been shifting slowly toward a more complex understanding of the world reminiscent of the 1960s. Early on, discrete policies oriented toward affecting the behavior of income transfer recipients were grafted onto the primary cash and in-kind entitlement programs. These new policy thrusts were primarily designed to facilitate labor force attachment though programs such as the Wisconsin Learnfare and Ohio LEAP initiatives, which pushed the agenda into broader behavioral domains (Long, Wood, and Kopp 1994; Long et al. 1996). The purpose and design of these new programs lent themselves to evaluations based on the types of classic social experiments associated with the large evaluation firms such as Mathematica Policy Research (MPR), the Manpower Demonstration Research Corporation (MDRC), Urban Institute, and Abt Associates. The implementation literature of this period is best represented by the work of Malcolm Goggin and colleagues (1990) as well as Richard Matland.

By the mid- to late 1990s, the social policy world was as institutionally complicated as it had been a generation earlier. Not surprisingly, the fundamental implementation question had shifted. No longer did the academic community focus on why there were institutional breakdowns in achieving federal intent. The locus of program and policy control itself was shifting downward. In at least some respects, both program purpose and processes increasingly were in the hands of state and local authorities. Given this devolution, a whole new set of implementation issues burst onto the scene with renewed urgency. What was going on at the operational level where programs and people interfaced, and how did this relate to what should have been going on? This latest period of reform ushered in a new social policy era, qualitatively different from what had come before. Local programs and processes increasingly became important objects of inquiry in their own right.

As detailed in chapter 1, this newest era of social welfare encompasses varied and multiple goals, and encompasses multiple target populations while introducing complex, behavior-focused programs that tend to be dynamic and longitudinal—seeking fundamental change over time in those served. Effective welfare workers in the emerging era must eschew bureaucratic rules and adopt professional norms. Many now function in agencies defined by porous boundaries as complex interagency agreements and one-stop models emerge. Malleable institutional forms that respond quickly to new challenges and that are more entrepreneurial in their approaches frequently supplant traditionally static and risk-aversive welfare systems. Distinct program and funding streams that are characteristic of the "silo" approach to social policy are being merged into networks of social assistance.

In this new era of social assistance, there is a tendency for passion and purpose to replace policy and protocols as the center of social policy. Increasingly, frontline workers in the better welfare agencies, when asked how they deal with certain clients or challenges, say they do "whatever it takes" (Kaplan 2002). This transition reflects recognition that programs designed to transform behavior follow a certain logic determined by the nature of the core goals rather than by a lower level of a hierarchical organization seeking to thwart public purposes. Income transfer programs can be run centrally, but it is challenging to run service programs this way.

The technological imperative embodied within the new world of welfare, where services are designed to alter behavior as opposed to simply provide income support, would benefit from more, not less, rigorous inquiry. Moreover, the needed rigor extends beyond classical experiments and observational analyses using national data sets to include rigorous research to understand and interpret the operational aspects of programs and policies as they relate to program goals, implementation policies, and outcomes.

Conceptual Framework for Future Implementation and Process Analysis

A convenient way to conceptualize the policy intervention process and its links with critical information needs is to relate policy and its implementation to a theory of change or impact. Figure 12.1 illustrates the relational approach with a framework that builds on the 40-year history of program and policy analysis research outlined above. The major advance reflected in this framework is its ability to accommodate the more complex and varied demands of today's policymakers and practitioners and the taxpaying public for scientific evidence to guide decisionmaking. Policymakers are demanding evidence to substantiate the extent and nature of social welfare problems warranting public intervention (box 2A) and to guide the translation of the problems into concrete policy goals and

Figure 12.1. Theory of Change or Impact

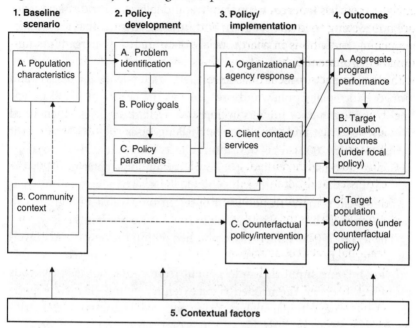

intervention strategies (boxes 2B and 2C). Practitioners are eager for assistance in moving most efficiently and effectively from policy to practice (box 2C to boxes 3A and 3B). And the policymakers, practitioners, and the public are demanding sound monitoring for accountability and evaluation to substantiate the effectiveness of the public policy initiatives (boxes 4A and 4B as well as comparisons of box 4B with 4C).

Social welfare policy research will thrive in this new environment to the extent that researchers embrace the information needs of policymakers and practitioners and adapt their research methods to provide focused, credible information to support decisionmaking and practice. In large part this means that future research will be more goal focused than it has been in the past. It also will be much more interdisciplinary. It will address policy-driven questions and use multiple information sources and analysis methods to address them. Indeed, the myriad research advances presented in previous chapters of this book, as well as more traditional impact evaluation methods,[1] will be fused in various combinations in the next generation of welfare policy research initiatives.

This anticipated explosion of research questions and tailored choices of analytic methods emerges from the sheer complexity of the policies and programs being tried and from the uncertainties associated with what is happening and who is in charge. In this amorphous policy and institutional environment, a host of questions beyond the traditional concern with client impacts present themselves.

- How does policy intent develop and become codified? If there is less structure and more participation in the development of rules, how do things really work?
- How does codified intent get translated and modified as purpose is expressed at different levels of the system? Goal leakage can occur as each level of implementers interprets and shapes policy.
- How creative is the use of discretion at the local level, what organizational forms develop, and what service delivery modes and professional practices actually emerge?
- What is the nature of the worker(s)–client(s) interface? In the new world of welfare, what is their interaction and how does the idiosyncratic nature of that relationship determine (as opposed to merely reflect) policy?

These types of questions reflect both macro and micro concerns. How is policy developed (macro)? How is policy managed (macro and micro)? And how is policy executed at the ground level (micro)? It is important to explore each level of concerns if we are to fully understand the emerging social safety net. A different mix of evaluation methods is best suited to each level of inquiries.

The Iron Triangle: Clear Goals, Answerable Questions, and Sound Methods

The key to sound evaluation is having clear goals for the study, using those goals to guide the specification of the research questions, then using information sources and analysis methods appropriate to answering the questions with rigor. Historically, the nexus of available data and the likelihood that the analyst can use those data to produce an interesting and publishable paper has guided much of the social welfare research. In today's world, support for research and—to a lesser extent—its "publishability" depend increasingly on its prospective utility in informing future policy-making or practice.

To this end, it is important that the evaluator be clear about the ultimate goal of the research. For example, is its primary goal to clarify the nature of the problem warranting public attention? Is it to empower a program or service agency to do its job better and/or to solidify or preserve its political and/or financial support? Is its primary goal to improve street-level performance? Is the goal to monitor compliance with program and policy directives? Is the intent to help guide expansion or replication efforts? Is the intent to measure program or policy effectiveness and to relate the outcomes of a policy or intervention to other possible uses of public funds?

To a large extent, the goals vary in predictable patterns across the various research consumer groups. Policymakers tend to be most interested in the front-end and back-end goals—clarifying the problems warranting public intervention and having evidence of the likely response to the application of various policy levers and programs. Program directors are the primary consumers of research for empowerment purposes. Frontline workers and their supervisors are the primary consumers of research directed at improving street-level performance. And policymakers and program directors share an interest in facilitating program expansion and/or replication.

The appropriateness and power of various analytic methods depend critically on the research questions being addressed. In large part, the changing client base for research and a corresponding sea change in the salient research questions have stimulated generational changes in our approaches to implementation and process analysis (Kaplan and Corbett, chapter 4, this volume). Until recently, programs themselves rarely entered the pool of research consumers. Yet, over the past decade, a number of forces have prompted greater interest in research by the program community, including the heightened demand for accountability by funders, the revealed utility of research to the practitioners, and increased attention by researchers to serving multiple consumer groups, including practitioners.[2]

Broadening the consumer pool affects our research strategy through expanding the study goals and thus the research questions to include those that are best answered through performance and street-level operational analysis, which were discussed by Mead (chapter 6) and Brodkin (chapter 7), respectively. Such analyses supplement the more traditional process and implementation studies that have provided the contextual support for impact evaluations (Sherwood and Doolittle, chapter 9, this volume) or simply served as contextual analysis to illuminate our understanding of welfare program performance (Holcomb and Nightingale, chapter 3, this volume; Lurie, chapter 5, this volume).

Ethnography is probably the newest methodology applied to welfare policy analysis (Edin, chapter 8, this volume). It is especially powerful in adding a human face to problems and their solutions. Ethnography also can be especially valuable in helping us understand policy and intervention strategies from the client's perspective.

The progressive development of implementation and process analysis in response to the changing consumer environment has not only generated a broader array of analytic strategies but also prompted improved technologies and standards for the collection and processing of data (Edin, chapter 8; Charlesworth and Born, chapter 10; and Goerge, chapter 11, this volume). Depending on the research questions, the critical information may be largely external to the program or policy implementation. However, increasingly over the past 15 years, we also have begun to harness the power of administrative data, often in ways that have had the side benefit of prompting improved recording and use of information at the program level.

What has been generically referred to as implementation and process analysis in this volume carries many other labels among researchers—for example, empowerment analysis, outcomes analysis, performance analysis, monitoring analysis, contextual analysis, and ethnography. The previous chapters in this volume illustrate the power of permeating the boundaries of these more narrowly defined analytic approaches in deference to the information needs motivating the analysis. The remainder of this chapter illustrates the mixing and matching strategies that may be appropriate to meeting the goals of various research consumer groups. Specifically, we focus on four consumer groups: (1) practitioners and program directors, (2) policymakers, (3) impact analysts and their clients, and (4) scientific and academic interests.

Implementation Research in Support of Programs and Practice

Practitioners need sound data to aid in the management of their programs and for external accountability. Indeed it is this need that drives the design, management, and products of their administrative data systems, as noted by Goerge (chapter 11). More formal research, whether conducted internally or through a research partnership, can be valuable in guiding internal operational decisions as well as in providing information critical to maintaining and/or expanding support. Examples of useful questions to pursue include the following:

- Is the policy/intervention targeting the right population? If not, why, and what could be done about it?
- Is the agency getting the target population in the door and effectively serving them? If not, why not, and how could that be addressed?
- Is the client population receptive to the intervention? If not, why not, and what could be done to improve receptivity?
- How well are outcomes aligned with goals? Where they are not well aligned, why not, and how could alignment be achieved?
- How smooth are operations, for example, in staff recruitment, support, and retention; office climate; and program costs and operational efficiency? What are the concerns and what could be done to address them?

These types of questions could be addressed through blending the type of bottom-up, street-level research strategy Brodkin uses (chapter 7) with Mead's performance analysis (chapter 6) and Edin's ethnographic methods (chapter 8). Indeed, in many respects, this type of blended research strategy mirrors Sherwood's and Doolittle's (chapter 9) description of the way implementation research methods commonly are employed in studies designed to complement impact analyses.

What is not illustrated in the preceding chapters of this volume is the way one meets the needs of the practitioner when conducting standalone research *solely* for that audience. In this case, one would simply sharpen the focus on the questions that are of most direct relevance to the practitioner and program management. This would entail "smart" analysis of their administrative data to allow documentation and monitoring of client contact, program services, and client outcomes (boxes 3B and 4A in figure 12.1), in relation to agency investment (box 3A). Adding some of the contextual information one would gather through the types of in-depth client interviews that are common in ethnographic research like that discussed by Edin (chapter 8) also can help. In other policy arenas, this type of analysis, conducted primarily for the programs and practitioner staff, encompasses advocacy goals and bears the label "empowerment analysis."[3]

Implementation Research in Support of Policymakers' Needs

Policymakers need information to focus their attention on the appropriate policy goals and to aid in the establishment of sensible policy parameters; they need research for accountability purposes; and they need research to identify gaps in coverage or effectiveness. Examples of the types of questions policymakers grapple with are the following:

- What are the social policy concerns? What is the nature and level of need warranting public policy attention?
- What policies or interventions are likely to be effective in promoting the intended response?
- What policy parameters are likely to result in the intended intervention being delivered?
- What are effective accountability measures?
- Are there more cost-effective strategies for achieving the policy goals?

Traditional social and demographic analysis is the primary tool used for need assessments (Rossi and Freeman 1993). The type of aggregate program performance analysis discussed by Mead (chapter 6) can be an extremely powerful way to provide ongoing indicators of the correspondence between the aggregate policy goals (box 2B in figure 12.1) and program outcomes (box 4A). This type of analysis also can be used to examine the relationship between that correspondence and the population served (box 1A), aggregate client contact and services (box 3B), and underlying contextual factors (box 5).

Particularly in cases where current policies do not eliminate the social welfare concern, it can be valuable to apply a blend of the other implementation analysis strategies discussed in previous chapters to aid in reshaping policy. For example, the types of field network studies Lurie discusses (chapter 5) can provide important information about possible slippage between policy parameters and organizational response. The implementation research paired with impact analyses described by Sherwood and Doolittle (chapter 9) can illuminate issues of differential effectiveness of interventions across population subgroups, in different social and economic contexts, and with different methods or levels of implementation.[4] And ethnographic research such as that Edin describes (chapter 8) can provide valuable information on the clients' receptivity and response to the interventions resulting from particular policies.

Cost analysis and cost-effectiveness analysis depends on the types of impact and implementation research outlined by Sherwood and Doolittle, supplemented by more rigorous analysis of cost information.[5] The combination of these methods allows one to examine the consequences for the costs of implementing policies under different social or economic circumstances, for different client groups, and with different partnership arrangements, for example. However, without the rigor of impact analyses, it is not possible to conduct a benefit-cost assessment of the policies (see examples in Levin 1993; Maynard 1996; McConnell and Glazerman 2001).

Implementation Research in Support of Impact Analysis

A primary goal of impact analysis is to serve the need of policymakers to judge the overall success of current or prospective new policies. However, impact analysis also is important in scientific research designed to advance the development and application of economic, social, and political theory. Companion implementation studies are the vehicle for documenting the context in which the policies were tested; for examining the sensitivity of the impact estimates to variability in that context, in the "street level" manner in which the policy was implemented, and in the target group served; and for guiding the development of expansion, improvement, replication strategies, or a combination.

The questions central to this type of supportive implementation study are those integral to the various linkages in the theory of change or impact between policy parameters (box 2C in figure 12.1), organizational or agency response (box 3A), client contact and services (box 3B), and program impacts (box 4B–box 4C). Following the examples of Holcomb and Nightingale (chapter 3) and Sherwood and Doolittle (chapter 9), the following are examples of the particular questions that analysis for this purpose might address:

- What is the organizational response to the policy parameters? What was the nature of the policies/interventions implemented? What is the extent and nature of variability in response and what accounts for it?

- What are the critical factors in achieving this level of implementation? What would be required to address gaps between the policy goals and the organizational response?
- What are the numbers and characteristics of the clients reached through the interventions? What accounts for the profile of clients reached?
- What was the actual level and nature of clients' exposure to the intervention? How much variability is there and what accounts for that variability?
- What outcomes resulted for those clients with different characteristics and/or exposures?
- How do outcomes for different categories of clients compare with what would be expected had the intervention not occurred?

As is well illustrated by Sherwood and Doolittle (chapter 9), the most effective strategies for addressing these types of questions involve blending the research strategies illustrated throughout this volume. Most notably, there is a strong role for adapting the type of street-level analysis Brodkin (chapter 7) describes to a similar analysis viewed through the lens of the client rather than the agency worker. Similarly, the up-close and in-depth ethnographic methods described by Edin (chapter 8) are useful ways to examine the correspondence (or lack thereof) between client needs and expectations and the goals of the policy and its resulting intervention. Much of the supporting statistical analysis entails micro-level applications of models similar to the aggregate program analysis Mead (chapter 6) applies to judge overall program performance and goal attainment.

Implementation Research in Support of Scholarly Interests

The most important condition for the continued refinement of implementation analysis methods and for their assuming a place in the methods training for social scientists is that the academic community recognize these methods as integral to the development and application of economic, political, and social theories. To this end, it is important for the research to support inductive analysis, be applied explicitly in the development and testing of theory, and be featured prominently in the applied research and reporting. To date, there has not been widespread application of the methods outlined in this volume for any but the third of these purposes. In part, this reflects the fact that such research is too costly to conduct without external support and, to date, support has been most available for component studies within large demonstration evaluation projects. However, we may now have accumulated adequate implementation databases to support more secondary analyses that would serve more development and testing of theories.

Certainly one place where the rear-view mirror approach to analysis described by Kaplan and Corbett (chapter 4) seems appropriate is in testing theories of change and in developing new theories to guide future demonstration and evaluation efforts. Indeed, the rich blend of methods illustrated in this volume validates the importance of the early waves of implementation analysis, described by Kaplan and Corbett as the top-down and bottom-up approaches, while also offering clear illustrations of the value of a mix-and-match approach, tailored to the particular concerns of the research consumers.

The challenge for the academic community of implementation researchers is to better codify their methods and data sources in a way that facilitates the emergence of more consensuses on the standards of evidence. We may be on the cusp of a fourth wave of implementation research, which could have stature in the academy. Among the critical next steps would be those of developing a common vocabulary, a shared appreciation for the unique and overlapping benefits of various strategies, and standards for evidence in support of theory, practice, and policy development and refinement.

Building Bridges of Support

There is a strong foundation for implementation research in support of social welfare policy development, implementation, and operations. The road traveled to attain this foundation has taught us important lessons we should apply as we seek to capitalize further on these achievements. First, we need to remember that the most productive research projects have involved strong partnerships among key representatives of policy interests, the agencies charged with implementing the policies, the clients affected by the policies, and the research team. Partnering with policymakers is critical to ensuring appropriate framing of the questions and dissemination of findings.

The process of building and supporting partnerships with programs can improve the practical utility of the research and, in return, may improve access to the information needed to accomplish the study goals. Insofar as the research is all about how policy trickles down to the clients, it is helpful if they too are willing partners in contributing to improving policy development and administration. Finally, researchers need to adopt a noncompetitive, highly collaborative approach to the evaluation. They need to expend as much effort working to learn from the areas where the policies are not yet achieving their intended goals as typically is devoted to making news when forward progress is achieved.

A related avenue for advancing the field is to build on and contribute to the wealth of information generated through policy implementation. In many cases, administrative data offer a reliable and reproducible source of information for analysis, thus minimizing the need to burden staff or clients with new data collection. Moreover, there may be productive legacies of administrative data analysis from the research, as noted by both Rabb and Winstead (chapter 2) and Goerge (chapter 11).

A third strategy for continued progress is to commit to further breaking down the methodological silos by working from the research question to the information needs and sources and finally to pairing the information sources with the strongest methods for analysis. In many cases, this will bring the implementation, performance, and impact analysts onto a common team and possibly even extend the skills and experiences of analysts to enable more of them to work across these methods.

Finally, the researchers should make concerted efforts to address the multiple consumer groups—official and unofficial—in their reporting. This will require using multiple reporting formats and documents, insofar as the various research consumer groups have somewhat different interests and speak somewhat different languages. However, commitment to this goal will force the researchers to broaden their inquiry to encompass the multiple perspectives, with the reward being greater support for and utility of the product.

Implementation Research in Search of a Future

The body of work summarized in this book represents a conscious effort begun in the mid-1990s to think through the analytic methods we were applying to document and understand the ongoing transformation of the social safety net. With support from the Foundation for Child

Development and its then-president, Barbara B. Blum, the Institute for Research on Poverty at the University of Wisconsin-Madison and the National Center for Children in Poverty at Columbia University's Mailman School of Public Health organized a set of events where knowledge producers and consumers might speculate on the nature of their respective crafts and what the future might entail (see Institute for Research on Poverty 1996).

One aspect of that overall effort involved a set of meetings among practitioners and, to some extent, users of implementation research in the field of social welfare. The gatherings proved revealing. Scholars and researchers using traditional evaluative techniques—for example, randomized experiments or nonexperimental analyses using contemporary estimation techniques—have a variety of venues through which to share their craft and their work. Their work is respected and their methods generally are understood and continually are being refined. Those engaged in implementation research often face a different professional terrain. Their work is often misunderstood and undervalued. They do not have many venues through which to share common problems and frustrations or develop their craft and skills. There is not even a shared language and vocabulary for describing this work.

As noted, there have been bursts of interest in implementation research over the past several decades. Although these discrete bursts of interest have resulted in enhancements to the literature, they have not resulted in a sustained effort or in the development of a coherent group of implementation research scholars. Ideally, efforts to create this community of interest will be renewed and strengthened. We need more venues for bringing together practitioners in this diverse field. And since this particular work represents a modest advancement of the field, there remains a need for additional publications on methods. Such steps could lessen the sense of isolation and uncertainty among those who practice these methods and expand and improve further the products.

There is a strong argument to be made that research and evaluation is too important to be left to researchers and evaluators. There is considerable value in developing a much more intimate relationship between knowledge producers and knowledge consumers. Without open and honest communication between these very different cultures, we risk evaluating yesterday's questions. We need forums where those developing policy and running programs can shape the research agendas that are pursued purportedly on their behalf.

Our social policy world continues to change. Whether we fully understand those changes will, in part, be dictated by the analytic tools and methods we employ in our research. The quality and appropriateness of those tools in large measure depends on the investments we are prepared to make.

NOTES

1. By design, this volume does not address impact analysis methods, as these methods are well established and more concrete than are the methods for process and implementation research. See Orr (1999) for an excellent discussion of impact analysis methods and their application to welfare and employment program initiatives.

2. The impetus for addressing practitioner needs derived primarily from a need of researchers to secure buy-in among their focal program staff. However, researchers quickly learned that there were other benefits to servicing these needs, including broadening the utility of the research and developing a more comprehensive and convincing articulation of the practical implications of the research findings.

3. One also would employ strategies other than the field network teams to collect the data for this type of analysis. Charlesworth and Born (chapter 10) provide a good discussion of myriad strategies for gathering information to inform researchers about the various linkages in the process from policy development to client outcomes.

4. This recommendation is at odds with the suggestion by deLeon (1999) and discussed by Kaplan and Corbett (chapter 4) for a fourth wave of implementation research that would advise us to continue to "accept simple implementation descriptions, without demanding predictive capability." It seems we already have moved beyond this point in practice. We simply have not developed a consistent vocabulary, shared appreciation for the unique and overlapping benefits of various strategies, and common standards for analysis and reporting.

5. Greenberg and Appenzeller (1998) provide a step-by-step guide to program cost analysis.

REFERENCES

deLeon, Peter. 1999. "The Missing Link Revisited: Contemporary Implementation Research." *Policy Studies Review* 16(3–4):311–38.

Derthick, Martha. 1972. *New Towns In-Town: Why a Federal Program Failed.* Washington, D.C.: The Urban Institute.

Goggin, Malcolm, Ann Bowman, James Lester, and Laurence O'Toole. 1990. *Implementation Theory and Practice: Toward a Third Generation.* New York: Harper Collins.

Greenberg, David, and Ute Appenzeller. 1998. *Cost Analysis Step by Step.* New York: Manpower Demonstration Research Corporation.

Hollister, Robinson, Peter Kemper, and Rebecca Maynard. 1984. *The National Supported Work Demonstration*. Madison: University of Wisconsin Press.

Institute for Research on Poverty. 1996. *Focus* 18(1):1–87. Special issue.

Kaplan, Thomas. 2002. "Whatever We Have Been Doing: Policy Control over TANF." *Focus* 22(1):35–38.

Levin, Henry M. 1993. "The Economics of Education for At-Risk Students." In *Essays on the Economics of Education,* edited by Emily P. Hoffman (11–33). Kalamazoo, Mich.: W. E. Upjohn Institute.

Long, David, Robert Wood, and Hilary Kopp. 1994. *LEAP: The Educational Effects of LEAP and Enhanced Services in Cleveland*. New York: Manpower Demonstration Research Corporation.

Long, David, Judith M. Gueron, Robert G. Wood, Rebecca Fisher, and Veronica Fellerath. 1996. *LEAP: Three-Year Impacts of Ohio's Welfare Initiative to Improve School Attendance Among Teenage Parents*. New York: Manpower Demonstration Research Corporation.

Maynard, Rebecca. 1996. "The Costs of Adolescent Childbearing." In *Kids Having Kids: Economic Costs and Social Consequences,* edited by Rebecca Maynard (285–335). Washington, D.C.: Urban Institute Press.

Mazmanian, Daniel, and Paul Sabatier. 1983. *Implementation and Public Policy*. Glenview, Ill.: Scott, Foresman.

McConnell, Sheena, and Steven Glazerman. 2001. *Evaluating the Benefits and Costs of the Job Corps Program*. Washington, D.C.: Mathematica Policy Research.

O'Connell, Alice. 2001. *Poverty Knowledge*. Princeton, N.J.: Princeton University Press.

Orr, Larry L. 1999. *Social Experiments: Evaluating Public Programs with Experimental Methods*. Thousand Oaks, Calif.: Sage Publications.

Pressman, Jeffrey L., and Aaron Wildavsky. 1973. *Implementation*. Berkeley: University of California Press.

Rossi, Peter H., and Howard E. Freeman. 1993. *Evaluation: A Systematic Approach*. Newbury Park, Calif.: Sage Publications.

About the Editors

Thomas Corbett has emeritus status at the University of Wisconsin, Madison, and remains an active affiliate with the Institute for Research on Poverty, where until recently, he served as associate director. He has long studied trends in welfare reform and how to better understand them. He has worked on reform issues at all levels of government and continues to work with a number of states through networks of senior state welfare officials in the Midwest and on the West Coast.

Mary Clare Lennon is a senior research fellow at the National Center for Children in Poverty (NCCP) at Columbia University's Mailman School of Public Health. From 1997 to 2000, she was director for research at NCCP's Research Forum on Children, Families, and the New Federalism. Lennon has been on the faculty of the Mailman School since 1987 and is currently associate professor of clinical sociomedical sciences. Her current research focuses on social policy, family economic security, and child well-being.

About the Contributors

Catherine Born is research associate professor at the University of Maryland School of Social Work and director of the multidisciplinary Family Welfare Research and Training Group, which for more than 20 years has provided research, training, and technical assistance services to the Maryland public human services community and board members of the National Association for Welfare Research and Statistics. She has published materials on such topics as recidivism and the child welfare experiences of TANF leavers, agency-university partnerships, and social work education.

Evelyn Z. Brodkin is associate professor at the University of Chicago, School of Social Service Administration, and lecturer in the Law School. Her major research interests include the politics of the welfare state, social policy, street-level organizations, and public management. She is codirector of the Project on the Public Economy of Work and a faculty associate of the Joint Center for Poverty Research.

Leanne Charlesworth has extensive experience with data collection in child welfare and welfare settings. Most recently, she directed a welfare reform implementation study focusing on intrastate variation in Maryland.

Fred Doolittle is vice president and deputy director of the Department of Education, Children, and Youth at the Manpower Demonstration Research Corporation (MDRC). Since his arrival at MDRC in 1986, he has worked on studies of welfare and employment reforms, with a special emphasis on programs serving youth. Recent publications include *Matching Applicants with Services: Initial Assessments in the Milwaukee County W-2 Program,* with Susan Gooden and Ben Glispie (MDRC, 2001) and *Fathers' Fair Share,* with Earl Johnson and Ann Levine (Russell Sage Foundation, 1999).

Kathryn Edin is an associate professor of sociology at Northwestern University and faculty fellow at the Institute for Policy Research. She is best known for her influential book *Making Ends Meet: How Single Mothers Survive Welfare and Low-Wage Work,* coauthored with Laura Lein (Russell Sage Foundation, 1997), which details the economic and social circumstances of working and welfare-reliant single mothers. Her research interests include poverty and social inequality, family and gender, and public policy. Currently, she is co–principal investigator for several qualitative, longitudinal, and ethnographic projects.

Robert M. Goerge is a research fellow at the Chapin Hall Center for Children at the University of Chicago and a faculty associate at the Northwestern University/UC Joint Center for Poverty Research. Central to Dr. Goerge's research is the goal of improving the available information on all children and families, particularly those who are poor, abused, or neglected or who have disabilities. A special interest is the issue of children receiving multiple services or benefits from multiple providers or agencies.

Pamela A. Holcomb is a senior research associate at the Urban Institute. Her research has concentrated on issues of evaluating and implementing social programs, particularly in the area of welfare reform. She has written extensively on welfare, welfare reform, institutional performance, and social services. She also was an analyst on special detail at the Office of the Assistant Secretary of Planning and Evaluation, Department of Health and Human Services (1995–1997), where she worked specifically on welfare reform issues and policy development, and was a congressional fellow at the House of Representatives and the Senate.

Thomas Kaplan is associate director and senior scientist at the Institute for Research on Poverty, University of Wisconsin, Madison. He has served as principal investigator for research projects on social policy and the evaluation of welfare reform programs and has written extensively on the implementation of recent welfare reforms. For 15 years he worked in Wisconsin state government, serving as deputy budget director, planning director, and director of Medicaid HMO programs in the state's Department of Health and Social Services.

Irene Lurie is a professor in the Rockefeller College Department of Public Administration and Policy at the University at Albany, State University of New York, and a research associate at the Rockefeller Institute of Government. She has examined welfare programs at the federal, state, and local levels, including a 10-state study of the implementation of the Family Support Act of 1988. She is currently studying the TANF implementation at the front lines of welfare and workforce agencies.

Rebecca A. Maynard is university trustee chair professor of education and social policy at the University of Pennsylvania. Her research focuses on education and welfare policy, with a particular emphasis on the design and field testing of innovative strategies to improve outcomes for poor children and their families. She has directed numerous large-scale demonstration evaluations, including evaluations of employment and training programs, alternative schools, dropout prevention initiatives, teen pregnancy prevention programs, and youth risk avoidance strategies.

Lawrence M. Mead is professor of politics at New York University. He is an expert on the problems of poverty and welfare in the United States, including the politics and implementation of welfare reform programs. His works include *Beyond Entitlement* (Free Press, 1986), *The New Politics of Poverty* (Basic Books, 1992) and *The New Paternalism* (Brookings Institution Press, 1997).

Demetra Smith Nightingale is a principal research associate and director of the Welfare and Training Research Program at the Urban Institute. Currently she is also adjunct professor of public policy at the George Washington University. Her research focuses on employment, welfare, and social policy, and she serves on numerous advisory groups, boards, and task forces. Among her publications are *The Work Alternative: Welfare Reform and the Realities of the Job Market*, coedited with Robert Haveman (1995); *The Government We Deserve: Responsive Democracy and Changing Expectations*, with C. Eugene Steuerle, Edward M. Gramlich, and Hugh Heclo (1998); and *The Low-Wage Labor Market: Challenges and Opportunities for Self-Sufficiency*, coedited with Kelleen Kaye (2000), all from the Urban Institute.

Joel Rabb is chief of the Bureau of Program Integration and Coordination in the Office of Family Stability at the Ohio Department of Human Services. He has been involved in planning the recent organizational and policy changes to implement welfare reform in Ohio. In his 18 years at the Department, he has been involved in developing, implementing, and evaluating policies affecting child welfare, child care, public assistance, food stamps, teen parents, and employment programs. He is currently developing and implementing an outcome management system for county offices in Ohio.

Kay E. Sherwood is a consultant and writer on social policy and education as well as evaluation issues. She has recently completed two teaching cases on evaluations of foundation initiatives for the Evaluation Roundtable, a foundation-sponsored project to improve evaluation practice in philanthropy, and is beginning work on a formative evaluation of a national foundation's community partners grant-making program.

Don Winstead is the deputy assistant secretary for human services policy with the Office of the Assistant Secretary for Planning and Evaluation, U.S. Department of Health and Human Services. At the time chapter 2 was written, Winstead was welfare reform administrator with the Florida Department of Children and Families. He worked in Florida for 30 years serving in a variety of positions, from frontline caseworker to deputy secretary.

Index

academics/academicians, 316
  tension between government and,
    121–122
  working with, 92–93
accountability, 154–155, 311
Adams, Charles Francis, 57
administrative data, 237–238, 281–282,
  296–297
  definition, 285–287
  obstacles in identification and access
    to, 294–295
  promise of, 287–290
  quality of, 292–294
  scope of, 290–292
  structure of, for research purposes,
    295–296
  ways of collecting, 286
  and welfare reform research, 282–285
agency information, staff, and data
  barriers to, 35–36
Agranoff, Robert, 85
Aid to Families with Dependent Children
  (AFDC), 30–31, 108
Aid to Families with Dependent Children
  (AFDC) waiver programs
  history of evaluation expectations,
    4–7
Assessing the New Federalism, 47

backward mapping, 62–63
Bailey, Stephen, 58–60
benefit-cost study, 222–223, 314
Brodkin, Evelyn Z., 148, 153, 154

case study approach, 60–61
Center for Employment Training (CET),
  201
change, theory of, 45, 307–308
child support. *See* Parents' Fair Share
client-based ethnographic research, 78,
  165–167, 191
  how to do, 177
    asking the right questions, 182–184
    data-gathering techniques, 179–182
    multimethod study design issues,
      186
    nailing it down, 184–186
    sampling, 177–179
  importance of client-centered qualita-
    tive component, 167–168
  program/policy's fit in context of
    clients' lives, 170–177
  what clients are hearing, 168–170
  recent examples, 186–190
collaborative model of manager-
  researcher interaction, 25–26

Commons, John R., 57
compliance model, 147, 150, 151
    problems with, 147–148
computer-assisted telephone interview-
    ing (CATI), 247–249
computer-based information systems. See
    information systems
confidentiality, 112, 121
content analysis of existing documents,
    268–269
    advantages and disadvantages,
        269–270
    issues to consider, 272
    sample secondary analysis items, 271
    use in welfare policy implementation
        research, 270–272
contractual model of manager-researcher
    interaction, 26
cost-effectiveness analysis, 222–223, 314
covert noncompliance, 174

data collection approaches, 235, 239–240,
    272–276
    strengths and limitations, 275
databases. See administrative data
"deep dish" analysis, 160
deLeon, Peter, 65–66
Derthick, Martha, 58–60, 69n.3
Devers, Kelly J., 41
direct observation. See observation
Duncan, Greg, 190

earnings disregard, 31–32
Elementary and Secondary Education
    Act, 58, 59
Elmore, Richard, 62–63, 154
Employment Security Automated
    Reporting System (ESARS), 109
Employment Service and Work Incentive
    program, 119
Employment Service (ES), 108, 124
empowerment analysis, 313
equipment, program, 221
ethnographic research, client-based. See
    client-based ethnographic research
ethnographies, 177–178, 311
evaluation findings, most useful way to
    present, 36–37

evaluation resources, rating in-state vs.
    out-of-state, 35
evaluation(s). See also specific topics
    external vs. internal (agency), 34–35
    key to sound, 309–311
evaluator activism, 198

facilities, program, 221
"fair test" of program/policy, 199–203
Family Support Act (FSA), 109, 138
Family Transition Program (FTP), 29–30
    earnings disregard, 31–32
    sanctions policy, 30–31
field network evaluation, 85
field network studies, 75–76, 81–84, 256
    analytical framework and research
        design, 89–92
    comparative case studies, 84–86
    critique, 99–104
    data analysis, 96–99
    data collection, 94–96
    purposes, 86–87
    staffing and managing, 92–94
    unit of analysis, 87–89
financing, and replication of successful
    impact studies, 222–223
focus group guide items, sample, 267, 268
focus groups, 179–181, 237, 262–264
    advantages and disadvantages,
        264–266
    issues to consider, 268
    use in welfare implementation
        research, 266–268

General Accounting Office (GAO), 85
Gibson, Christine, 190
goal clarity, 61, 66
Goggin, Malcolm, 64
governance, 218–221
Greater Avenues for Independence
    (GAIN) study, 244, 249, 255, 261

impact analysis, 2–6, 34, 215, 314–315
    vs. performance analysis, 134–136
impact sample
    how it was drawn, 215
    size, 215

impact studies, 78–80, 107, 193–196, 227–228
  "black box" problem with, 135
  conditions needed for strong, 197–199
  intervention's likelihood of making a difference, 197–199
  program/policy's receiving fair test, 199–203
  program's producing a real service difference, 203–206
  explanation of impact results, 206–209
  based on theories, methods, and quirks of impact analysis, 215
  perspectives of program staff and target group members and, 216
  results of similar interventions/ research as guide to, 212–215
  site variation and, 216–217
  theory of impacts as guide to, 209–212
  and implementation research methodology, 224–226
  managing time sensitivity and multiple-site problems, 226–227
  questions of implementation research in, 196–223
  replication of successful, 217–223
implementation
  hierarchical concept of, 60
  top-down vs. bottom-up approaches to, 62, 63, 66, 89
  variations in, 200–201
implementation analysis, 1, 18–19
  defined, 40–42
  disciplinary contributions to, 46–49
  ethnographic research as tool for. See client-based ethnographic research
  limitations, 53–54
  and process analysis, conceptual framework for future, 307–309, 311
  theory of change or impact, 307–308
  theoretical dimensions, 42–46
  translation of proposal into program, 2–4
  types most helpful to managers, 33–34
Implementation (Pressman and Wildavsky), 146

implementation studies, 18–20. See also research; specific topics
  common features and research and design issues, 49–51
  types of, 43
  impact evaluation vs. stand-alone, 34
  knowledge- and theory-based, 45, 52–53
Implementation Theory and Practice (Goggin et al.), 64
information systems, 221–222, 290
Institute for Research on Poverty (IRP), xi–xiii
institutional analysis, 43
interview(s), 179–183, 236, 240–241. See also telephone surveys
  of administrators, 111–114
  guidelines for conducting, 112–114
  advantages and disadvantages, 158–159, 241–243
  issues to consider, 246
  sample questions by type of, 243, 244
  use in welfare policy implementation research, 243–247

Job Club model, 209
job clubs, 152–153
Job Opportunities and Basic Skills Training Program (JOBS), 83, 87, 88, 93, 94, 97–100, 102, 103, 109, 125, 128, 248, 256
  actual vs. predicted percentage of cases closed, 118–119
  analytical framework for implementation study, 90, 91
  percentage of clients entering jobs, 117
Job Service. See Employment Service
Job Training Partnership Act (JTPA), 94–96, 108, 109, 120
  adjustment of JTPA welfare employment standard, 120–121
Johnson, Earl, 187–188

key-word-in-context (KWIC) lists, 269

Learning, Earning, and Parenting (LEAP) program, 26–29

Learning, Earning, and Parenting (LEAP) (*continued*)
   changing policy based on early findings, 28–29
   helping provide information to key constituencies, 29
Lipsky, Michael, 62, 149
Lynn, Laurence, 65

macro-implementation approach, 46–48
mail surveys. *See also* questionnaires, self-administered
   advantages, 252
   issues to consider, 256–257
   sample items, 255
Management and Evaluation Project (MEP), 122–123
management information system (MIS), 221, 225
management perspectives on evaluation
   strategic *vs.* operational levels, 21–23
managers, public program, 21
   effective interaction between evaluators and, 32–33
   models of interaction between researchers and, 25–26
   research used by, 26–32
   types of implementation analysis most helpful to, 33–34
Manpower Demonstration Research Corporation (MDRC), 27, 29, 31, 32, 107, 132, 136, 245, 250, 290
marketing, 222
Matland, Richard, 62
Mazmanian, Daniel, 61, 68
micro-implementation approaches, 48. *See also* street-level analysis
Mosher, Edith, 58–60

Nathan, Richard, 65, 83–86
National Center for Children in Poverty (NCCP), xi
Nelson, Richard R., 69n.5
net costs, 222
net impact evaluation. *See* impact studies
New Hope, 188–190, 206, 208
noncompliance, covert, 174

observation (form of research), 43, 236–237, 257–259

advantages and disadvantages, 259–260
   issues to consider, 262
   use in welfare policy implementation research, 260–262
observation guide items, sample, 261
Ohio Department of Human Services (ODHS), 27, 29
Okun, Arthur, 81–82, 84
O'Toole, Lawrence, 64, 65

Parents' Fair Share (PFS), 186–188
participatory model of manager-researcher interaction, 25
performance analysis, 76–77, 107–108
   audiences, 137–139
   field interviewing, 111–114
   vs. impact evaluation, 134–136
   vs. other methodologies, 136–137
   past research, 108–111
   performance standards, 118–121
   practical problems, 121
      clearance, 121–123
      data availability, 123–126
   pros and cons, 134–137
   selection bias, 129–132
   standards for studies, 132–134
   statistical analysis, 115–118
   statistical problems, 126–129
Personal Responsibility and Work Opportunity Reconciliation Act (PRWORA), xii, 2, 7, 9, 12n.1, 66–67, 109, 289
policy, welfare, 303–304
   history, 23–25
   new, 7–9
      implications for evaluation, 9–11
policy content and analytic methods, 40
   years of interplay between, 304–307
policy production, understanding new modes of, 155–156
policymakers, 303
   implementation research in support of the needs of, 313–314
   research used by, 26–32
pregnancies, unwed, 67. *See also* teen parents
Pressman, Jeffrey, 58–60
probing in interviews, 182–183

program management, 43. *See also* management
program participation, 225
program typologies, developing, 44
Project on Devolution and Urban Change, 168–170, 175, 179, 186
Project on the Public Economy of Work, 156, 157, 161n.3

questionnaires, self-administered, 236, 251–252
  advantages and disadvantages, 252–254
  construction of, 253
  issues to consider, 256–257
  sample items, 255
  use in welfare policy implementation research, 254–257

Radin, Beryl A., 85
random assignment, point of, 215
rear-view mirror approach to analysis, 316
reasonable theory criterion, 198–199
reform, welfare. *See* welfare reform
Request for Proposals (RFP), 26, 35
research (implementation), 18–20, 303–304. *See also* implementation studies; *specific topics*
  building bridges of support, 316–317
  challenges for, in welfare reform environment, 51–54
  cost of, and decisionmaking, 35
  first generation, 58–60
  implications for study of welfare reform, 65–68
  in search of a future, 317–319
  second generation, 60–64
  in support of impact analysis, 314–315
  in support of programs and practice, 311–313
  in support of scholarly interests, 315–316
  third generation, 64–65
research methodology, implementation impact studies and, 224–226
research questions, consistent, 272–273
researchers
  barriers they must overcome, 35–36

models of interaction between public managers and, 25–26

Sabatier, Paul, 61–63, 68
secondary analysis. *See* content analysis of existing documents
Service Delivery Areas (SDAs), 120, 121
site variation, and implementation and impact, 195–196, 215–217
sites, multiple, 227
social assistance, era of, 306–307
sponsors of implementation studies, 52–53
staffing, 218
Stone, Deborah, 66
street-level analysis in policy evaluation, 48, 150–151
Street-Level Bureaucracy (Lipsky), 149
street-level bureaucracy model, 149–150
street-level research, 77–78, 145–146
  methodological issues, 156–157
    case selection, 157
    research techniques, 158–159
  practical benefits, 154–155
  pros, cons, and considerations, 159–160

target group, reaching, 199–200
teen parent cases, identifying, 27–28
teen parents, 26–29
  developing uniform method of calculating bonuses and sanctions to, 28
  measuring the effectiveness of case management of, 28
telephone surveys, 236
  advantages and disadvantages, 248–249
  computer-assisted telephone interviewing, 247–249
  issues to consider, 250–251
  sample survey items, 251
  use in welfare policy implementation research, 249–251
Temporary Assistance for Needy Families (TANF), 10, 68, 87, 97–100, 109, 124, 125, 290, 291
Temporary Assistance for Needy Families (TANF) study, 7, 83, 84, 86, 88, 93–95, 102, 103
  analytical framework for, 90, 91

threshold criterion, 197–198
time lag between intervention and findings, 207–208
time sensitivity (of audience for implementation findings), 195
 quality of findings *vs.* demand for
 speed, 54
tractability of (original) policy problem,
 61, 68
Turner, Jason, 67

Urban Change project. *See* Project on
 Devolution and Urban Change
Urban Institute information/records, 288
Urban Institute (UI) studies, 46, 47, 116,
 119, 122, 141n.22

waivers and waiver evaluations, 5–6, 29
War on Poverty, 58–60, 304
welfare. *See specific topics*
welfare reform, lessons from implementation research for study of, 65–68
welfare reform research, administrative
 data and, 282–285
Wildavsky, Aaron, 58–60
Work Incentive program (WIN),
 108–110, 124, 128
Working Toward Independence, 10

Yin, Robert K., 97–101